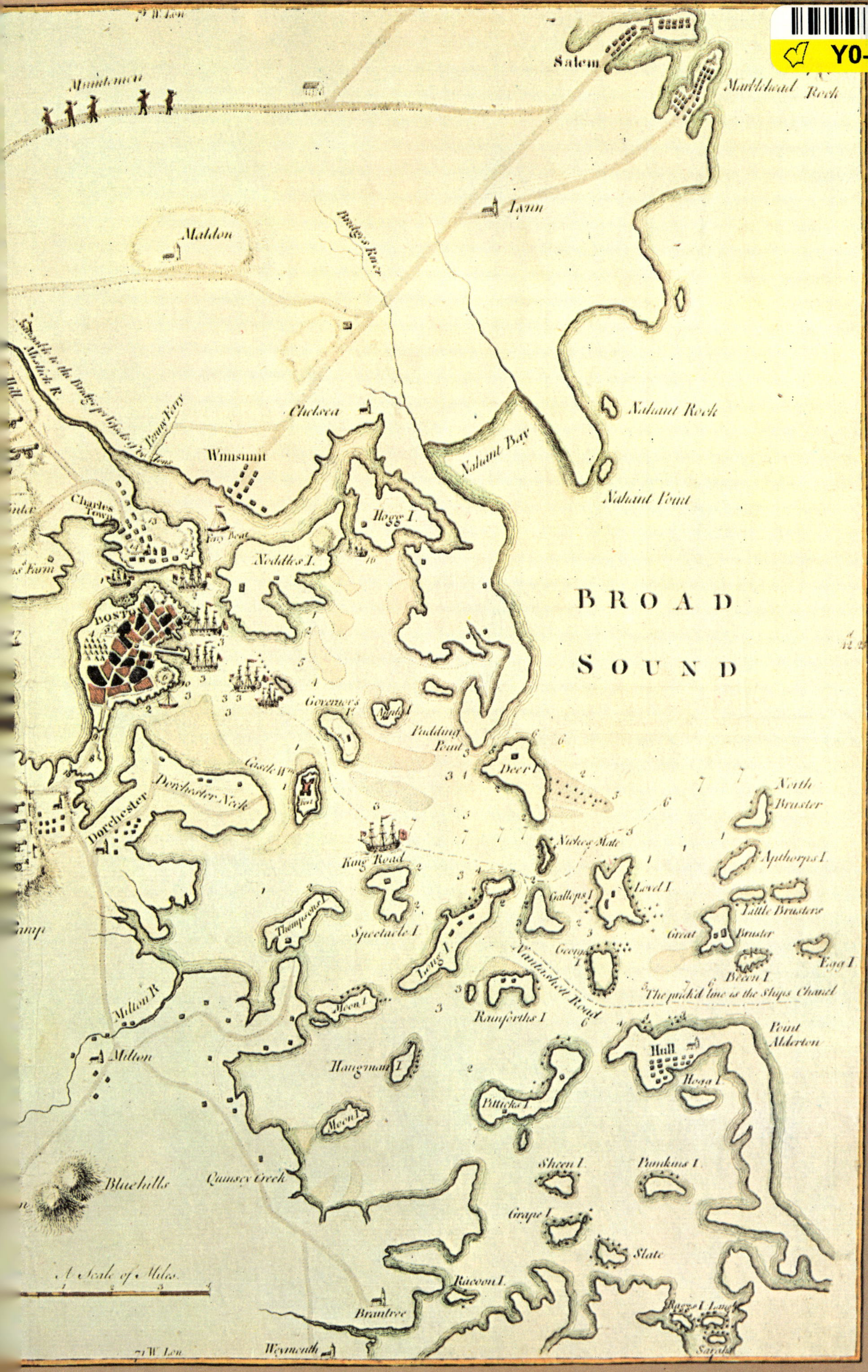

John Carter Brown Library

The Golden Book of

THE
AMERICAN
REVOLUTION

The Golden Book of THE AMERICAN REVOLUTION

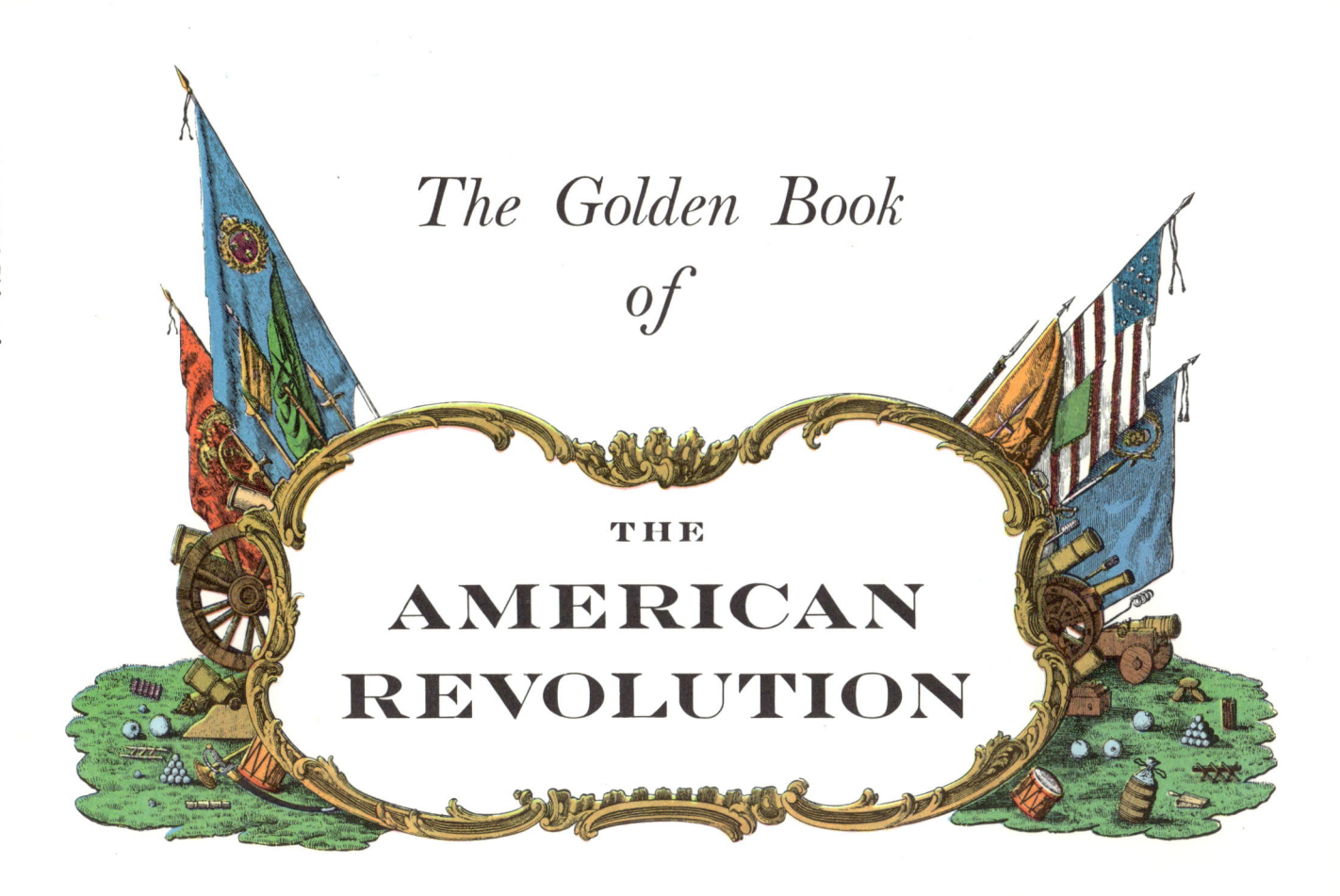

State Capitol, Richmond

ADAPTED FOR YOUNG READERS

by Fred Cook

from *The American Heritage Book of The Revolution*
by the Editors of AMERICAN HERITAGE
with narrative by BRUCE LANCASTER

INTRODUCTION BY BRUCE CATTON

GOLDEN PRESS • NEW YORK
Western Publishing Company, Inc.
Racine, Wisconsin

Alexander Hamilton

Title page of Thomas Paine's Common Sense

The first stars and stripes carried by an American army

1754 cartoon by Benjamin Franklin

CONTENTS

Introduction by Bruce Catton	6
Before the War	9
The War Begins	17
First Campaigns	31
The Day of Freedom	41
Arms and Men	57
The Darkest Hours	81

GOLDEN, A GOLDEN BOOK® and GOLDEN PRESS® are trademarks of Western Publishing Company, Inc.

Seventh Printing, 1974

Copyright © 1959, 1958 by American Heritage Publishing Company, Inc. All rights reserved under Berne and Pan-American Copyright Conventions. Reproduction in whole or in part without permission is prohibited. Printed in the U.S.A. by Western Publishing Company, Inc. Published by Golden Press, New York. Library of Congress Catalog Card Number: 73-89050

18th-century "new cleared" American farm

The Making of an Army   99

The Turning Point   113

The Quest for Allies   125

The War at Sea   132

Frontiers Aflame   149

Struggle for the South   163

The World Turned Upside Down   179

Index   192

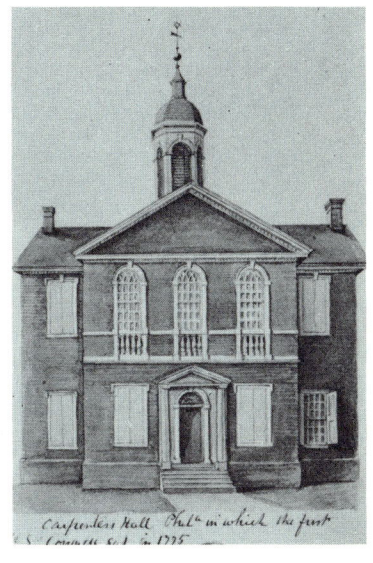

Carpenters' Hall, Philadelphia, where the first U.S. Congress sat in 1775

Drawing from a 1769 broadside

PICTURE CREDITS: Opposite page, top to bottom, 1. Museum of the City of New York 2. Library of Congress 4. Library of Congress. This page, top to bottom, 1. Patrick Campbell, *Travels*, 1793; Reserve Div., New York Public Library 2. Historical Society of Pennsylvania 3. New-York Historical Society 4. New York Public Library.

Troops at Valley Forge

This old engraving illustrates the growth of a farm in 18th-century America. After the land had been cleared, a cabin was built. Then water power was put to use, and a permanent house (right) was built.

INTRODUCTION

by Bruce Catton

We had our American Revolution nearly two centuries ago, and the years have done something to it. The legends remain, and the statues and the grassy earthworks and the great body of tradition, but a good deal of the reality has been filtered out. When we look back we see Washington crossing the Delaware on a cold winter night, or kneeling in prayer in the snow of Valley Forge; we see the Minuteman, or the lanky Virginia rifleman picturesque in fringed buckskin; but somehow it all seems to be out of a pageant, and neither Washington nor the men who followed him quite come alive for us.

This is a pity, because the central reality in this great act that brought a nation to its birth was the living, aspiring, struggling people who were immediately involved in it. A romantic haze has settled down over the whole affair, and when we look through it the facts tend to be a little blurred. And what is most worth remembering—the thing that so often escapes us—is the fact that like all of history's wars the war of the American Revolution was a hard, wearing, bloody, and tragic business—a struggle to the death that we came very close to losing.

It was a struggle, furthermore, that was fought out by people very much like ourselves; which is to say that they were often confused, usually divided in sentiment, and now and then rather badly discouraged about the possible outcome of the tremendous task they had undertaken. It comes as a shock to realize how many Americans in 1775 were actually opposed to independence and a break with King George III. A good many historians believe that no more than a third of the provincials were active patriots; and they estimate that another third were Loyalists, with the remaining third uncommitted. To continue with the arithmetic a little farther, it is clear that a good many of the people who believed in independence were not always eager to fight for it. When the war began the colonies contained about two and one-half million men, women, and children — a population which should have yielded some seven hundred thousand men capable of bearing arms. Yet in 1780, only one year before the crucial battle at Yorktown, the Continental Army and the state militia together contained no more than one-sixteenth of the country's available manpower.

But all of this says nothing more than that the people of the Revolutionary period were extremely human. Enough of them, in the end, were willing to fight and die for what they believed in to make the dream of independence and freedom come true, and we who look back at them owe them a debt whose size is almost beyond our comprehension. They did not have a very easy time of it, and if they got confused and discouraged now and then it is not to be wondered at.

For behind the great struggle with the professional armies of Great Britain there was the unending struggle between patriot and Loyalist, a civil war just as real and as bitter as the one which broke in 1861. And although the principal battles were decided along the eastern seaboard, the fighting on the frontiers, along the rim of American civilization, was, if anything, even more violent, and it continued in many areas long after the peace treaty with England was signed.

Furthermore, although the Revolution was a civil war it was also, after 1778, something very much like a world war as well. The fighting extended from the West Indies to India, and at times England itself was in as much danger of invasion as in the year of the Spanish Armada.

Sometimes it is hard to see how the Americans could have won if the Revolution had not turned into a world war—that is, if France had not intervened in the wake of the surrender of Burgoyne's army—and yet there was an unconquerable toughness at the core of the American effort. The farmers and shopkeepers of Massachusetts and Pennsylvania and South Carolina and the other colonies were hard men to beat, and they went quite a way on their own, without any help from anyone but themselves. They knew very little about European methods of warfare (and despite all of the tales about frontier riflemen fighting Indian-fashion from behind trees, most of the great Revolutionary battles *were* fought according to the European style) and they were poorly equipped, usually ill-fed, and almost constantly badly clothed; but fighting against the world's greatest power they managed not only to hold off disaster but usually to give a little better than they got.

Somewhere, in the course of more than six bitter years of warfare, those Americans worked something out. They began to see, amidst the monotony and discomfort and acute danger and suffering of constant campaigning, that they were somehow more than just the soldiers of the separate colonies. Somewhere, through their efforts—because of their efforts, because of what they learned while they were making the efforts—a nation was born. As South Carolina's Christopher Gadsden had urged before the fighting even started, they began to see that "There ought to be no more New England men, no New Yorkers . . . but all of us Americans!" That came, and finally independence came after it, as it had to come once the vision had truly taken hold.

This book is an attempt to give flesh and blood to the war that gave us our independence, to get back to the reality beneath the legend—not only in words, but also, as far as it is possible, through pictures drawn and painted by men who lived through those times. If it provides a clearer understanding of the Revolution—if it breathes a little life into the legend of the men who provided us with our freedom—it will have served its purpose.

At the end of the French and Indian War, American settlers streamed west in search of land. These pioneers are shown following Daniel Boone's trail through the Cumberland Gap.

Washington University; Courtesy *Time*

Paul Revere aroused Americans with this picture of the Boston Massacre. Actually, five men were killed, not seven as the legend states, and the rioters in front of the State House (center) were not the meek innocents Revere shows.

BEFORE THE WAR

"The Revolution was effected before the war commenced. The Revolution was in the minds and hearts of the people.... This radical change in the principles, opinions, sentiments, and affections of the people was the real American Revolution."

JOHN ADAMS—1818

In the middle of the eighteenth century, King George III and his ministers in London levied a series of unpopular taxes upon the Thirteen Colonies. Colonial opposition to these taxes was violent. And opposition only made the Crown more stern, more rigid. The differences between the colonists and the mother country might have been settled, but in the fall of 1768 an event occurred that virtually made war, still seven years away, a certainty.

In the last days of September, a large British fleet worked its way in from the sea past the low, green island of Boston Harbor. The decks of the ships were bright with scarlet uniforms. On October 1, 1768, anchors plunged into the harbor waters, and longboats put out from the sides of the vessels and rowed to the Long Wharf. There they landed files of British soldiers. Boston was being occupied by a British army as if it were a conquered, enemy city.

In 1768, a British fleet anchored in Boston Harbor "as for a regular Siege." Scarlet-clad troops landed on the Long Wharf for an "insolent parade" up King Street, as shown here in Paul Revere's engraving.

Du Pont Winterthur Museum; Courtesy *Life*

Colonial Williamsburg

King George III is shown in his coronation robes in this portrait painted by Allan Ramsay.

There were 4,000 redcoats in the occupying army. They had been sent by the British government as the result of earlier riots and disturbances. The tax acts had been unpopular throughout the colonies, but nowhere so unpopular as in Boston. There, rioting mobs had nearly taken Lieutenant Governor Thomas Hutchinson's mansion apart; they had stoned the houses of British colonial officials; they had dragged the official barge of the Customs Collector ashore, had paraded it through the streets, and, finally, had burned it. In England, the government decided to put an end to such demonstrations. And so it sent to Boston so many soldiers that there was nearly one redcoat to every four inhabitants.

It was the kind of action almost certain to make worse the very situation it was supposed to cure. Force usually leads to counter-force, tempers mount, violence breaks out. In Boston, the process began the first day. The colonial city did not have barracks for so many troops; therefore, the British commanders had to seize the quarters they needed. One regiment pitched its tents on the Common. Another forced entry into the town's prize meetingplace, Faneuil Hall, and still other soldiers were quartered in the State House itself. Even these measures did not provide housing for all the troops, and so individual soldiers were placed in the homes of citizens, who were given no choice about taking them in.

Such high-handed actions made the soldiers unpopular with the citizens of Boston from the start, and friction between the townsfolk and the military constantly increased. The British troops were badly paid, badly fed. Many hired out in their spare time for unskilled jobs at the lowest possible wages. This took work—and money—out of the hands of the laborers of Boston. A man made jobless by such unfair competition was an angry man, and fights broke out between the civilians and the soldiers.

There were other annoyances. Leading citizens of the town, on their way home from a

City of Boston Loan, Boston Museum of Fine Arts
Revolutionary leader Samuel Adams stirred up the colonists against the British by giving thundering speeches and commissioning broadsides and ballads.

night meeting or social gathering, were stopped on the streets and forced to explain their activities. Young officers sometimes raised the temperatures of Bostonians by marching bands past the churches, where they would whang and tootle away with massed drums and fifes during meeting time. Each side seemed to take childish delight in provoking the other, and it was inevitable that one final episode would lead to bloodshed.

The time came on the evening of March 5, 1770. In the year-and-a-half of the occupation,

Benjamin Franklin was brought before the Privy Council in London, in 1774, for releasing letters of Thomas Hutchinson, Royal Governor of Massachusetts, which hinted that "English liberties" were being restricted in America. Sam Adams had circulated them without Franklin's knowledge.

the pressures upon the British troops had mounted. Constant clashes with the townspeople had led the British command to send part of the original 4,000 troops to Halifax in Nova Scotia. The hope obviously was that, with fewer soldiers in town, there would be fewer fights. But actually, as long as any soldiers remained, quarrels were inevitable. The troops still in the city felt their weakness, and this feeling doubtless played its part in the tragic events of this early March night.

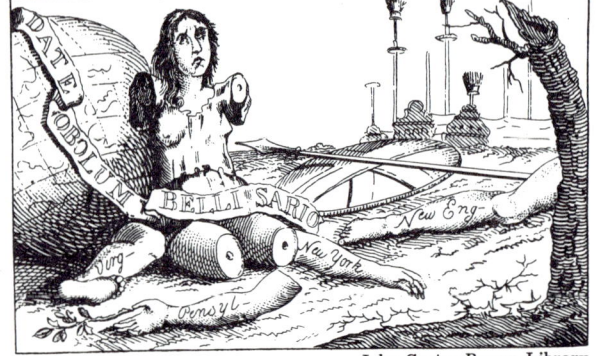

The trouble started when a group of small boys began to throw snowballs at a forlorn British sentry standing guard near the Custom House. Soon, they were joined by rowdies and port toughs. A squad of duty-troops swarmed out of the nearby barracks to help the guard. The mob, excited, pressed closer.

Captain Preston of the 29th British Regiment raced to the scene and ran up and down

Franklin drew this cartoon in 1767. It shows the plight of Britain, maimed by loss of her colonies.

the line of soldiers, trying to keep them under control. He shoved down muskets, pushed aside bayonets, shouted to his men not to fire—not to fire—not to *fire!*

The very repetition of the order probably undid its purpose. In the end, just one word—*fire!*—registered with the troops. A nervous finger tightened on a trigger. The first shot led to another and yet another. Before the ragged firing ended, five figures lay dead in the slush of King Street. Others had been wounded.

Still the mob and the soldiers faced each other. The war might have begun then and there, had it not been for Lieutenant Governor Thomas Hutchinson, who quickly forced his way through the crowd to the State House. He managed to quiet the angry throng, promising that the matter would be settled legally, in the courtroom. Slowly the crowd drifted off, carrying away its dead; the British soldiers returned to their barracks. And the "Boston Massacre" was history.

The whole affair might have been forgotten quickly except for one man, Samuel Adams. Samuel was a distant cousin of John Adams, the lawyer and solid citizen who was to become the second President of the United States. Many of the more staid citizens of the town looked down upon Sam Adams—and with some reason. Though he had been educated at Harvard, he was shabby in appearance, careless with money, and he had a bad head for business. He hated King George; he hated foreign tyranny. Quite early he had seen the possibilities in Boston's waterfront mobs and had organized them into a patriotic group known as the Sons of Liberty. He was a born revolutionist and propagandist, and the events of March 5 gave him a golden opportunity.

Under Sam Adams' skillful juggling, the firing on the crowd in King Street became a deliberate massacre. The port toughs became noble martyrs who had been shot down in cold blood by hireling, foreign troops. Sam Adams saw to it that speech after speech was

The Boston Massacre occurred in front of the old State House, at center in this painting. At right, behind the carriage, is the British Coffee House, a favorite with English officers.

Massachusetts Historical Society

made on the theme. He turned out broadsides and ballads. He created such a popular uproar that he forced the removal of two regiments from the city to lonely Castle William in Boston Harbor. By such tactics, he turned the shooting of March 5 into a grim anniversary, marked each year by solemn ceremonies that insured the public would not forget.

Throughout the other colonies, Sam Adams' version of the Boston Massacre was the one that reached the public. Sam was a principal figure in the Committees of Correspondence, set up by patriot leaders to keep in touch with each other, and he made certain that the news from Boston was spread in such a manner as to arouse public anger and stir the spirit of revolt. The public temper that resulted led, before long, to a second act of violence.

In June, 1772, His Majesty's armed schooner *Gaspée* was chasing smugglers at night through the waters of Rhode Island's Narragansett Bay. The smugglers knew the channels better than the officers of the *Gaspée* did, and the revenue cutter ran aground.

Abraham Whipple, a leading seaman and merchant in Providence, raised several boatloads of volunteers and rowed down the bay to the spot where the *Gaspée* was stranded. Stealing up quietly out of the night, the Rhode Islanders swarmed over the low sides of the schooner and set her afire.

The Boston Massacre and the burning of the *Gaspée* were two incidents in a chain-reaction of violence that now approached its climax. In London, the British ministry decided to help the financially hard-hit East India Company by imposing a tax on tea. The company was to be given a monopoly of the tea trade with the American colonies. The price was so carefully rigged that, even with the tax, the Americans would pay less for the East India Company's tea than for the tea being smuggled into the colonies from other sources.

Because of this cheaper price, the British expected no difficulty, but they had overlooked a couple of important facts. First, Americans hated monopolies. Second, the agents appointed to handle the tea shipments in the colonies were all either relatives of colonial governors or governmental favorites. Again, Sam Adams went into action, pointing out that a tax on tea was still a tax, and that the whole arrangement would benefit a privileged inner circle. Soon, throughout the colonies, public opinion hardened into one clear resolve: the tea should not be sold.

Rhode Island seamen pull away from the grounded British revenue cutter Gaspée, *which they have set on fire. This action, in 1772, was one of the most daring and war-like in the period just before the Revolution.*

Rhode Island Historical Society

Patriots dressed as Indians dumped chests of tea into the Boston harbor while crowds cheered on the wharf. The Boston Tea Party shocked England and cost the colonies some of their best friends.

In all the ports to which the tea was shipped there was trouble, but nowhere was there the kind of trouble that Sam Adams stirred up in Boston. There, three tea ships sailed into the harbor, ready to land their cargoes. On the night of December 16, 1773, some 150 Boston patriots, many wearing Indian head-dresses, with faces blackened, boarded the ships. They brushed aside the members of the crews who were inclined to resist. Surprisingly, the patriots were helped by others, and in a few swift minutes, they seized 342 chests of tea and dumped them into the harbor.

The action produced an "electrical shock" of giant proportions in England. None of the previous incidents had so united British opinion against the colonists. One Englishman stated flatly that this was "the most wanton and unprovoked insult offered to the civil power that is recorded in history." And the British government acted with a harshness that made war inevitable.

It passed the Boston Port Bill. The effect was to close the port of Boston to all trade. Even the shortest ferry-run could not be made across the harbor. Supplies for the city had to be shipped to such neighboring ports as Salem and Marblehead, then transported by wagon across the narrow neck that linked Boston with the mainland. To make certain that this stern measure was enforced, additional regiments of infantry were poured into the city, and the Royal Navy closed off the harbor. Boston was faced with ruin and starvation. The city was to suffer until its citizens had paid for all the tea dumped into the harbor—plus duties that would have been received by His Majesty's Customs had the tea been landed and sold.

Boston had no intention of paying. It set itself to endure. And Sam Adams spread the story of the city's plight through the colonies.

Anger swept the Atlantic seaboard. Every port city—New York, Philadelphia, Baltimore, Williamsburg, Charleston—could see itself as another Boston, cut off from trade, strangled at the whim of a foreign ministry. In an effort to help Boston, Charleston sent money and rice; from New York and Connecticut, convoys of sheep wound overland. The British Crown, by its harshness, had united the colonists in a common cause. The revolution that moderate men had hoped would never come was being born, in John Adams' phrase, "in the minds and hearts of the people."

Collection of Gilbert Darlington

The spirit of revolt spread from Boston through all the colonies. This painting shows patriots in 1776 pulling down the statue of George III in New York.

THE WAR BEGINS

"I cannot but lament . . . the impending Calamities Britain and her Colonies are about to suffer . . . Passion governs and she never governs wisely. . ."

BENJAMIN FRANKLIN—February 5, 1775

Boston was now an armed camp. General Thomas Gage, the British commander, ruled a city in which hundreds, perhaps thousands, had been thrown out of work by the Port Bill. Hardship made men bitter, and the Boston Sons of Liberty kept the printing presses busy turning out leaflets ever more violent in tone. Surprisingly, Gage ignored them. Perhaps he counted on the Port Bill to starve the city into submission. If so, he was mistaken.

For Boston was being fed by supplies smuggled in at night from the surrounding countryside. And in that countryside, the example of Boston was proving all that was needed to call men to arms. An army was being formed—an army of volunteers.

In Waltham, in Dedham, in all the little towns ringing Boston, farmers and villagers began to drill in the fields. Gage's younger officers, leading their troops on mild route marches across Boston Neck and through the buzzing countryside, laughed at the drilling yokels. But others saw the determined purpose behind the clumsiness; here was an army of colonials actively forming to resist the army of the Crown—something that had never happened before.

With force gathering to meet force, an explosion was bound to come. It almost happened in September, 1774, when one of Gage's routine marches suddenly turned serious. A few scarlet-coated companies, swinging into Cambridge across the Charles River from Boston, seized powder and arms belonging to the Province. They went on to Charlestown, grabbed more supplies and returned to Boston.

This little success was, in the end, a costly one for the British. The raid had shown up the weakness of the Province, and the patriots were determined to be better prepared in the future. The Provincial Congress, meeting illegally in Cambridge, set up a Committee of Safety headed by John Hancock, the wealthy Boston merchant. The committee was given the power to call out the entire militia of the colony, and special groups were formed in each militia unit—men who could be counted on to spring to arms at a minute's notice. So the Minutemen were born.

During the winter of 1774–75, the battle lines on both sides were drawn. John Hancock's Committee of Safety voted that "all kinds of warlike stores be purchased sufficient for an army of fifteen thousand men." The supplies were to be stored in the village of Concord, deep in the countryside beyond the normal reach of Gage. With spring, however, the British commander increased the size of his marching units and sent them out farther from Boston. On one occasion young Lord Percy led a full brigade through Watertown and Cambridge, and the Provincial Congress, meeting in Concord, took counter-action. It ordered that, whenever as many as 500 troops should march out of Boston, "an Army of Observation" should be immediately formed "to act *solely on the defensive* so long as it can be justified on the Principles of Reason and Self-Preservation and *no longer.*"

17

General Thomas Gage was commander of the British forces in America when the war broke out.

Collection of R. V. C. Bodley

Those defiant words meant war.

It was not long in coming. On April 15, 1775, Dr. Joseph Warren and other patriot leaders in Boston learned that Gage was preparing to send his grenadier and light infantry companies, some 700 men, on some mysterious extra maneuver. Why? For what purpose? The patriot leaders could only guess, but they guessed shrewdly.

Sam Adams and John Hancock were in Lexington, lodging with the Reverend Jonas Clarke. Lexington was close to Concord, where the Provincial Congress was meeting, and where arms were stored. Did Gage hope to arrest the two patriot leaders and seize the stores in one swoop? It seemed likely, and so the patriots in Boston sent a warning.

Their messenger was a remarkable man—Paul Revere. Revere was an expert in many crafts. Chiefly a silversmith, he was also a volunteer militiaman, a dentist, engraver, car-

Paul Revere, an expert silversmith, is shown at his workshop bench in this 1765 portrait by Copley.

toonist, goldsmith, inventor, and, above all, a trusted express rider for Sam Adams' Sons of Liberty. Revere had carried many messages for Sam Adams, but none as important as the one he carried now. He warned Lexington that Gage was about to move, and Lexington passed the word to Concord, where villagers labored night and day packing the hidden stores and moving them out of reach. As for Paul Revere, he returned to Boston to wait for the British march to begin.

The alarm came on the night of April 18. Revere was asleep in his house on the North Square when patriot messengers aroused him, spirited him past British guardposts, and rowed him across the Charles, almost under the stern of H.M.S. *Somerset,* swinging slowly in the tide. In Boston, two lanterns glowed from the spire of Old North Church—the signal agreed upon that the British were out and that

Boston Museum of Fine Arts; Courtesy *Time*

18

they would move by water across the Charles, not by land across Boston Neck.

A horse was waiting on the Cambridge shore, and Revere mounted and galloped inland. As he rode through the night, he spread the alarm. Reaching Lexington, he warned Adams and Hancock, then rode for Concord. Halfway there, he was captured by a mounted British patrol, part of a thin screen Gage had flung out to the north to stop just such messengers as Revere on just such missions. Revere was held prisoner only a short time, but his night's work was done. The word he had carried "to every Middlesex village and farm" spread in all directions. The countryside was coming angrily alive.

The British, not yet aware that the alarm had been given, moved slowly and sluggishly from the south. The command of the expedition had been given to fat, slow-witted Colonel Francis Smith of the 10th Lincolnshires. The troops were ferried across the Charles, were landed in knee-deep water, were kept standing for two bone-chilling hours. Then, finally, the march began. Near Lexington, the marching troops caught dim glimpses of armed men hurrying across the dark fields on either side, and officers sent back word that a Rebel force was massing near the town. Even Colonel Smith sensed that he might be in for trouble, and he got off a message to Boston, asking for reinforcements.

This done, the British pressed forward. Their advance unit was led by Major John Pitcairn,

One of the lanterns which were hung in the spire of Boston's Old North Church

of the Royal Marines, one of the most capable and respected of the British officers, and Smith's second in command. Day was just breaking, clear and warm, with apple blossoms a misty white in the roadside orchards, when Pitcairn and his men wound down the curving hill past Munroe's Tavern into Lexington.

Two companies, the Minute and the Alarm, had been drawn up to receive them near Lexington Green. Lexington's Captain John Parker took stock of the situation, saw that he was heavily outnumbered, and started to disperse his men. Major Pitcairn, who had orders to disarm quietly any militia encountered, swung his troops from column into line and ordered them "on no account to Fire or even attempt it without orders."

But, as before at the Boston Massacre, the tension was too much. Someone fired.

Concord Antiquarian Society

Map showing route of Paul Revere's famous midnight ride

This engraving, made by Amos Doolittle, a Connecticut militiaman, captures crudely but accurately the action at Lexington Green. The militia is shown fleeing after a volley from British Major Pitcairn's advance guard.

Pitcairn's own report suggested that the first shot came from an American straggler near the edge of the Green. Whoever fired, that one shot was all that was needed to start a war. Several British volleys crashed out in response. Powder smoke coiled heavily across the Green. Possessed by battle fury, the British regulars broke ranks, charged with the bayonet, and only with difficulty were bullied back into line. The Americans fled, Colonel Smith came up with the main body, and the British pressed on for Concord. They had no casualties. But behind them on the Green, they left eight American dead—the first victims of a long, long war.

In Concord, some hundred-odd militiamen had waited through the dark early-morning hours. When word came of the fighting at Lexington, they set out to meet the British, fifes and drums at their head. From the brow of a low hill, they caught sight of the British force, realized it was too big for them to fight, and so turned around and marched back again —almost like an escort of honor for the regulars coming along the road some hundred rods behind them. Minuteman Amos Barrett later recalled this pageant-like return to Concord: "we . . . marchd before them with our Droms and fifes agoing . . . we had grand musick."

The militia retreated through the town of Concord, crossed the Concord River and went

These are the pistols Major Pitcairn lost in the British retreat from Concord.

on to the high muster ground beyond. Smith and Pitcairn occupied the town without a shot having been fired and sent out men to search for the Rebel stores. Three companies of light infantry were left to hold the North Bridge. Beyond the bridge, on the high ground, the militia were being reinforced by volunteers from neighboring towns. As they gathered, someone saw smoke rising beyond the trees, and the rumor spread (a false one, as it turned out) that Concord was being put to the torch. The militia, headed by Captain Isaac Davis of Acton, started down the hill toward the bridge.

This time there was no question about who fired first. The British light infantry touched off several ragged volleys. One of the first musket balls killed Captain Davis. His men fanned out, took cover, and opened up a hot fire on the British troops. These British soldiers were veterans, hardened fighters, but few officers were with them to keep them fighting. They broke and fled back into Concord.

The militia made no attempt to pursue. They simply went on to a hill overlooking the town and waited—and wondered. Colonel Smith brought his scattered forces together, delayed until some time after noon, and then, too late, headed back on the road to Lexington. The hours he had lost had given militia companies from distant towns time to join up. Still, nothing happened. There was no firing.

Then, at a bridge near the junction of the Bedford and Lexington Roads, the last files of the British wheeled about, probably without orders, and fired a farewell volley. Thus began the real fight of the nineteenth of April, 1775.

From path and road and field, the militia closed in on the British column. They fired from behind stone walls, houses, woodpiles, and sheds. Men ran out of ammunition and went home. Men were killed. Others were frightened by whistling bullets and gave up the fight. But more men, more companies, kept arriving, so that the British marched through "a Veritable Furnass of Musquetry." The British tried to stand, but Colonel Smith was

Another of Amos Doolittle's engravings shows Colonel Smith and Major Pitcairn studying the countryside from a Concord cemetery while their regiments march into town.

Connecticut Historical Society; Courtesy Life

Amos Doolittle shows the militiamen (at left) firing on the British at North Bridge, beyond Concord. This began the British retreat through a hostile countryside to Lexington.

wounded, and Pitcairn lost his horse and pistols. The retreat became a rout, with red-coated veterans throwing away arms and equipment as they ran.

The militia closed in tighter and tighter. Disaster loomed. Then, just beyond Lexington Green, the panic-stricken British troops caught sight of a relief column led by Lord Percy. The two forces joined, and the entire body, now some 2,000 strong, resumed the retreat. Every step of the way, the British were badgered by the swarming militia with whom the regulars could not come to grips. Through town after town, the retreating column was hounded relentlessly until finally it flung itself down panting and spent on the little hills above Charlestown, safe at last under the guns of the Royal Navy.

Gage's official report listed only 73 killed and 174 wounded. This meant that only one out of every 300 American bullets had found its target. As for the patriots, they had lost 49 killed and 41 wounded. But the significance of Lexington and Concord was not to be found in any toll of dead and wounded. The significance lay in the simple fact that rank amateurs—townsmen, professional men, farmers—had stood up and fought veteran troops and seen them run. They had answered a call and risked their lives because they deeply believed in a cause. And because they had, an old order died, and this day of the nineteenth of April, 1775, marked a turning point in the life of an entire continent.

The spirit of the day was perhaps best expressed by the glow of campfires that ringed the British army on Charlestown heights on this night of April 19. For the men who had chased the British through the countryside were not finished. They stayed, watching and guarding the foe. Many, it is true, quit and went home at the end of the day's adventure, but hundreds more came and took their places. They made an army.

In the days that followed, while express riders galloped furiously to the south with the news of Lexington and Concord, a rough organization was set up. Artemas Ward, senior

This cartoon shows British soldiers looting and setting fire to houses on the retreat to Boston.

General of the Massachusetts Army, was given command of the forces ringing Boston. Companies came in from New Hampshire and Connecticut and Rhode Island. Despite local jealousies, they put themselves under Ward's command, and, by this act, they formed for the first time, not a Massachusetts army, but a New England army. And all the time General Gage, sitting quietly in Boston, made no move to interfere, thus allowing the Rebels to strengthen and unite.

Throughout the colonies, wherever the news of fighting spread, men were on the march. Less than a month after Lexington and Concord, in the early hours of May 10, 1775, a wild, yelling rush of men poured into Fort Ticonderoga at the narrow south end of Lake Champlain. Captain De la Place and a skimpy garrison, holding the fort for the Crown, were roused from sleep and bundled off, prisoners of war.

The surprise blow had been struck by two ill-matched commanders, each jealous of the

John Carter Brown Library

other. One was tall, swaggering Ethan Allen, born in Connecticut but lately a resident of the Hampshire grants, now Vermont. The other was the highly ambitious Colonel Benedict Arnold, a Connecticut officer who had come west with troops supplied by Massachusetts. Allen, who had been given authority

Doolittle shows the retreat, with Minutemen firing at the British from behind stone walls.
Albany Institute of History and Art

23

Joseph Dixon Crucible Co.

Henry Knox's heroic feat in hauling 59 heavy cannon from Fort Ticonderoga to Boston is shown in the above painting. These views of the Rebel lines circling Boston (below) were sketched from Beacon Hill by a

24

by Connecticut, and Arnold, who held command in Massachusetts, had seized a fort in New York. As the legal-minded tried to figure out to whom the captured fort should belong, new events were taking shape near Boston.

Two masses of high ground commanded Boston—the heights of Dorchester and Roxbury to the southwest, and those of Charlestown on the north just across the Charles River. Military sense called for the placing of guns on the southern heights, from which artillery could sweep the narrow Neck linking the city to the mainland and bombard the waterfront. The American commanders considered the two choices and decided to occupy first the low twin hills in Charlestown, where farmers named Breed and Bunker grazed their cattle.

The decision risked terrible disaster. Charlestown Peninsula, shaped much like Boston itself, was a fat polliwog swelling out into the water. It was tied to the shore by a long narrow tail, often overflowed by the Mystic River on one side, the Charles on the other. A garrison on the exposed peninsula could be cut off easily by landing parties from the King's ships in the harbor, there for just that purpose.

Despite this, on the evening of June 16, a force of patriots was sent out from Cambridge to dig in on the Charlestown hills. Bad planning marked the project from the start. No steps were taken to relieve or back up the troops; no food or water was sent with them; and, worst of all, they had no ammunition reserve in case the British tried to interfere.

These oversights were bad enough, but error was added to them. Artemas Ward had ordered his men to fortify Bunker's Hill, the higher peak, but instead they went on to Breed's Hill, closer to the water, closer to the guns of the Royal Navy, closer to the beaches where hostile troops might land.

All night the patriots dug, and by dawn an earthwork redoubt circled the top of Breed's Hill. A smaller earthwork and a rail fence ran down the left side of the hill to the Mystic River. Sunrise showed the British in Boston what had taken place overnight. Where there had been a green, unpeopled knob, there was now fresh-turned earth, swarming with furiously digging men. The British stared in surprise—and stirred themselves to act.

Now they, too, made errors. Though the narrow Charlestown Neck behind the hills could easily be cut and the whole lot of Rebels bagged, pride demanded a direct attack in front. The guns of the fleet opened up, and round shot went darting and skittering among the still-laboring men on Breed's Hill. Nothing usually scares green troops as much as artillery fire, but these troops did not scare.

The June morning wore on. Along the Boston waterfront barges and longboats filled with scarlet-clad regulars. Drums pounded, fifes shrilled, and a floating pageant lurched out across the Charles River, oars splashing in the sun. The warships in the river stepped up their fire, the barges grounded, and the troops swarmed ashore on the Charlestown beaches.

British officer. Dorchester Heights is visible in the first panel at left. The large house in the second section is John Hancock's. Bunker's and Breed's hills rise to the right of the steeple in the fourth panel.

Massachusetts Historical Society

Sir William Howe, commanding the landing force, studied the slope ahead of him. He noted its tangle of rail fences, the clumps of blackberry and blueberry bushes—and at the crest, the bristling, strangely quiet main redoubt. He realized that perhaps his job wouldn't be so easy after all, and he sent back for more men. They reached him quickly. Among the new troops was Major John Pitcairn, heading a detachment of Royal Marines on what was to be his last assignment.

The mass of men on the beaches shifted, shuffled—and the assault started. Long scarlet and white lines, three deep, climbed up the slope of the hill. The June sun beat down on troops carrying unwieldy 125-pound loads, including three days' rations and blankets.

On Breed's Hill, the raw American troops faced alone this menacing advance by the best soldiers of the day. Those untried patriots must have felt sheer terror. But they had strong leaders. Colonel William Prescott and Dr.

26

Final action at Breed's Hill is shown in John Trumbull's painting. The leading patriot, Dr. Joseph Warren, was a major casualty. Major Pitcairn (center) is carried from the field mortally wounded.

Yale University Art Gallery; Courtesy *World Book Encyclopedia,*
©Field Enterprises Educational Corp.

Joseph Warren were calm and inspiring men. So were Thomas Knowlton and John Stark, heading their Connecticut and New Hampshire troops along the down-hill line behind the rail fence. One might have expected the patriots to loose one ragged volley and flee. But these men were determined. A gray-haired farmer prayed aloud, thanking the Lord he had been spared to fight this day. And he and his fellows waited as the redcoats came closer and closer, until faces could be distinguished, and little details stood out, like the brass matchboxes on the chests of the grenadiers.

No one knows who gave the order to fire. Only one thing is certain: the British were less than fifteen paces from the lines, bayonet points sharp in the sun, when one ripping volley was poured into their faces. Bearskin caps flew into the air; bright uniforms were strewn over the trampled green of the grass. And the patriots, peering above earthworks and the rail fence, watched in disbelief as the British ranks were shattered, swept away, and sent pounding back down the hill.

On the beaches, the British reformed. On they came again, marching up that deadly slope with measured step, toward the waiting muskets. Again a blaze of fire came out to meet them; again the smart ranks were shredded, driven back in bloody wreckage and defeat. The slopes of Breed's Hill were littered with scarlet and white forms, unmoving in the bright sun.

On the hill, the Americans watched the thinned-out companies form again, and wondered if any troops could rally after two such murderous smashings. The answer came quickly. Drums beat once more. Wounded officers, some with arms in slings, or heads bandaged, sang out their orders, grimly ignoring the fact, as one wrote, that "Some had only eight or nine men a Company left; some only three, four or five." But they formed, what was left of them, and started up the hill again.

Behind the defenses, nervous and exhausted men waited for them. These were men who had marched and dug all night, who had driven back two fierce attacks, and who now were at the end of their resources. They felt their cartridge boxes. Four rounds left? No, only two. In some cases none at all. And they did not have bayonets.

27

Still they stood their ground. And still the British came on through the smoky dusk, faces set, breath sobbing in their throats. Again, a deadly sheet of flame, weaker this time, swept out from the rim of the redoubt. A second ragged blast followed. Then silence. Grenadiers, light infantry, line companies—all with their bayonets eager—were over the earthworks and in among the defenders, clubbing and stabbing.

A massacre seemed certain. But those raw defenders of Breed's Hill did not panic. They fought stubbornly with clubbed guns, drew off slowly, and made an orderly retreat—first to nearby Bunker's Hill, black with men so poorly armed they had taken no part in the battle, and then across the narrow Charlestown Neck to the safe mainland beyond.

So General William Howe had won an almost useless peninsula at horrible cost. Out of some 2,300 British troops who had been thrown into the three attacks, nearly half—a shocking 1,054—were dead or wounded. This terrible slaughter left an indelible mark on the minds of British commanders. No officer who witnessed it would ever blot it from memory. No officer who witnessed it would ever again want to send his men against entrenched, prepared Rebel troops.

As for Artemas Ward's men, they had lost some 500 killed and wounded, most of them in that last wild rush when they were out of ammunition. Among the dead was the much-loved Dr. Joseph Warren. For both sides, June 17, 1775, was a crucial day. The British, in winning, had suffered a tremendous shock, and the Americans, in losing, had emerged with renewed determination—a spirit that was to be strengthened by an even greater event that had just taken place in far-off Philadelphia.

There the Second Continental Congress was in session. It had before it an appeal from Massachusetts to adopt the New England army blockading Boston as an *American* army and to set up a civil government to handle all the affairs of the colonies. The suggestion was debated, and, in the end, it was John Adams who pointed the way. He urged the Congress not only to create a "Grand American Army," but to appoint a Virginian to command it—George Washington. Congress approved and on June 16, 1775—the day before the Battle of Breed's Hill—Washington was named commander-in-chief of the Continental Army.

Sixteen days later, on the rain-soaked Sunday of July 2, 1775, Washington rode into camp at Cambridge to take over the command from Artemas Ward. In the weeks that followed, the first American army began to take shape under his guiding hand. All this time, Gage sat quietly in Boston doing nothing, just as he had sat quietly doing nothing after Lexington and Concord. Perhaps he—and Howe, who succeeded him in October—hoped that the blockading army would just get tired of it all and go away. And so the British, though they had a powerful army of some 10,000 men, contented themselves with firing occasional cannon shots at the American lines, and now and then undertaking a raid or skirmish.

While the British held back from putting heavy pressure on poorly organized patriot forces, lights burned late in Washington's headquarters. The problems that flowed across his desk were tremendous. Most serious was the fact that nearly his whole army had enlisted for only eight months. By the end of the year, these enlistments would all expire, and there would be no army, unless Washington could keep the men in the ranks or enlist new men to take their places. He and his officers persuaded a large number of the veterans to stay. Short-term militia were called to the lines to fill the places of those who left. Recruiting officers beat their drums in distant towns and hamlets. By these means—and thanks to the inactivity of Howe—an army was kept together, and the period of greatest danger passed.

Washington immediately sought a way to drive the British out of Boston. If only he had

In this engraving of the Battle of Breed's Hill, Boston is at right; Charlestown, at center, is afire from the British cannonade. At left, the Rebel line breaks a British thrust.

artillery, he could place heavy guns on Dorchester Heights and shell the redcoats out. But where was he to get such cannon? There was only one source—the guns that Ethan Allen and Benedict Arnold had seized in Fort Ticonderoga on Lake Champlain. Henry Knox, a bookseller who had taught himself engineering and artillery, volunteered to go west and see what could be done.

Knox faced a stupendous task. Cannon that weighed tons had to be dragged through the ice and snow, across mountains, through an almost roadless wilderness, from Lake Champlain to eastern Massachusetts.

From dawn to sunset, day in and day out, Knox and his men labored to haul the heavy guns across the Taconics, along the very edge of the Berkshire Hills, and on into Great Barrington in Massachusetts. It was a masterful feat. From Framingham, Knox finally wrote to Washington that he had arrived with 59 pieces of ordnance—a "noble train of artillery."

Knox's feat decided the fate of Boston. Washington acted swiftly and on the morning of March 5, 1776, the crests of Dorchester Heights, bare at sundown, were crowned with works and heavy guns. With those guns in place, the British could not hold the city.

Howe made one weak attempt at a breakout. He massed his men for an attack on the heights, but a terrific storm swept up the bay and battered his landing craft. Abandoning his plans, he loaded his garrison into the ships of his fleet and sailed away. On March 17, the Americans poured into the city.

The next day, Washington entered Boston and attended divine worship, the first to be held under the new flag of the colonies—thirteen red and white stripes with the Union Jack in the canton. As he listened to the sermon he must have worried about the future. For Howe's flotilla was still visible off Nantasket Roads, and Washington must have wondered where its menacing sails would next be sighted.

General Montgomery dying in the arms of his soldiers at Quebec. This painting by Trumbull captures the spirit of the desperate Rebel assault.

FIRST CAMPAIGNS

"The Sun never shined on a cause of greater worth. 'Tis not the affair of a City, a County, a Province, or a Kingdom; but of a Continent—of at least one eighth part of the habitable Globe."

THOMAS PAINE, January, 1776

The cause which Thomas Paine described so eloquently was spreading far indeed from the immediate area of Boston, where the Revolution had started. Truly, it was "not the affair of a City, a County, a Province," for in the fall of 1775 the conflict that had begun at Lexington and Concord was stretching far to the north into Canada and was soon to spread far south into the Carolinas.

The northern front was the one that first drew the attention of the rebelling colonists. Canada was a huge land that, they knew, could be of great importance to their cause. When the French still held Canada, it had been a vast enemy fortress from which Indian war parties had been sent to raid the frontier. If the British were to keep Canada, the same thing could happen again. But if Canada could be conquered—or if its people could be persuaded to join the rebelling colonies—this threat would be wiped out. The British would lose a valuable base.

And so, quite early, the Continental Congress sent to General Philip Schuyler, who com-

This 1758 print of Quebec shows the government buildings and the churches of the Upper Town and, below them, the steep slopes to the Lower Town, where the Americans made their attack.

Stokes Collection, N.Y. Public Library

Arnold began his march to Quebec with 1,100 men. About half of them, sick and nearly starved, conquered the rapids, swamps, and the numbing cold. The 350-mile march took six weeks.

manded the American forces in the north, a strange letter. It urged Schuyler to invade Canada "if [he] finds it practicable, and that it will not be disagreeable to the Canadians." Always there was that half-expressed hope that the invasion would not really be an invasion, that perhaps the Canadians would welcome it.

Schuyler held command in a vital area. An ideal water route stretches south from the St. Lawrence River clear to New York City—a chain of lakes and rivers: the Richelieu River, Lake Champlain, Lake George and the Hudson River. In a day when there were no roads through the wilderness, such connecting bodies of water were perfect for the movement of troops, heavy guns and supplies. If the British could drive all the way south from Canada, they could split New England from the other colonies. But if the Americans could beat the British to the punch, they could use the same waterways to invade Canada.

This was the early hope. Schuyler's headquarters had hardly received the half-order for invasion when a warning came that the British were planning to move. Sir Guy Carleton, the British commander in Canada, was building some good-sized ships at the northern end of Lake Champlain. Obviously, the vessels were intended to carry Carleton's troops and supplies in an invasion of New York State.

Map at right shows routes of the two American invasion forces that met at Quebec in December, 1775.

General Richard Montgomery, Schuyler's second in command, acted promptly to meet the threat. Montgomery was probably one of the ablest of the American generals. He was the son of a British baronet, he had been a member of Parliament, and he had served in the British army, acquiring the professional military training that so many American leaders lacked. A vigorous officer, he now rounded up all the available troops and started north up the chain of lakes.

Schuyler joined him, and the little army made a landing along the Richelieu River, the northern water exit from Lake Champlain. Everything went wrong. Guns and supply wagons had to be dragged through forests, through swamps, across ledges. Schuyler's health, always delicate, broke under the hardships, and the full command fell to Montgomery. Some of the poorly trained American officers argued and haggled over his orders instead of obeying them. Supplies ran short. Torrential rains fell.

To all these trials and hardships was added a stubborn British resistance. Carleton had constructed a fort at St. John's to block the Americans' path across the relatively narrow stretch of ground to Montreal. The fort was garrisoned by Royal troops, an artillery detail, and Canadian militia. Montgomery's attacking force was too weak to carry the works by assault, so the Americans had to sit down to a long and tiresome siege. Montgomery had hoped to carry the fort in five days, but instead it held out until November 2, 1775—two long months.

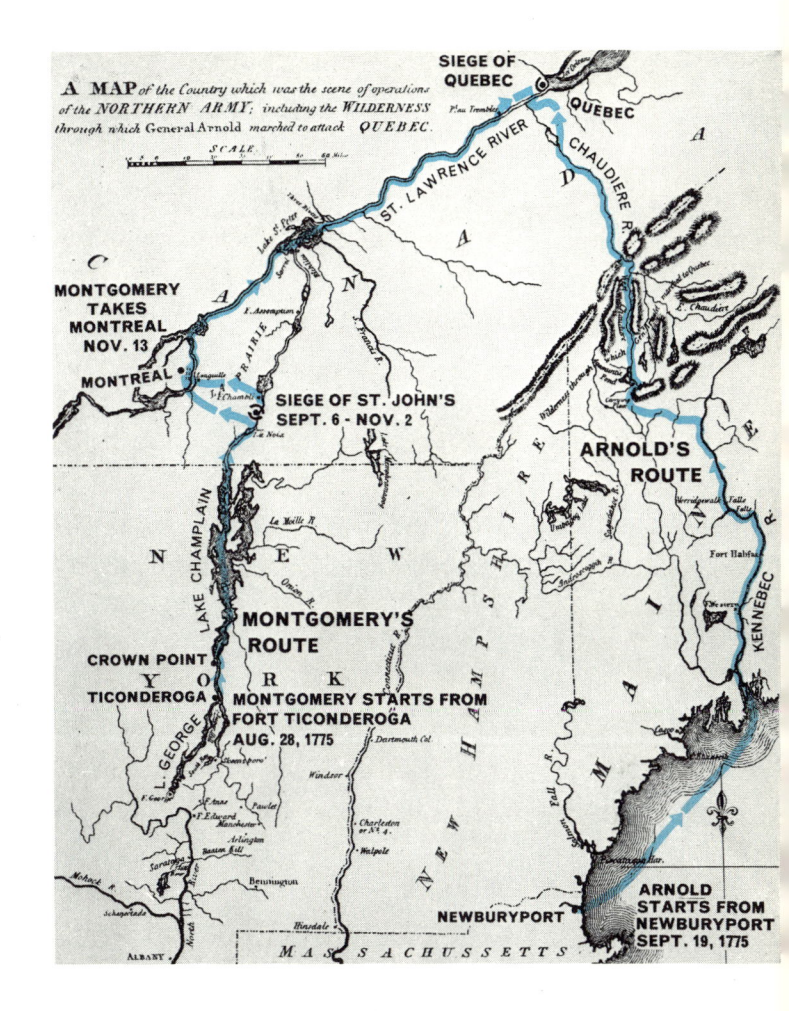

The delay was all-important. Montgomery now faced the prospect of invading Canada in the worst season of the year, the frigid northern winter. A lesser man might have given up the whole project, but Montgomery re-equipped his tattered troops with supplies

American attack on Quebec (left) was cloaked by a "thick small snow" driven by "outrageous winds."

33

While this contemporary print is not strictly accurate in detail, it does show the steep, rocky trail around Cape Diamond (left) that Montgomery's men followed until they were halted by a blast of cannon fire.

taken at St. John's, and on November 5 moved out along the ragged corduroy road that led to the St. Lawrence and Montreal. As one of the weary soldiers later recalled: "Under our Feet was Snow and Ice and Water, over our Heads Clouds Snow and rain, before us the mountains appeared all white with Snow and Ice." But they pressed on "to new Sieges and new Conquests."

Montreal fell to the Americans on November 13, but the biggest prize in the city was missed —Sir Guy Carleton. One of the ablest of the British generals, Carleton was the brains and soul of British resistance in Canada. He escaped by boat, virtually alone, and reached Quebec, a fortress city built on high cliffs above the St. Lawrence. There he prepared to meet the American invaders.

Montgomery had so few troops that he could never have attempted an attack against such a stronghold as Quebec. But a second force—sent out by Washington from his headquarters outside Boston—was about to join him. The commander-in-chief had studied the maps and had noted what seemed like a good invasion route up Maine's Kennebec River, across land to the Dead River, up this to the Height of Land on the Canadian border, and then down the Chaudière River to its mouth, almost opposite Quebec.

Some 1,100 men were assembled for this expedition, and the command was given to the restless, ambitious Benedict Arnold. With Arnold went some of the best soldiers and officers in the army—such men as the huge Captain Daniel Morgan, commanding his Virginia and Pennsylvania riflemen, and Lieutenant Colonel Christopher Greene, a cousin of General Nathanael Greene.

The invasion that had looked so easy on the map was ill-starred from the beginning. The start from Cambridge was delayed until Sep-

Map at right shows the positions and tactics of the two fleets during the Battle of Valcour Island.

tember 13, a date dangerously late to begin moving an army through the Maine wilderness. The bateaux, the flat-bottomed boats made to carry troops and supplies along the rivers, had been built of green wood and flung together so hastily that they leaked and began to fall to pieces. The rivers that had looked like highways on the map were filled with fierce rapids. Boats were smashed, supplies lost. Then winter came.

When Arnold checked his bearings, deep in the remote Maine wilds, he found that he had already spent double the time estimated for the whole trip, he had used up more than half his provisions—and he was not even close to Canada. Men began boiling rawhide and eating it. At Dead River on October 15, Colonel

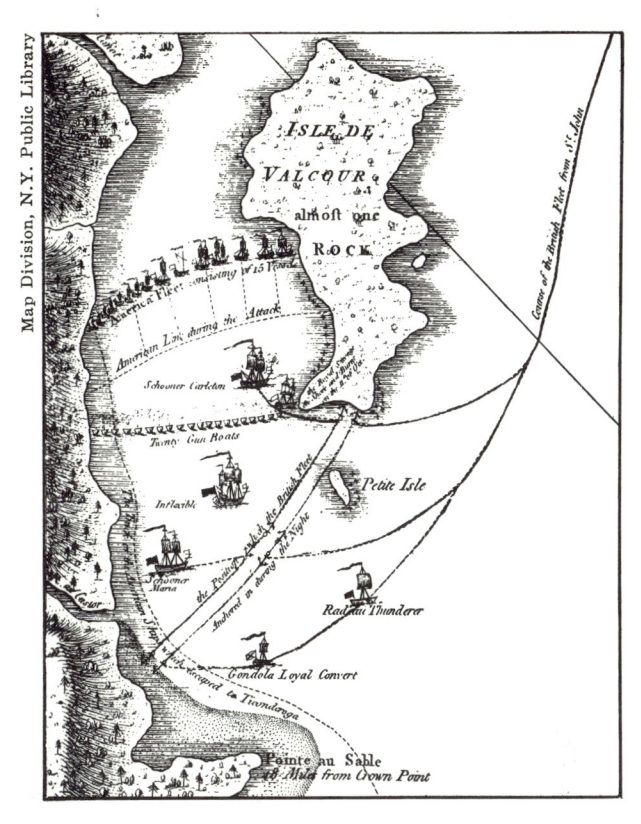

"Commander Arnold" is the central figure in the water color below. Bottom panel shows the ships with which he tried to block the British advance in the Battle of Valcour Island.

Greene's command supped on candles, stewed into a kind of water-gruel. Here, too, a Connecticut division rebelled at the hardships, quit, and went back home. But Arnold, a fierce, driving leader, and the rest of his men, a determined band, pressed on.

There was snow at the Great Carrying Place over the Height of Land, and men weak with hunger staggered under the load of the few remaining bateaux. Private George Morrison of the Pennsylvania Rifles wrote afterward that men fell from sheer exhaustion. If a man tried to help a fallen comrade, he lost his footing. "At length the wretches raise themselves up . . . wade through the mire to the foot of the next steep and gaze up at its summit, contemplating what they must suffer before they reach it," Morrison wrote. "They attempt it, catching at every twig and shrub they can lay hold of—their feet fly from them—they fall down—to rise no more."

Still the survivors staggered on, and on November 8, little more than skeletons, they pushed down the last stretches of the Chaudière and came out on the St. Lawrence opposite Quebec. They had completed one of the most terrible and magnificent marches in military history. But the march, with all its sufferings, had only led them to the main problem—the capture of Quebec.

Arnold and Montgomery joined forces. Together they hardly made up an army. Arnold had some 650 men, Montgomery less than 400, and between them they had no cannon with which to batter down the walls of Quebec. There Carleton, with 1,300 well-fed, well-equipped men, waited their attack.

The two American commanders consulted and agreed to take the last desperate chance left to them—to carry Quebec by direct assault. Montgomery would strike from the west, close along the river, following the road that still winds at the base of the towering cliffs. Arnold would come in from the east. They would meet

Arnold anchored his ships in the channel between Valcour Island and the mainland. The powerful ships in the foreground are British warships, which were

in the heart of the Lower Town, and together they would storm up the twisting slope that led into the Upper Town, the heart of Quebec.

The attempt was set for December 31. Snow swirled in blinding sheets across the cliffs of Quebec. At the west end of the Lower Town, a barricade had been erected. Behind it was a blockhouse with a little battery of three-pounders. One of the tiny cannon had been loaded with deadly grapeshot, and a glowing linstock was kept handy, ready to fire the piece at an instant's notice.

In the black, blizzard-filled night, British Sergeant Hugh McQuarters saw a movement along the track in front of the barricade. Some fifty yards away, a shadowy mass halted. One man came forward slowly, followed by two or three others. McQuarters dropped his glowing linstock into the breech of the loaded cannon. A stunning explosion shattered the night, and grapeshot in a deadly hail swept away those dark objects standing in the snow. This one murderous blast halted Montgomery's attack. The General himself had been killed by the winging grapeshot. And his men retreated.

Arnold, attacking the town from the east, also met with disaster. His men charged in, penetrated the Lower Town, but were caught and lost in a tangle of twisting streets under the sheer cliffs. Arnold himself was wounded, and some of his best men, Morgan and Greene among them, were trapped and forced to surrender. The rest of Arnold's little force withdrew, and the invasion of Canada died on the blizzard-swept cliffs of Quebec.

Retreat was all that was left. The next summer found the Americans under Arnold pressed all the way back to Crown Point and Ticonderoga. And it found Carleton, reinforced by a British fleet and strengthened by British and hired Hessian troops, launching an attack of his own up Lake Champlain. Arnold, with a hastily constructed, makeshift fleet, tried to block the southward sweep of Carleton.

forced to round the point of the island and beat upwind to reach Arnold. The small craft stretched in a line across the channel mouth are British gunboats.

Hopelessly outnumbered, the Americans fought with the kind of fury and desperation that seemed typical of battles led by Arnold. Carleton fell upon them on October 11, 1776, at their anchorage in the shelter of Valcour Island. The British had larger ships and heavier cannon and expert Navy sailors to handle both, but for two days Arnold battled them furiously. Then, his fleet smashed down to the last canoe, he and a handful of his men escaped to shore. The invasion route up the lake lay open to Carleton. But because winter was almost at hand, he decided not to strike until next year and returned to Canada.

Meanwhile, fighting burst out far to the south in the Carolinas. British planners had high hopes for the South. There was strong Tory sentiment among the Scottish Highlanders who had settled in the Carolina hill country, and if these allies could be joined by British regulars, the southern colonies might fall. With this hope in mind, a British army under General Henry Clinton and a fleet to transport it under Admiral Sir Peter Parker were sent to the southern coast.

Unfortunately for the British, their Tory allies in North Carolina did not wait. An army 1,500 strong massed in February, and started its march to the coast. At Moore's Creek they were met by a patriot force of 1,000 men under Colonels Richard Caswell and John Alexander Lillington. The patriots were entrenched just beyond Moore's Creek Bridge, and when the Tories crossed, they were stopped by a hail of bullets. Only thirty men were killed, but more than half the Tory army was captured. This collapse weakened the Tory movement in the South for years to come.

As a result, when Clinton and Parker arrived off the coast in March, their allies already had been beaten. The two commanders held long conferences and finally decided to attack Charleston, South Carolina, the largest port in the South. A worse decision, from the British standpoint, could hardly have been made, for up to this time South Carolina had taken no part in the war. There was a chance, slim perhaps, that the colony might have remained neutral, but there was no doubt what Carolinians would do once they were attacked by a British fleet and army. They would fight fiercely.

On June 4, 1776, ten British warships and thirty transports dropped anchor off Charleston Bar. Clinton and his top army and navy officers went into a planning huddle that lasted for a week. And ashore the men of Charleston made grim preparations to receive the British.

Forts had been built on two long, sandy islands—Sullivan's and James—to guard the harbor mouth. Dwellings and warehouses along the waterfront that might have blocked

John Blake White's painting shows the interior of Fort Moultrie at the height of the battle with the British fleet in 1776. The 7,000 cannon balls fired at the fort caused only 36 American casualties.

38

off a field of fire were ruthlessly torn down. Regiments, led by some of the best men in South Carolina, drilled for the defense. Colonel Christopher Gadsden commanded the 1st, Colonel William Moultrie the 2nd. Under Moultrie was a little-known major from a plantation on the Santee River—a frail, swarthy man who spoke little, but of whom much was to be heard. His name was Francis Marion.

Such were the men who met the attack launched by Clinton and Parker on June 28, 1776. The week of British planning led only to blunders. Clinton's 2,500 troops landed on Long Island, an extension of Sullivan's Island, believing they could advance down it and join in the attack on the earthwork fort defended by Moultrie. But the narrow channel between Long Island and Sullivan's Island was too deep to wade across. The result was that the redcoats never did get into the battle.

This left everything to the Navy. Admiral Parker brought his warships up the channel and launched a "furious and incessant cannonade." Inside the casements American gunners, under the cool direction of Moultrie, manned their cannon and fired back steadily.

In the confusion of battle, some of the British ships went aground. Others got out of formation and masked each other's fire. And all the time Moultrie's gunners poured out a thunderous hail of roundshot that tore great gaps in the sides of ships, splintered spars and masts, and felled crews and officers at their posts.

At day's end, Parker's battered warships limped slowly out of reach of Fort Moultrie's well-served cannon. They lay off the coast for several days more, but the attack was not renewed. Clinton and his troops were taken aboard the transports, and the entire fleet set sail for New York—and a new British endeavor.

The Capitol, Washington

The drafting committee, headed by Thomas Jefferson, submits the Declaration of Independence to the Continental Congress for decision.

THE DAY OF FREEDOM

"We hold these truths to be self-evident, that all men are created equal, that they are endowed by their Creator with certain unalienable Rights, that among these are Life, Liberty, and the pursuit of Happiness."
   THE DECLARATION OF INDEPENDENCE

In the beginning, only a few leaders of the thirteen colonies wanted independence. Many more were horrified at the very thought of it. All that winter of 1775–76, while Washington's army ringed Boston and Benedict Arnold battered at the gates of Quebec, the delegates to the Continental Congress in Philadelphia argued about the steps the colonies should take.

In the State House, twin fireplaces blazed as John Hancock presided over the endless, tense debates. Delegates shouted for the floor, made hot objections, passed hastily scrawled notes from row to row. During the recesses, they paced the central corridor, arguing, pleading, storming at one another. They still debated, as they walked along Market Street, each man worried about the future of those thirteen colonies that some were beginning to call states.

They were following a blind trail, with no signposts to guide them. At war with the mother country, many of them still hoped that wrongs could be righted, that peace could be made, and that they could return to the British family. Others, more realistic, knew that for ten years they had been on a road that could lead to only one destination—independence.

To understand the problems and the doubts and worries that beset the patriot leaders, one must go back to the beginning . . .

Baltimore, as sketched in 1752 by John Moale, had fewer than 50 houses and some 200 inhabitants. By 1776, the city had grown so fast it was ninth in size in the colonies.

Stokes Collection, N.Y. Public Library

Rice fields and indigo plantations had made Charleston wealthy.

Charleston Library Society

In the mid-years of the eighteenth century, England had fought a world war against her old enemies, France and Spain. In 1759, General James Wolfe stormed the heights of Quebec and wrested all Canada from the French. In this same year—"the year of miracles," as it was known in England—victory followed closely upon victory, and when George III came to the throne in 1760, England's enemies everywhere were badly beaten. The Peace of Paris in 1763 confirmed what British arms had won. Canada, Florida, and all the lands east of the Mississippi were taken from France and Spain.

The victory had two important effects. During the long conflict known in America as the French and Indian War, England and the two million-odd colonists strung out along the Atlantic seaboard had been one against a common enemy. Now, suddenly, there was no enemy. The American colonies were safe and prospering. Great Britain, however, had come out of her long world war with a national debt of some 130 million pounds sterling—a crippling burden. And more burdens were to come.

England had acquired a world empire, but it was largely an undeveloped empire that would continue for years to drain the British treasury. It was fine for the American colonists that they no longer had to worry about Indian war parties sent out by the French in Canada, but Great Britain had to garrison Canada.

While planters and their families lived gaily in Charleston, the slaves on whom their wealth depended labored in the fields. In this picture by an unknown artist, Negroes dance after the day's work.

Abby Aldrich Rockefeller Folk Art Collection; Courtesy *Ladies Home Journal*

On Sundays, Virginia's widely separated planters met at churches like Bruton Parish in Williamsburg. Here they worshipped and, after the religious service, discussed business and politics.

British statesmen estimated that 10,000 regulars would be needed to keep America secure and make certain the French did not try to recapture it. Who was to pay the price?

To the British government it seemed only logical that the Americans should be taxed, to pay at least part of the cost of their own security. In deciding this, the British overlooked the fact that the Americans had paid heavily during the war. The last successful campaigns against the French had been financed largely by Massachusetts and New York; Pennsylvania had also spent heavily—and none of the colonies had been repaid. Ignoring this, the British went ahead with their tax plans.

The collection of Royal customs, long a joke, was tightened. The largely forgotten Acts of Trade and Navigation were dusted off and ordered enforced. This meant that the colonies could trade only with Great Britain or British possessions. It was a ruling that, for many, meant business ruin. For example, New England for years had shipped dried fish, lumber and naval stores to West Indian islands be-

Settlers moved steadily west, turning the wilderness into prosperous farms like the one pictured here at right.

This is New York in the 1750's. In the foreground of the picture are nine British ships, probably privateers, at anchor in the East River. At the far left is a French vessel captured by the English during the Seven Years' War. On the shore, at center, a straggling militia company parades below the steeple of Trinity Church. At far left the British Union Jack flies over Fort George.

longing to France, Spain, Holland, Denmark and Great Britain. Her ships had brought back molasses to be made into rum. By 1750, Massachusetts alone was exporting more than two million gallons a year. Now New Englanders were suddenly told they could trade only with the British islands in the West Indies. These

44

islands could neither supply all the molasses the colonies needed nor buy all the goods the colonies had to export. New England faced ruin, and a gale of protest swept through the northern colonies.

The South, which had no interest in the rum trade, was silent—but not for long. In 1765, the British passed the Stamp Act. This placed a direct tax on all sorts of licenses, publications, and legal papers. Each had to bear a revenue stamp. Now, the South joined the North in angry protest. In Virginia, Patrick Henry made a fiery speech that came close to treason, and the legislature adopted the Virginia Resolves.

Patrick Henry

Colonial Williamsburg

Independence Hall

Thomas Paine

Boston Museum of Fine Arts

John Hancock

These stated firmly that only Virginians could tax Virginians.

Opposition to the Stamp Act led to a colonial Congress. It met in New York in October, 1765, and its members were stirred by the bold words of South Carolina's Christopher Gadsden. He called on the delegates to "stand on the broad and common ground of natural and inherent rights . . . as men and the descendants of Englishmen! There ought to be no more New England men, no New Yorkers . . . but all of us Americans!" In the end, the Congress passed a Declaration of Rights and Grievances. Its main point was that only the colonists themselves could levy taxes on the colonies.

In the years that followed the colonies and the mother country continued to clash on the issue of taxation. Great Britain insisted on the right to tax; the colonists, just as stubbornly, held that this must be their right alone. When the Stamp Act and the so-called Sugar Act were repealed, Britain tried a new tax method in the Townshend Acts. These imposed duties on articles shipped into America such as paper, lead, glass, paint—and tea.

Coupled with the outcry against taxes was a concern on the part of many Americans about the nibbling away of basic liberties. The Towns-

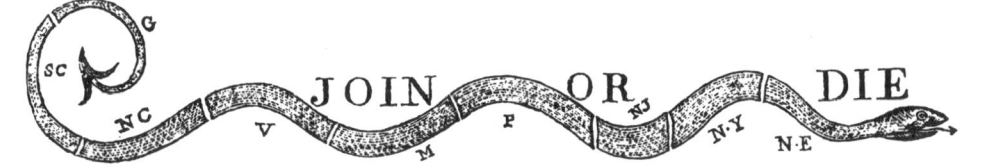

American Antiquarian Society

Library of Congress

Paul Revere designed the "Join or Die" device (above) for a patriot newspaper. Tories and Whigs often came to blows (left) at local town meetings.

46

hend Acts, for instance, provided for Writs of Assistance—in reality, blank search warrants giving officers of the Crown the right to invade any man's home with or without cause. The Townshend Acts, too, provided that the duties collected should be used to pay the salaries of judges and colonial officials. This meant that the colonists would be deprived of control of their own affairs, that they might be ruled in the end by a few favored families and a few favored government officials.

This concern with the loss of liberties reached its peak after Boston held its tea party and Parliament passed measures so stern that the colonies could see themselves becoming little more than slave states.

It was not just that Boston was occupied by the British army. Under the new laws, any Royal officer accused of a capital crime, such as murder in putting down a riot or collecting revenue, would be sent to England for trial. Acquittal could almost be taken for granted; therefore, the act seemed to give agents of the Crown a free hand in using violence. In addition, the Governor's council was to be Crown-appointed and responsible only to the Crown; the attorney general, judges, sheriffs, and justices of the peace were to be named by the Royal governor. Even juries were to be selected by a Crown-appointed sheriff.

These measures, along with the Port Bill that closed Boston, became known to the colonists as the "Intolerable Acts." They were aimed against Massachusetts alone, but all of the colonies knew that, if these severe measures succeeded in Massachusetts, they would be used elsewhere. Banding together in common cause, the colonies sent delegates to the First Continental Congress in Philadelphia in September, 1774. Once more, as the Stamp Act Congress had done in 1765, the delegates stated the colonies' strong insistence on basic rights—the rights to life, liberty, and property, the rights of their Assemblies alone to tax and to decide governmental policy. They declared

Roger Sherman
Yale University Art Gallery

John Adams
Independence Hall

John Dickinson
Independence Hall

the Intolerable Acts of Parliament illegal, and they backed the right of the people of Massachusetts to set up their own government, to gather arms, to raise a militia.

Britain remained adamant, and so the next year, when the Second Continental Congress met in Philadelphia, the delegates had to deal with the problems of war and independence.

Such were the events that led to those bitter debates in the winter of 1775–76. A strong bloc of conservatives approved resistance, but fought the idea of independence. Their view was best expressed by John Dickinson of Pennsylvania, who in 1767 had written a series of strong essays on colonial rights, but who considered independence sheer madness. Such men believed that the Crown had been wrong, that its acts must be resisted; but in the end they wanted to see the colonies reunited with England.

Other men, such as John Adams and Chris-

Patrick Henry denounces the Stamp Act in Virginia's House of Burgesses.

Stamp Act cartoon printed in the Pennsylvania Journal, *in 1765*

The stamp, which was to be affixed to all licenses and legal papers.

The engraving below pictures a Tory strung up on a liberty pole during the Stamp Act uproar.

topher Gadsden, felt that relations with the mother country, so violently broken, could never be repaired. The war, as they saw it, could have only one outcome—the beginning of a new nation.

Meanwhile, one of the most important documents ever written in America was capturing the popular imagination. It was a little 47-page pamphlet entitled *Common Sense.* And it was written by an Englishman, Thomas Paine, who had come to the colonies recently, under the sponsorship of Benjamin Franklin.

Some of Paine's attacks on the British government and on the King himself were too wild for even the most radical of the American leaders. But there were other words in *Common Sense* that rang with high ideals and that, once read or heard, could never be forgotten. Words such as: "O ye that love mankind! Ye that dare oppose not only the tyranny but the tyrant, stand forth! Every spot of the old world is overrun with oppression. Freedom hath been

48

hunted round the globe. Asia and Africa have long expelled her. Europe regards her like a stranger, and England hath given her warning to depart. O receive the fugitive, and prepare in time an asylum for mankind!"

Across the final page of *Common Sense* ran the daring words: THE FREE AND INDEPENDENT STATES OF AMERICA.

Paine won powerful support for the cause of independence. And on the political front, two other events helped persuade those who were still doubtful.

In January, 1776, the text of George III's October message to Parliament reached America. The Royal address ripped out at the "desperate conspiracy" aimed at establishing "an independent Empire" in the colonies. It made clear that the Royal temper was worn out. It called for severe steps and announced that Hessian troops had been hired from rulers in Germany to help put down the rebellion in America. It was a harsh speech that showed even the more conservative that they could not look to the King for justice.

A further nudge to the cautious in making up their minds came in a hint of help from abroad. France and Spain, both smarting from their defeat in 1763, saw in the American war a chance to get even with their old enemy, Great Britain. Secretly they began shipping powder and supplies to America through an innocent-looking private trading firm, Hortalez et Cie. It is doubtful that any member of Congress was misled about the nobility of French intentions, but the prospect of such help could not fail to stiffen the spines of those considering such a daring step as independence.

All of these forces were combining to shove the Rebels in the path that they must take, when, in the spring of 1776, Congress named a committee to study the resolutions being sent to it by various Provincial Congresses. The committee was to weave the views of the colonies into one resolution for action. Mem-

This British print, published two weeks after the Stamp Act's repeal, shows the Act's originator, George Grenville, cradling his dead "child." In the background, three ships await "goods NOW ship'd for America," as the warehouse sign proclaims.

John Carter Brown Library

49

The "Olive Branch" petition on this page was the colonists' last effort to make peace. Humble in tone, the document was signed by the patriot leaders in July, 1775, after fighting had begun. But King George III refused to receive it, and so drove many American conservatives to the side of those who wanted independence. The Declaration of Independence followed a year later. The following pages reproduce Jefferson's own copy of the Declaration, including marginal notes and comments by John Adams and Benjamin Franklin.

Manuscript Division, N.Y. Public Library

bers of the committee began to meet regularly at a newly built house at Seventh and Market Streets. There, its youngest member—tall, red-haired, rawboned Thomas Jefferson, the squire of Monticello in Virginia—played host to his fellow committeemen in the second-floor living room which he had rented in Philadelphia.

Meeting with Jefferson were the wise, unruffled Benjamin Franklin; determined John Adams, the heart and soul of the independence movement; Roger Sherman of Connecticut, a careful man whose last doubts had been swept away by the wave of popular sentiment; and Robert Livingston, the wealthy New Yorker whose mind was not yet quite made up. Soon, by general agreement, the task of shaping the resolution that the committee was to present to

(Continued on page 55)

A Declaration by the Representatives of the UNITED STATES OF AMERICA, in General Congress assembled.

When in the course of human events it becomes necessary for one people to dissolve the political bands which have connected them with another, and to assume among the powers of the earth the separate and equal station to which the laws of nature & of nature's god entitle them, a decent respect to the opinions of mankind requires that they should declare the causes which impel them to the separation.

We hold these truths to be self-evident; that all men are created equal, that they are endowed by their creator with inherent & inalienable rights, that among these are life, liberty, & the pursuit of happiness; that to secure these rights, governments are instituted among men, deriving their just powers from the consent of the governed; that whenever any form of government becomes destructive of these ends, it is the right of the people to alter or to abolish it, & to institute new government, laying it's foundation on such principles & organising it's powers in such form, as to them shall seem most likely to effect their safety & happiness. prudence indeed will dictate that governments long established should not be changed for light & transient causes: and accordingly all experience hath shewn that mankind are more disposed to suffer while evils are sufferable, than to right themselves by abolishing the forms to which they are accustomed. but when a long train of abuses & usurpations [begun at a distinguished period, &] pursuing invariably the same object, evinces a design to reduce them under absolute Despotism, it is their right, it is their duty, to throw off such government, & to provide new guards for their future security. such has been the patient sufferance of these colonies; & such is now the necessity which constrains them to expunge their former systems of government. the history of the present king of Great Britain is a history of unremitting injuries and usurpations, [among which appears no solitary fact to contradict the uniform tenor of the rest, but all have] in direct object the establishment of an absolute tyranny over these states. to prove this, let facts be submitted to a candid world, [for the truth of which we pledge a faith yet unsullied by falsehood.]

he has refused his assent to laws the most wholesome and necessary for the public good:

he has forbidden his governors to pass laws of immediate & pressing importance, unless suspended in their operation till his assent should be obtained; and when so suspended, he has utterly neglected to attend to them.

he has refused to pass other laws for the accomodation of large districts of people unless those people would relinquish the right of representation in the legislature, a right inestimable to them, & formidable to tyrants only:

dissolved Representative houses repeatedly & continually for opposing with manly firmness his invasions on the rights of the people:

he has refused for a long time after such dissolutions to cause others to be elected, *mr Adams

whereby the legislative powers, incapable of annihilation, have returned to the people at large for their exercise, the state remaining in the mean time exposed to all the dangers of invasion from without & convulsions within:

has endeavored to prevent the population of these states; for that purpose obstructing the laws for naturalization of foreigners; refusing to pass others to encourage their migrations hither; & raising the conditions of new appropriations of lands:

he has suffered the administration of justice totally to cease in some of these states, refusing his assent to laws for establishing judiciary powers:

he has made [our] judges dependant on his will alone, for the tenure of their offices, the + & payment and amount of their salaries: † Dr Franklin

he has erected a multitude of new offices [by a self-assumed power,] & sent hither swarms of officers to harrass our people & eat out their substance:

he has kept among us in times of peace, standing armies [& ships of war] without the consent of our legislatures

he has affected to render the military, independent of & superior to the civil power:

he has combined with others to subject us to a jurisdiction foreign to our constitutions and unacknoleged by our laws; giving his assent to their acts of pretended legislation, for quartering large bodies of armed troops among us;

for protecting them by a mock-trial from punishment for any murders which they should commit on the inhabitants of these states;

for cutting off our trade with all parts of the world;

for imposing taxes on us without our consent;

for depriving us in many cases of the benefits of trial by jury;

for transporting us beyond seas to be tried for pretended offences:

for abolishing the free system of English laws in a neighboring province, establishing therein an arbitrary government, and enlarging it's boundaries so as to render it at once an example & fit instrument for introducing the same

abolishing our most valuable Laws

for taking away our charters & altering fundamentally the forms of our governments:

for suspending our own legislatures & declaring themselves invested with power to legislate for us in all cases whatsoever:

he has abdicated government here, by declaring us out of his protection & waging war against us [withdrawing his governors, & declaring us out of his allegiance & protection:]

he has plundered our seas, ravaged our coasts, burnt our towns & destroyed the lives of our people:

he is at this time transporting large armies of Scotch and other foreign mercenaries to compleat the works of death, desolation & tyranny already begun with circumstances of cruelty & perfidy scarcely paralleled in the most barbarous ages, and totally unworthy the head of a civilized nation:

he has constrained others, taken captives on the high seas to bear arms against their country, to become the executioners of their friends & brethren, or to fall themselves by their hands.

he has endeavored to bring on the inhabitants of our frontiers the merciless Indian savages, whose known rule of warfare is an undistinguished destruction of all ages, sexes, & conditions [of existence:]

[he has incited treasonable insurrections of our fellow-citizens, with the allurements of forfeiture & confiscation of our property:

he has waged cruel war against human nature itself, violating it's most sacred rights of life & liberty in the persons of a distant people who never offended him, captivating & carrying them into slavery in another hemisphere, or to incur miserable death in their transportation thither. this piratical warfare, the opprobrium of infidel powers, is the warfare of the Christian king of Great Britain. determined to keep open a market where MEN should be bought & sold, he has prostituted his negative for suppressing every legislative attempt to prohibit or to restrain this execrable commerce: and that this assemblage of horrors might want no fact of distinguished die, he is now exciting those very people to rise in arms among us, and to purchase that liberty of which he has deprived them, by murdering the people upon whom he also obtruded them: thus paying off former crimes committed against the liberties of one people, with crimes which he urges them to commit against the lives of another.]

in every stage of these oppressions we have petitioned for redress in the most humble terms; our repeated petitions have been answered only by repeated injuries. a prince whose character is thus marked by every act which may define a tyrant, is unfit to be the ruler of a people who mean to be free. future ages will scarce believe that the hardiness of one man, adventured within the short compass of twelve years to lay a foundation so broad & undisguised, for tyranny over a people fostered & fixed in principles of freedom.

Nor have we been wanting in attentions to our British brethren. we have warned them from time to time of attempts by their legislature to extend an unwarrantable jurisdiction over [these our ~~states~~]. we have reminded them of the circumstances of our emigration & settlement here, [no one of which could warrant so strange a pretension: that these were effected at the expence of our own blood & treasure, unassisted by the wealth or the strength of Great Britain: that in constituting indeed our several forms of government, we had adopted one common king, thereby laying a foundation for perpetual league & amity with them: but that submission to their ~~parliament, was no part of our constitution, nor ever in idea, if history may be credited: and~~] we have appealed to their native justice & magnanimity, [as well as to the ties of our common kindred to disavow these usurpations which [were likely to] interrupt our correspondence & connection. they too have been deaf to the voice of justice & of consanguinity, [& when occasions have been given them, by the regular course of their laws, of removing from their councils the disturbers of our harmony, they have by their free election re-established them in power. at this very time too they are permitting their chief magistrate to send over not only soldiers of our common blood, but Scotch & foreign mercenaries to invade & destroy us. these facts have given the last stab to agonizing affection, and manly spirit bids us to renounce for ever these unfeeling brethren. we must endeavor to forget our former love for them, and to hold them as we hold the rest of mankind, enemies in war, in peace friends. we might have been a free & a great people together; but a communication of grandeur & of freedom it seems is below their dignity. be it so, since they will have it. the road to ~~glory~~ & to glory & happiness is open to us too; we will tread it apart from them, and acquiesce in the necessity which denounces our ~~eternal~~ separation!

We therefore the representatives of the United States of America in General Congress assembled, do, in the name & by authority of the good people of these [states,] reject & renounce all allegiance & subjection to the kings of Great Britain & all others who may hereafter claim by, through, or under them; we utterly dissolve & break off all political connection which may ~~have~~ heretofore have subsisted between us & the people or parliament of Great Britain; and finally we do assert and declare these colonies to be free and independant states, and that as free & independant states they shall hereafter have full power to levy war, conclude peace, contract alliances, establish commerce, & to do all other acts and things which independant states may of right do. And for the support of this declaration we mutually pledge to each other our lives, our fortunes, & our sacred honour.

Congress was given to Thomas Jefferson. The tall, shy Virginian, only 33, protested that older and wiser heads would be better suited to the work, but John Adams waved aside all such arguments. The shrewd New Englander, representing Massachusetts, where all the trouble had started, wanted to keep himself in the background; at the same time, he was a warm admirer of Thomas Jefferson's keen mind and of his undoubted skill with words.

And so during the warm spring weeks, Thomas Jefferson talked earnestly with his colleagues and built, sentence by slow sentence, a soaring structure of words. It was his aim not only to proclaim the goal of independence, but to convince men everywhere of the rightness of the cause, to express the glory of the ideal. Occasionally, Franklin or Adams would suggest a change of phrase or the deletion of a too violent sentiment, but the spirit and the sense of the words remained Jefferson's.

It was on the first day of July, 1776, that the issue of independence was presented to the Congress for debate. The die-hard conservatives were shocked. John Dickinson argued against such a declaration with such passion and conviction that all but the stoutest radicals wavered. To proclaim independence, he said, would be "like destroying our house in winter . . . before we have got another shelter." He stressed the power of Britain, the weakness of the colonies. Then John Adams answered him. The text of his speech has been lost, but Jefferson recorded that Adams "came out with a power of thought and expression that moved us from our seats."

When the debate was over, the first roll call was taken. Some delegates were absent, and the vote was indecisive. But the next day, July 2, nearly all who had been absent were in their seats. A second vote was taken, and this time those favoring a declaration of independence carried the day.

The actual document that Jefferson had drafted was not presented to the Congress for

A portrait of Thomas Jefferson by C. W. Peale

At left, the ink stand used at the signing of the Declaration of Independence

consideration until two days later, July 4. It was a hot and breathless day, and delegates wiped perspiring foreheads as they studied the words. Each man had his own ideas, and each copy that was passed about the hall was scratched and marked with suggested changes. But the changes were relatively few and unimportant. In the end, the great Declaration of Independence was adopted very much as Jefferson had written it—adopted down to those last, proud words: "And for the support of this Declaration, with a firm reliance on the protection of divine Providence, we mutually pledge to each other our Lives, our Fortunes, and our Sacred Honour."

The great choice had been made.

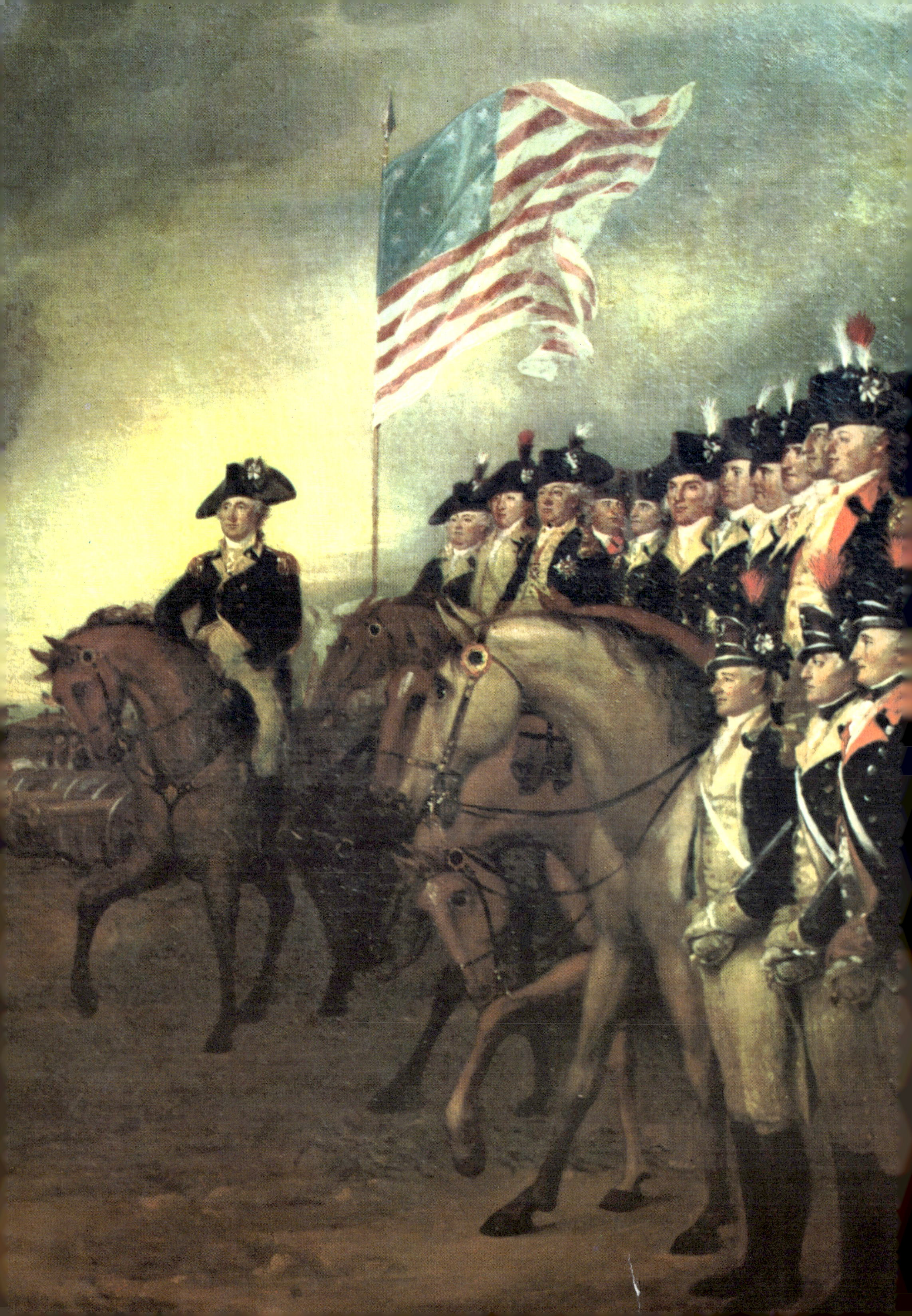

ARMS AND MEN

America's victory in the Revolutionary War was won against odds that seem truly staggering when one considers the contrast between the opposing armies: the Americans, almost to a man, were rank amateurs; the British and Hessians were highly trained professional soldiers.

The colonists had never organized a large and well-trained body of troops, because they distrusted standing armies. They preferred to rely on militia for their defense. When emergencies arose, extra volunteers were called out. These served for a single campaign, and when the campaign was ended, they returned to their homes and hung up their muskets. It was this tradition of short, spotty, emergency service that plagued George Washington throughout the war.

In the painting at left Washington and his officers watch the British surrender at Yorktown.

He wrestled with the problem in those first days at the siege of Boston, and he never really managed to solve it. Periodically, in crisis after crisis, short-term enlistments expired, and the men, despite the pleading of their officers, tramped back to their farms and firesides.

Most of the soldiers, in one way or another, had had a smattering of experience. Many had been exposed to simple drills at militia "training days." Others had seen limited service against the French and Indians. But Washington's first army was, as he observed, "a multitude of people . . . under very little discipline." The men, he said, "regarded an officer no more than a broomstick."

One reason for this lack of respect was that officers frequently were elected by their men and could be ousted by the vote of the men. Therefore, the officers had no real authority. Uniforms were few, ammunition scarce, and

British uniforms were elaborate. At left, a British grenadier officer; at right, a British drummer boy.

British Museum

A British drill manual shows the key positions for an infantryman. From left to right, it illustrates how to fix bayonet, charge, prime and load, fire, and "rest your firelock."

weapons (since they belonged to the men who carried them) were of every conceivable kind, age, type, and quality. Even the basic details of drill and camp routine were practically unknown.

The disadvantages of such an amateur army are even more apparent when one realizes that the tactics of the day called for troops to wheel into battle in precise and ordered ranks. To get large masses of men to march and fight in such perfect unison required long and hard training. Some authorities felt that five years were needed to turn a recruit into an accomplished soldier. Although smaller American units sometimes adopted woodland tactics and fought from shelter, the major land battles of the war were generally fought in the open, according to the rules of the European system, where the well-trained British had all the advantage.

The British, of course, were not without their own problems. Commissions in the infantry and cavalry were obtained not by merit but by purchase, and the result was that the quality of officers was generally low. Noncommissioned professionals, who were fine soldiers but too few in number, drilled the men. All too often the men in the ranks were the worst elements of British society, recruited from jails and slums. Despite such drawbacks, the overwhelming weight of training, experience, skill, and equipment rested with the British—the army that lost the war.

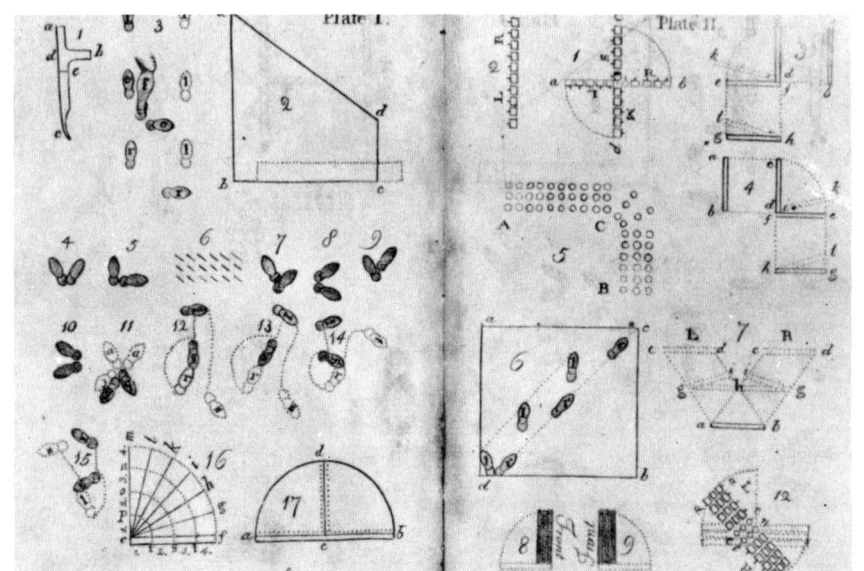

Timothy Pickering of Salem drew up this manual for colonial drillmasters after the Boston Tea Party. He called it An Easy Plan of Discipline for a Militia. *His drawings in Plate I at left show an all-purpose tool (top left) and, next to it, the positions of feet for firing; a pattern for making cartridges (2); motions for right, left and about face (7–11); and to the rear march (12–13). Plate II includes a diagram for wheeling by column of ranks (5); and offers an explanation of the oblique march (6).*

The 1775 engraving above pictures the sad state of the poorly paid British soldier "Exposed to the Horrors of War" in America while tradesmen at home live in comfort. Many British soldiers were recruited from jails and slums. The picture below shows a recruiting sergeant with a typically poor lot in tow.

THE INFANTRYMAN'S WEAPONS

The foot soldier, since earliest history, has usually been the man who won or lost a war, and the Revolution was no exception. That war belonged to the infantryman, and his chief weapon was the flintlock musket with its attached bayonet. The British redcoat was trained to fire rapidly, then charge with the cold steel —a method of fighting that the Americans had to learn and adopt.

In actual battle, an experienced commander drew up his battle line just out of effective enemy artillery range. This put the opposing forces about 500 yards apart. The attacking line formed, dressed ranks, and marched off toward the enemy as if on parade; and from that moment, victory or defeat depended largely on the discipline, training, and maneuverability of the attacking line.

The large-bore musket shot a lead ball, contained in a paper cartridge made up in advance. It was effective only up to 80 or 100 yards. "As to firing at a man at 200 yards . . . you may just as well fire at the moon," a British expert wrote.

This limited range put a premium on volley firing. The object was to march up close to the enemy, then to load and fire as swiftly as possible on command. The solid mass of troops made targets that were hard to miss, and aim was not as important as the sheer volume of fire power. Troops were taught to "load and fire fifteen times in three minutes and three-quarters." This meant a sustained fire of one shot every fifteen seconds, or about two effective volleys during an average charge.

Contrary to popular imagination, the American long rifle was not a major infantry weapon of the Revolution. Although it was extremely accurate at ranges up to 300 yards, it could not be equipped with a bayonet, and it took too long to reload. The rifle was used effectively in special situations, but the Americans, like the British, relied mainly on the musket.

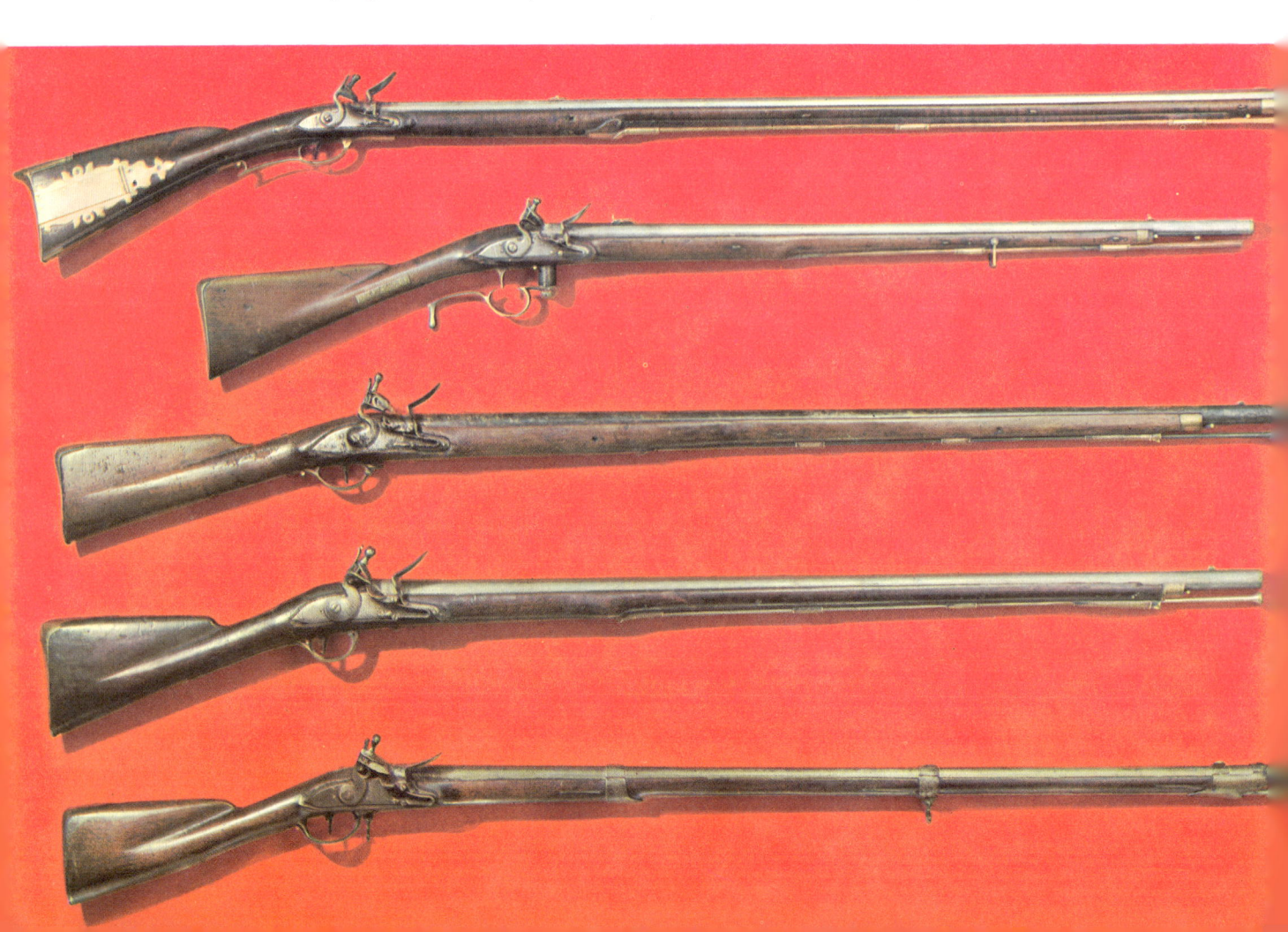

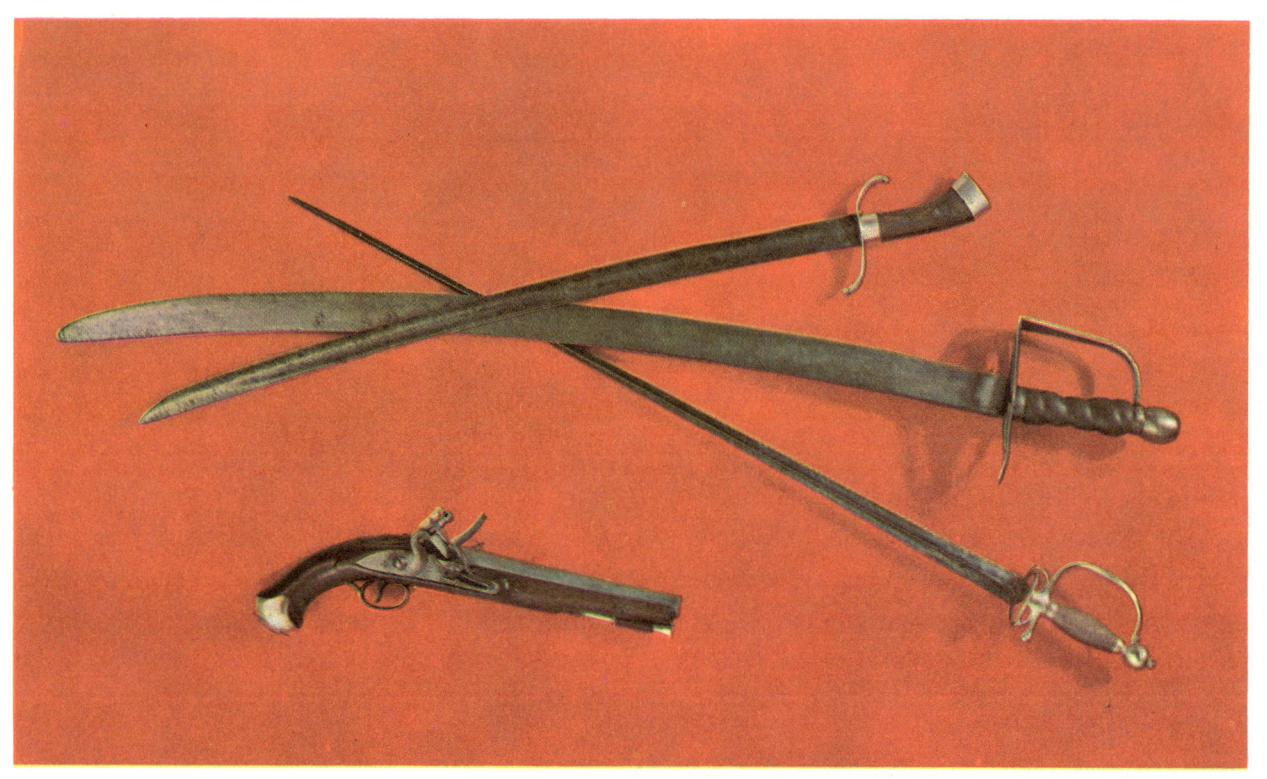

Typical Revolutionary weapons are shown in the pictures above and below. The three swords above were the most popular American types. The hunting sword *(top) and the* small sword *(bottom) were worn by officers; the* heavy saber *was favored by cavalrymen. The British* pistol *was also a cavalry weapon. Below (left to right), the* halberd *was carried mainly as a symbol of rank by sergeants, but the* spontoon *was still used in combat. The* tomahawk *was carried by American riflemen, who fought without bayonets, and was used by the infantry as an extra weapon. At right are a French and a British* bayonet *of the period.*

Guns of the Revolution are pictured left. The American rifle *(top) was also called the "Kentucky" or "Pennsylvania" rifle. The* Ferguson rifle *shown below it, invented by British Colonel Patrick Ferguson, was the only breech-loading, rapid-firing gun of the war, but not over 200 were used. Under the rifles are three muskets. First, the type of musket turned out by American gunsmiths and copied from the British "Brown Bess" below it. The "Brown Bess" musket was a .75-calibre smoothbore that got its name from its brown barrel, some 44 inches to 46 inches long. The* French infantry musket *at bottom is of the type shipped here in the first French munitions ships, and it replaced most American-made guns.*

Collection of Harold L. Peterson

This sketch, made on a powder horn, is a contemporary drawing showing an American field gun limbered up for the march.

ARTILLERY IN THE REVOLUTION

The Americans knew less about artillery and its uses than about any other arm. The reasons are simple: cannon were too heavy and too cumbersome to be dragged through the wilderness where the Indian wars were fought, and most of the Americans' experience of fighting prior to the time of the Revolution had been on the frontier.

When war broke out, the rebelling colonists had few cannon, and there were almost no trained gunners. Henry Knox, Washington's chief of artillery, was a bookseller whose knowledge of big guns came from reading British books.

The Rebels gradually added to their store of heavy guns. A large quantity of cannon was captured at Fort Ticonderoga; others were seized when British supply and munition ships were taken. In 1775, Pennsylvania and Massachusetts foundries began casting cannon, and when France began to back the cause of the colonists, French artillery was shipped to America.

Most fieldpieces ranged in size from tiny 3-pounders to huge 24-pounders, but the smaller

A drawing from the diary of the Revolutionary artist Charles Willson Peale shows how a cannon barrel was raised or lowered by means of an elevating screw.

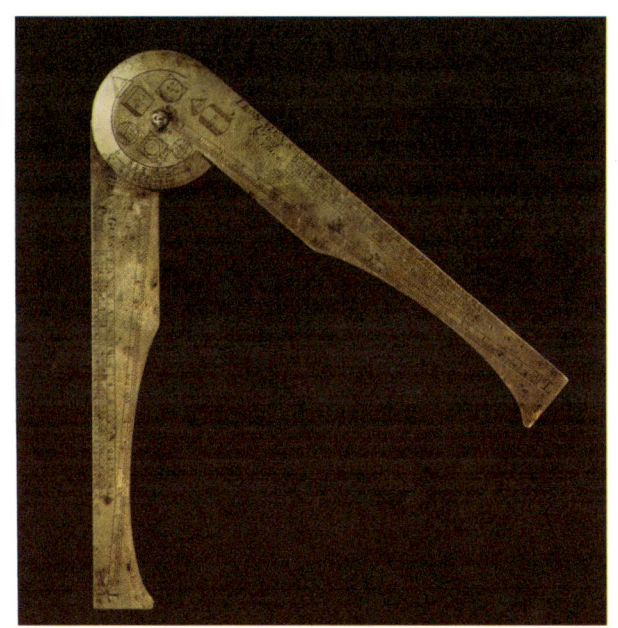

sizes were much more numerous than the larger. Horses and oxen hauled the heavy pieces to the battlefield. There cannoneers used dragropes to maneuver their pieces into position.

Since the artillery of the day had a comparatively short range, it was used not to lay down a barrage on troops massing behind distant lines, but rather to increase the firepower of defenders at the moment of attack. Then its effect on an enemy advancing in massed ranks was deadly. Under such circumstances, fieldpieces were wheeled into the front line with the infantry, and they were often used to protect an exposed flank or to smash an attack aimed at a gap left in defending lines by faulty alignment.

The picture at top, right, from Muller's Treatise of Artillery *shows fieldpieces and mortars common during the Revolution, as well as gunners' tools and methods of firing. The brass gunner's calipers at top left were used to measure gun bore and size of cannon balls. Ammunition for the Continental Army's guns was transported in horse-drawn wagons like that directly above. The wheels on this wagon have been reconstructed and should actually be larger.*

The Americans suffered, during the war, from powder shortages. Committees of Safety issued instructions for the manufacture of saltpeter and gunpowder. The drawing at right illustrates the manufacture of saltpeter.

63

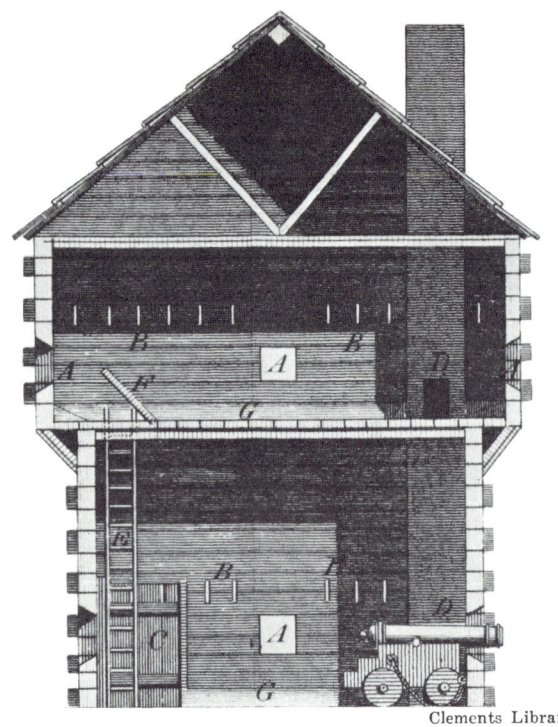

Thomas Anburey's plan for a blockhouse shows musket loopholes and cannon ports on both floors.

FIXED DEFENSES

Fortifications played a minor role in the Revolution, where the important battles were fought in the open. The Americans, indeed, had little knowledge of military engineering. When given the opportunity, they dug like beavers and threw up earthworks as they had on Breed's Hill. They also erected frontier blockhouses, two-story structures built of logs with the second story overhanging the first so that fire could be sprayed directly down on the heads of attackers. The log walls were pierced with loopholes for rifle fire, and sometimes small cannon were mounted in corner bastions. Such relatively simple fortifications,

At left is a cross section of a British redoubt built on Charlestown Peninsula after the Battle of Breed's Hill. The rare English print above, dating from the mid-eighteenth-century, shows a variety of military tools and methods of town fortification.

Fort Ticonderoga Museum

however, represented the limit of American military knowledge.

Until France's entry into the war, the Americans had no trained engineering officers. This lack was recognized as early as 1775 by John Adams. He wrote Henry Knox, asking "what skilful engineers you have in the army; and whether any of them . . . have seen service."

Most of the forts existing in the colonies were relics of the French and Indian wars. The solid masonry walls of Fort Ticonderoga were a rare example of the type of citadels designed by British and French engineers. The Americans themselves built no such strongholds.

65

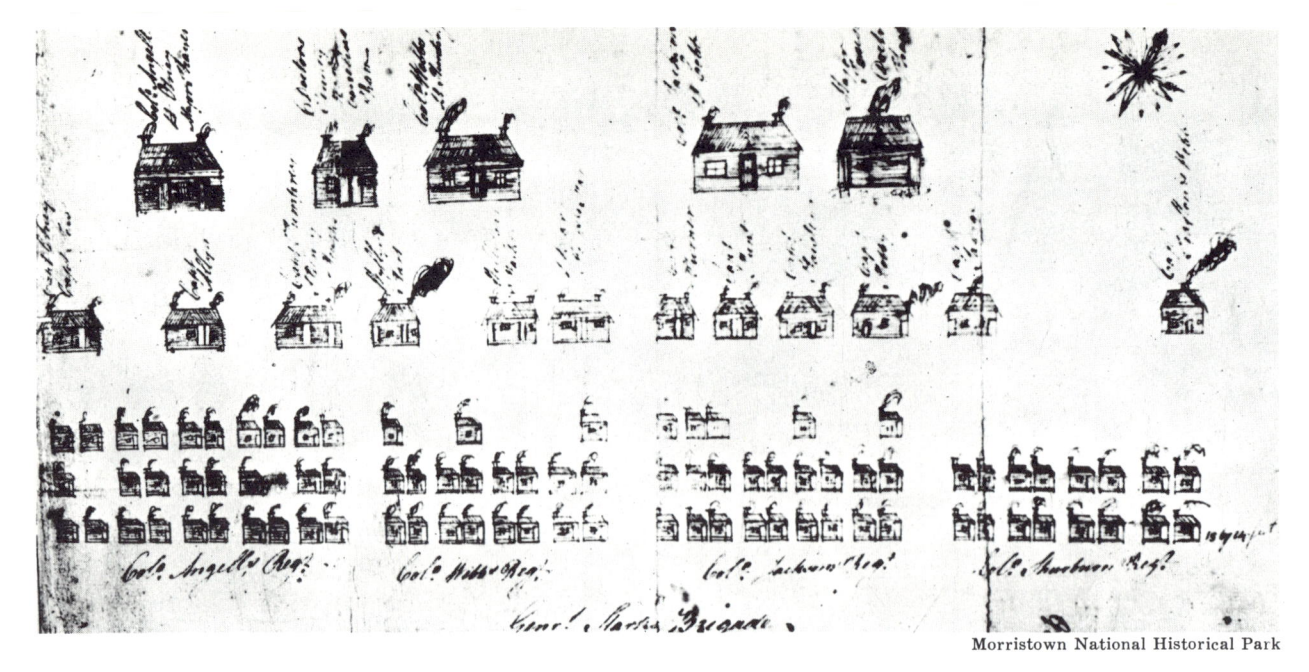

CAMPS AND PRISONS

Winter was a time of horror for the pitifully equipped Continental Army. Throughout the war, the troops lacked clothing, food, and shelter, and when winter came, disease and starvation swept the ranks.

Several times the army was so wasted away by its winter sufferings that Washington was reduced to a state, as he once wrote, "of scarce having any army at all." The horrors of Valley Forge during the winter of 1777–78 are well

Newgate, the American prison in Connecticut, was "commonly called Hell." Loyalists, often chained, worked the prison copper mine.

◄ *The sketch at left shows the winter camp of General Stark's brigade at Morristown. Each small hut held twelve soldiers. The larger ones were for officers.*

Dreadful conditions aboard the British prison ship Jersey *are shown in John Trumbull's sketch at right. Many Americans starved to death in its foul hold.*

Fordham University Library

known, but less well known is the fact that the previous winter at Morristown had been equally grim, and the winter of 1780, again at Morristown, was the worst of the war.

Typically, the army went into winter camp in the fall, after all chance of a major encounter with the enemy had passed. It pitched its tents on frozen ground, and the men, often "without shoes and stockings, and working half leg deep in the snow," set about felling trees for a crude "Log-house city." The huts they built were icy and damp. A dozen men were packed into each, and when disease struck, the place became a nightmare.

Yet Washington's veterans bore up under such conditions with great courage. He wrote on one occasion that his troops endured their distress "with as much fortitude as human nature is capable of."

If conditions in camp were horrible, military prisons were even worse. The British, shortly after they seized New York, gathered a fleet of rotting hulks, anchored them off the Brooklyn shore, and turned them into prison ships. American soldiers and sailors were packed into these foul hulks and died by the hundreds. Conditions in the American prison camps were almost equally bad, and on both sides a quick death in battle was often to be preferred to the agony of prison.

At left is a large British camp which was located near the present 204th Street in New York City.

New-York Historical Society

67

THE UNIFORMS AND EQUIPMENT OF AMERICAN INFANTRYMEN *are shown on these pages. The blue coat with white facings at right and the buff waistcoat and overalls beside it were worn by a soldier in the Continental Corps of Light Infantry in 1780. His leather cap had a bearskin crest and red feathered plume, while his shoes (top right) were the ordinary buckle type worn by civilians. His weapon was a French musket with bayonet, and he made cartridges out of paper, black powder, and ball (on vest). These were carried in a leather cartridge box (right center). His blanket was inside the red knapsack, on top of which are a pair of ice-creepers, used on winter marches, and a*

West Point Museum; Fort Ticonderoga; Newburgh (N.Y.) Museum; Photograph by Arnold Newman.

three-pronged holder for his rush light or candle. Just to the left of the lower part of the red knapsack are a flint and tinder box. The fringed, homespun linen hunting shirt and tricorn hat at left were worn by a rifleman. For his long rifle (shown on page 60) he carried powder horn, lead balls, and a shot pouch (lower left) instead of cartridges. Both the uniformed Continental and the rifleman carried a canteen (extreme left) and such items as folding knife and fork, fishhook, and sinkers. Both might also have had Continental money, clay pipe, sundial-compass, dice, lead for writing (on top of letter), small horn for salt, needle, scissors and the hunting knife below them.

THE AMERICAN INFANTRYMAN

A private in the Continental Army risked his life for less than $7.00 a month, and from this, the cost of his clothing was deducted. Congress ruled that uniforms "as much as possible" were to be brown, with different color facings to distinguish regiments, but in the war's early years, most units had no regular uniforms.

Only a few state regiments like the Delawares and the Marylanders were well uniformed and equipped. The average soldier turned out in his civilian clothes. The New Englanders who laid siege to Boston in 1775 wore "small-clothes, coming down and fastening just below the knee, and long stockings with cowhide shoes ornamented by large buckles." Homespun shirts and coats and waistcoats of various colors completed their dress.

In 1778, a shipment of uniforms—brown and blue coats with red facings—arrived from France. This was the first time that anything like a regular uniform for a large part of the army was possible.

About 1775, a German engraver made the fanciful picture above of the "very healthy and durable" American rifleman, basing it on a drawing by a Bavarian officer who had served with the British. At right, a 1784 drawing shows an American "sharpshooter" and, in brown, a regular of the Pennsylvania line.

In the Revolution, drums like the one above took the place of the modern bugle. Orders governing camp life routine and battle maneuvers were signaled on drums.

Most of the few illustrations of the day showing American uniforms appear on these pages. Above, a German engraving pictures riflemen in fringed, coarse cotton cloth, their leather hats lettered with the word "Congress." The caption says most of them were barefoot. At left is a British picture of an American general. His plumed cap was made from a hat on which the brim was turned up to make a "Liberty" cap-plate. The American pennant below appeared in a German book in 1784.

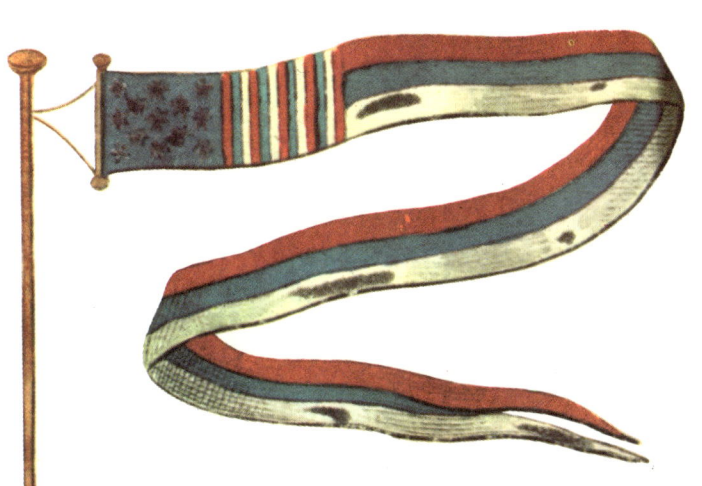

Collection of Mrs. John Nicholas Brown, except drum—Guilford Court House National Military Park

A FEW CRACK REGIMENTS HELD THE ARMY TOGETHER

At the heart of the Continental Army were a few gallant regiments that suffered and endured throughout the long course of the war. When the militia and the six-months enlistment men were going home, Washington could always count on this hard core of veterans. Without their toughness, courage, and loyalty, he could hardly have kept an army together, and the outcome of the war might have been far different.

The contrast between the militia and the stout-hearted regulars was made vivid for Washington at the Battle of Long Island. There he saw the militia flee, disappearing "almost by whole regiments," while Haslet's Delawares and Smallwood's Marylanders stood firm, holding off some of the finest troops of Europe. Afterwards, Washington wrote to Congress, declaring that "our liberties" might be lost "if their defence is left to any but a permanent standing army."

He never succeeded in building an army composed entirely of hardened veterans. Always he had to rely on militia to increase his force to fighting size. But in battle after battle, from war's beginning to war's end, a few Continental regiments stuck to their task and formed the center of American resistance.

The Maryland regiment (left) is shown departing from Annapolis on July 10, 1776, to join Washington. Their dress uniforms were actually scarlet and buff, not blue-green as in this painting, but at the Battle of Long Island they were clad sensibly in hunting shirts or smocks of a brownish color. They were commanded by William Smallwood, whose portrait appears above.

175th Infantry, Maryland National Guard

(Above) Regimental flag of the Philadelphia Light Horse Troop, another famous outfit that served throughout the war. The flag was carried in battle at Trenton, Princeton, Brandywine, and Germantown.

For example, the Delaware regiment that had seen its first fighting on Long Island was in the fight at Camden in 1780. It lost so many men that its few survivors were combined with Maryland companies to form a new regiment. Later still, its remaining veterans were organized into a crack light company.

Similarly, the Marylanders who had marched north under William Smallwood in 1776 to join Washington in New York were still with the American army that left Williamsburg, Virginia, in 1781, headed for the siege of Yorktown. They had fought through the early disasters, and they were there, still fighting, in the final moment of victory.

Regimental flag, 5th Foot

Regimental flag, 33rd Foot

Reserve, N.Y. Public Library

Regimental Flag, 9th Foot

Collection of Mrs. John Nicholas Brown

This British officer's uniform coat is faced with blue of the House of Hanover, indicating that he belongs to a Royal regiment. The coat's knee-length skirts are turned back for greater ease in marching. The contemporary illustration of a British camp shows the common soldiers' laundry drying on tents. At far right, camp followers cook a meal. The commander's three-part tent is at center. In the background are the sutlers', or butchers', tents. Camp guards patrol in the foreground, where the regiment's colors, drums, cannon, and stacked muskets can be seen.

THE BRITISH FOOT SOLDIER

The British army was the product of favoritism and harsh recruiting. Regiments were raised by a favored officer or gentleman who was paid by the Crown for each soldier he enlisted. The man with the influence to get himself a regiment was often a wealthy amateur who knew little of the art of war. He in turn sold lesser commissions to other gentlemen. The common soldiers were recruited in this fashion: "By lies they lured them, by liquor they tempted them, and when they were dead drunk they forced a shilling [signifying enlistment] into their fists." Unreliable the system was, but it secured hardened, often desperate, men who made good soldiers.

An English regiment had ten companies—eight for line service, one light infantry, and one known as the grenadiers. The grenadiers were picked for strength and courage. They were given detached duty or posts of honor in battle, while the fast light infantry was used for scouting or for skirmishing.

British uniforms were highly ornamental and impractical. Stiff collars and high leather cravats made it difficult to turn the head, and the awkward hats had no visor to shield the eyes. It often took a British soldier three hours a day to wash his white breeches and clean brightwork and belts; but this drudgery was part of the discipline that made him reliable in battle.

Collection of Mrs. John Nicholas Brown

These 1784 drawings of Germans show (top) the men of the Prinz Carl Regiment and (right) a grenadier of the Landgrave's Third Guard.

GERMAN MERCENARIES

The outbreak of war caught Great Britain with a relatively small standing army. Recruiting lagged, and the government fell back on the practice of hiring foreign troops—mercenaries as they were called—to help conquer the rebelling colonies.

It was a move that outraged the Americans and it helped to bring many of the hesitant into the patriot camp. The mood of the day found expression in the Declaration of Independence which denounced George III for an action "unworthy the Head of a civilized nation."

The King and his ministers first tried to hire troops in Russia, but when this attempt failed, they turned to the nearly 300 princes who ruled sections of Germany. A treaty with the Duke of Brunswick produced 4,300 men. The price was more than 11,517 British pounds—and twice that each year for the next two years. In addition, the Duke received "head money" of over 7 pounds for each man furnished and a similar payment for each one killed. Three wounded brought the Duke as much cash as one dead man.

Below, in blue and white, stand an officer, noncom, grenadier, private, and drummer of the Knyphausen Regiment. The jägers (right), former hunters and foresters, wore green. These fine troops carried rifles, and their deadly fire was greatly feared by Americans.

Collection of Mrs. John Nicholas Brown

In all, six German states—Brunswick, Hesse-Cassel, Hesse-Hanau, Waldeck, Anspach-Bayreuth and Anhalt-Zerbst—sent nearly 30,000 men to the colonies during the war. Of these, some 12,000 never returned home. Nearly 5,000 deserted to stay in the New World.

The principality of Hesse-Cassel furnished the best of the mercenaries, and so the title of "Hessians" came to be applied, quite inaccurately, to all of the German troops in British service. This loose usage of the name is understandable, however, since more than half of the troops came from Hesse-Cassel, whose greedy ruler stripped his kingdom of one out of every four able-bodied males. The unfortunate soldiers had nothing to say about their fate. They were shipped off to war like cattle, but they had been disciplined to fight well, whatever the cause. And this they did in America.

The miter-shaped brass hat at right belonged to a Hessian fusilier; the regimental flag below was captured at the Battle of Trenton.

Essex Institute

Historical Society of Pennsylvania

A broadside of the time describes Hessian outrages in New Jersey. Not all the atrocity stories were true, but the actions of Cornwallis' army turned many neutrals into patriots.

Reserve, N.Y. Public Library

Musicians, like those above, were always the most colorfully uniformed troops in armies of the period. Flanking these French drummers are (left) the flags of the Dillon and Metz Regiments, and (right) the Soissonnais and Auxonne Artillery.

THE ARMY OF LOUIS XVI OF FRANCE

The British redcoats made a splendid sight. So did the blue-coated Germans. But the most colorful of all the troops were the French.

Most impressive of these were the troops of Lauzun's Legion. They were an eye-filling sight, physically powerful men dressed in light blue jackets trimmed with yellow, yellow breeches, plumed caps, and fur-trimmed capes.

In addition to the Legion, there were four infantry regiments—the Soissonnais, in white and rose; the Bourbonnais, in white and black; the Saintonge, in white and green; and the Royal Deux-Ponts, in blue and yellow.

A dazzling sight were the French, but more important, they were veterans of European combat. Superbly trained and equipped, they were truly the flower of Louis XVI's French army, and their commander, the Comte de Rochambeau, was undoubtedly the best general France could have sent to America.

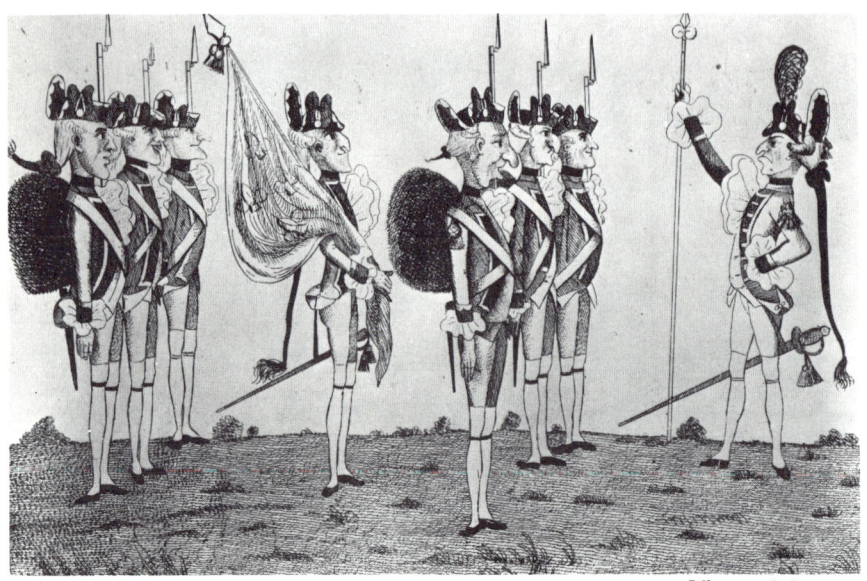

This cartoon (left) showing Rochambeau drilling his men is a 1781 British jibe at the elegance of French uniforms.

The French painting at right portrays (left to right) the uniforms of the Soissonnais, Limousin, and Bretagne troops.

Musée de Blérancourt

This painting by Thomas Sully shows Washington after the victory at Trenton.

THE DARKEST HOURS

"These are the times that try men's souls: the summer soldier and the sunshine patriot will, in this crisis, shrink from the service of his country; but he that stands it Now, deserves the love and thanks of man and woman."

THOMAS PAINE, *The Crisis*—December, 1776

All Boston rejoiced on the morning of March 18, 1776. The last British troops had left; the city was free.

George Washington guessed that the British would strike next against New York, and so even before he entered Boston to celebrate his victory, he started five regiments on the long road south. The bulk of his army quickly followed.

It soon became clear that Washington's guess had been good. The British were massing in tremendous force against New York. On the morning of June 29, Daniel McCurtin, peeping at sunrise through the windows of his sea-front house, was amazed to see, he later wrote, "something resembling a wood of pine trees trimmed . . . the whole Bay was as full of shipping as ever it could be. I . . . thought all London was afloat."

The "wood of pine trees trimmed" was the advance unit of the British fleet. By the following day, more than 100 ships had anchored. Almost daily other fleets arrived. On the decks of some were thousands of Hessian troops, hired by George III's agents in the German states for war against the colonies. From the South came Clinton and Cornwallis. They had been beaten off before Charleston, and they added their men to Howe's army. By late August, more than 500 dark hulls massed off the shores of Staten Island, a fleet that dwarfed in size and power the famed Spanish Armada. It had brought 32,000 seasoned, well-equipped troops —the largest force Great Britain had ever sent from her shores.

Washington had about 20,000 men. Some were members of brave and hardy outfits that were to become famous in the days ahead. There were John Glover's gnarled Marblehead seamen, known as "The Web-Footed Infantry," and John Haslet's stalwart Delaware Continentals, called "The Blue Hen's Chickens." These men could be counted on, and so could the staunch files of the Pennsylvania line, the Marylanders, the Virginia riflemen. But thousands of others in Washington's army were untrained militia. They were cocky now, because

The New York headquarters of George Washington were at No. 1 Broadway (building at left).

John Carter Brown Library

IN PROVINCIAL CONGRESS,
NEW-YORK, June 13, 1776.

WHEREAS this Congress have been informed by the Continental Congress, and have great Reason to believe that an Invasion of this Colony will very shortly be made.

RESOLVED UNANIMOUSLY, That it be, and it is hereby recommended to all the Officers in the Militia in this Colony, forthwith to review the same, and give Orders that they prepare themselves, and be ready to march whenever they may be called upon.

ORDERED, That the aforegoing Resolution be published in the public News-Papers, and printed in Hand-Bills to be distributed.

Extract from the Minutes,
ROBERT BENSON, Sec'ry.

A call for militia to meet Howe's New York attack

81

Sir William Howe wearing the Order of the Bath, awarded for his victory in the Battle of Long Island.

Collection of Mrs. John Nicholas Brown

they had chased the British out of Boston, but they had yet to stand the test of battle.

Adding to Washington's problem was the geography of the area he had to defend. Up and down the isle of Manhattan and across the East River on Long Island, soldiers dug trenches, threw up fortifications. But there was just too much to fortify. The Americans did not have a single warship to oppose the British armada, and it was impossible to guard every inch of shoreline. The long finger of Manhattan was washed on either side by the Hudson and East Rivers; beyond, on Long Island, were the heights of Brooklyn, lapped by deep harbor waters. The British with their powerful fleet could force their way up the rivers and land troops behind the American lines. Clearly, Brooklyn and Manhattan were potential death traps.

Wisdom called for retreat to the north, up into the rocky fastness of Westchester County where the British fleet could not follow. But Washington and his generals, amateurs in large-scale strategy, wanted to hold New York, and so they made a serious error: they divided their army, keeping part in Manhattan, sending the rest across the East River to Brooklyn. It was against Brooklyn that Howe finally moved.

The British frigates Rose *and* Phoenix, *with their tenders, force their way up the Hudson River in October, 1776. View is to the north, with Fort Lee at left, Fort Washington at right.*

U.S. Naval Academy Museum

The Royal Navy took control of the Hudson by sailing past poorly manned American shore batteries. Here the Rebels fail to destroy frigates Rose *and* Phoenix *with fire ships.*

Dawn broke clear and hot on August 22, with a breeze off the bay rippling the water and bending the wheat in the fields about New Utrecht and Flatbush on the Brooklyn shore. American lookouts gasped in awe as British frigates and bomb ketches spread their sails and stood over to the Long Island shore. A great procession of barges sculled slowly in their wakes—88 of them, carrying British and Hessian troops, shrill music soaring above them, sun winking bright on bayonets, on scarlet coats and blue coats and high brass helmets.

The invaders stormed ashore almost without opposition. The barges returned to Staten Island, loaded more troops, and came back again. All day the ferrying went on, and by nightfall 15,000 hardened soldiers, the best fighting men of their day, fanned out across the flatlands in front of the American lines.

Washington met the threat by sending more men across the East River into the bottleneck of Brooklyn. Half his army was now on one shore of the river, half on the other. Fortunately, Howe never seemed to realize how easily the Americans could be cut off by his fleet, and fortunately, too, adverse winds held back the British warships. But by August 25, Howe was ready.

He faced an American position with a strong center based on a fortified line running along Brooklyn Heights. Here Israel Putnam commanded. John Sullivan had charge of the left,

A warship of British Admiral "Black Dick" Howe's fleet is shown under sail off Manhattan in 1776.

83

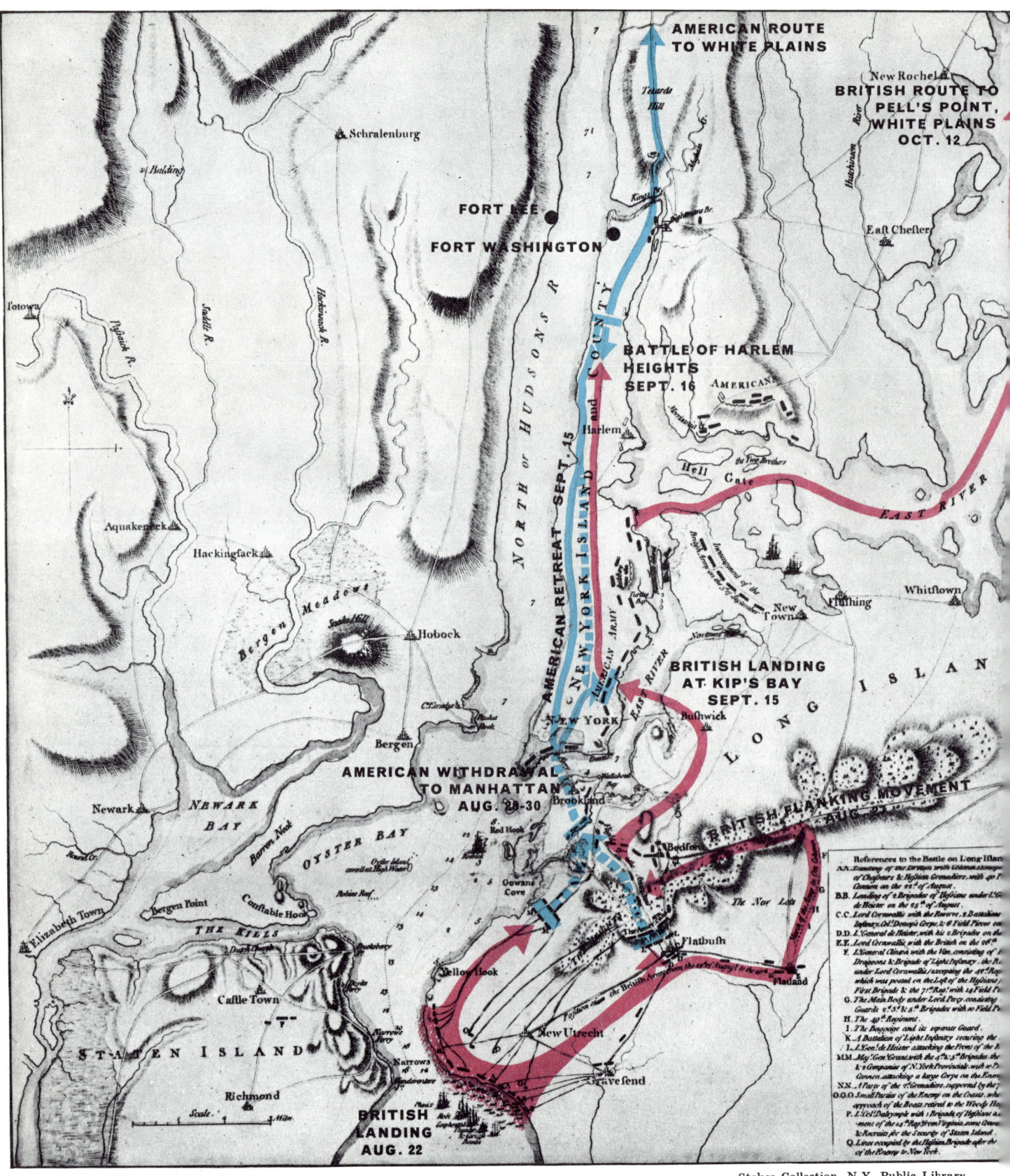

The movements of the opposing armies (British in red, American in blue) during the New York campaign are superimposed on the so-called "Howe War Plan" map, made in October, 1776.

A British officer, Archibald Robertson, sketched this view of the British fleet and camp on Staten Island in July, 1776. In the left background, beyond the forest of masts, is the dark tip of Long Island.

a line thrust forward from the center and straggling across farm and field until it ended uncertainly in woods. The right wing, also pushed out in front of the center, ran down to Gowanus Bay and was commanded by William Alexander of New Jersey, known to the Americans as Lord Stirling, because of his claim to a Scottish title. The Americans' hope was that Howe would attack their center, but Howe, remembering the slaughter of Breed's Hill, had no such intention. Instead, on the night of August 26, he prepared a surprise for Washington.

Under cover of darkness, a column of 10,000 British troops formed in the Flatlands area beyond the American lines. It curved away from the fortified American center, swung far to the north and found an undefended gap at Jamaica Pass. As the sun rose "with a Red and angry Glare," the British swept through the pass and smashed into the left and rear of the American

A German jäger corps officer shown (right) in full uniform. Below, a German cartoon pokes fun at an awkward Rebel soldier.

85

At Long Island, Maryland and Delaware Continentals retreat after holding back the British long enough to enable the rest of the army to escape.

defenses. The surprise and rout were complete. John Sullivan's entire left wing was crushed and broken, thrown back southward in defeat.

Minute by minute, the disaster mounted. On the whole American front there was only one bright spot. Lord Stirling, on the right, stood like a rock with the British army thundering down upon him. Smallwood's Marylanders and Haslet's "Blue Hens" from Delaware fought fiercely around the gray stone walls of the Cortelyou house near the banks of Gowanus Creek. Stirling sent most of his men across the creek to safety, then whirled and led a fierce charge on the British lines. The unexpected blow rocked the British back for an instant, but Stirling, engulfed in a sea of scarlet uniforms, was captured.

By noon the battle was over. The Americans had lost 1,000 men, and the rest had taken cover behind Putnam's earthworks. Howe, instead of striking hard and fast, sat down to write a glittering report about his victory. Actually, he had not accomplished much. He had swept away the poorly placed wings of the American army, but he had not destroyed it. Putnam still held Brooklyn Heights.

Behind the American lines, all was confusion. Men wandered up and down trying to find their shattered units. The shock of defeat had left the troops bewildered, disorganized. Only Washington appeared calm and confident. If doubt gnawed at him, he gave no hint of it as he set about the task of restoring order.

For two days, the armies faced each other. Head winds kept the British fleet from moving up the bay, but the weather could shift at any time. Washington saw that his army was hopelessly divided. On August 28 a howling, rain-lashing nor'easter broke, and Washington decided to leave Brooklyn under the protection of the storm.

He rounded up all the small craft on the waterfront, and on the night of August 29 he began the risky task of ferrying his army across the river under the very eyes of the British. Discovery would mean disaster, for an army in the midst of such a hazardous retreat cannot defend itself. Strict orders for silence were given, and units began to pull back stealthily from the forward lines. Fortunately, Washington had fine sailors in his infantry—the men of Israel Hutchinson's 27th Massachusetts from

Collection of William H. Duncan

Salem and the blue-coated, white-trousered Marbleheaders of John Glover. They were men who had lived in boats all their lives. Now, along the drenched wharves and beaches, they bent to the task of spiriting away an entire army.

For six consecutive hours, they rowed back and forth across the East River between the Brooklyn and Manhattan shores. Occasionally, order broke down on the beaches. Men panicked, brawled and fought to get aboard the boats; but these outbreaks were put down quickly, and quiet was restored. Toward morning came a moment of peril. The storm died away. But in its wake came a dense fog that covered shore and river. Through the fog, the seamen of Salem and Marblehead made their last trips. They had taken off 9,500 men and every piece of equipment except a few hopelessly rusted cannon. From the stern of one of the last of John Glover's boats to leave the Brooklyn shore, young Lieutenant Benjamin

Washington is the central figure in this picture of the skillful retreat from Long Island. So quietly did the Americans leave that Howe captured not an army but only three stragglers.

Tallmadge looked back and saw a very tall figure, cloaked and booted, coming down slippery steps with a blue Marblehead arm outstretched to guide him. George Washington was one of the last to leave.

The withdrawal had been a magnificent feat. So quietly had the Americans slipped away that the British and Hessians never suspected what was going on until four o'clock in the morning of the 30th—and then it was too late.

Washington had escaped, but still he was not safe. His position at the tip of Manhattan was much like that on Brooklyn Heights. There was still the danger that the British fleet would sail up the rivers and land troops behind the American lines. Yet Washington wanted so badly to hold New York that he hesitated for nearly two weeks. When he decided to retreat, it was almost too late. Howe was attacking.

The British general, whose favorite pace was the crawl, delayed on the Brooklyn shore until the morning of September 15. Then, finally, British warships slid up the Hudson and East Rivers. Frigates and gun ketches began to fire their salvoes. And at Kip's Bay, in the neighborhood of East 34th Street, barges grounded and Hessian grenadiers in towering helmets came bounding ashore. Only militia opposed them, and the militia, after one look at the enemy's gleaming bayonets, fled in panic. Howe, as usual, took his time. He moved slowly forward, and in the meadows south of the present Grand Central Station, he had his men ground their arms for a noon-day rest.

Once more Howe had missed an opportunity. Washington had most of his army drawn up in a strong position on Harlem Heights, a high cliff-like stretch of ground, north of the present 125th Street, extending to the Hudson River. But far down at the tip of Manhattan were Israel Putnam and Henry Knox, with some 4,000 men and mounds of priceless ordnance and supplies. A quick cross-island thrust by Howe would have cut off Putnam and Knox, but Howe had no speed in him, and the Americans raced to safety.

Fort Washington (on high ground, center) was attacked from three directions. Hessians stormed the fort itself. British troops, ferried by boat up the Harlem River in the foreground, attacked the outposts. In the right background, below the New Jersey Palisades, the British frigate Pearl *shelled American positions from the Hudson.*

They escaped by the slimmest of margins. While they came at a forced march up the west side of the island, Howe at last moved toward Harlem Heights. The two forces, heading for the same point, were separated from each other by the long, broken, and wooded stretch which is now Central Park. Neither column was aware of the other. British flankers at one point fanned into the woods, but they never got a clear look beyond, never glimpsed the exhausted men of Putnam and Knox as they spilled over the heights to safety behind the American lines.

Cornwallis' troops are shown landing from boats in the Hudson and climbing the Palisades to attack Fort Lee. Thomas Davies, a British officer, painted this water color.

This map shows Fort Washington, at the top, and the area where the Battle of Harlem Heights took place.

Howe simply assembled his army before the heights and then sat down to wait and to think.

Washington was thinking, too. A huge hollow, that looked as if it had been scooped from the earth by some gigantic trowel, slanted off from the American front toward the west. On the morning of September 16, Washington pushed 100 picked Connecticut Rangers into this funnel, called the Hollow Way. The Rangers made contact with British light infantry, fired, and battled sturdily.

Long Island and Kip's Bay had given the British false ideas. They charged headlong, expecting the Americans to run as they had run before. Up on Harlem Heights, Washington saw the chance to turn the Hollow Way into a trap. Orders rang out. Rhode Islanders, infantry from Massachusetts, Virginia riflemen charged down into the hollow. The scarlet lines were met, checked! And this time not from behind stone walls, but in open fighting. More troops swept down from the heights. Washington threw in the same militiamen who had run for their lives at Kip's Bay just the day before, and this time they stood and fought. This time it was the British who ran—through a field of buckwheat on the present site of Barnard College, through an orchard, with Americans at their heels. Howe rushed up British and Hessian reserves, and Washington, not daring to risk a full-scale battle, broke off the action. His men had won a skirmish, and though the victory was small, it was enough to boost their

American troops at Harlem Heights were treated to a rare sight—British regulars in flight. Here the 42nd Highlanders, the famous Black Watch, are retreating under heavy fire.

morale. They knew now that they could fight in the open; they had done it, and they had seen the British run.

Once more Howe wasted his days. For a full month, he did nothing. On September 21, a disastrous fire leveled much of New York behind him, costing him more in equipment than Washington's army had. For Washington, the period of waiting was even worse. He had lost valuable stores in Manhattan. He lacked supplies and materiel of war, the number of desertions was rising, and always there was the menace of that huge British fleet in the Hudson, if Howe ever got around to using it. Washington's officers urged a new retreat into Westchester, and on October 16 Washington agreed.

His withdrawal was painfully slow. Carts were shaky, horses famished. Supplies had to be leapfrogged in short hauls that wasted time. Howe stirred sluggishly and followed. He moved up the East River, and put troops ashore at Pell's Point, intending to get behind Washington. John Glover's men fought off the landing party long enough for Washington to get his troops together in a defensive position at White Plains. Howe attacked him there on October 28, and charged the American right with cavalry in the first action of its kind in the war. Again the Americans broke. Again Howe did not pursue.

Instead, he swung south and struck at two forts that Washington had left behind him. They were built on rocky heights on opposite sides of the Hudson—Fort Washington on the New York shore, Fort Lee on the Jersey Palisades. Washington had hoped their guns would control the river, but British warships had forced their way past the forts, and now both were in danger.

On November 16, Howe mounted an all-out attack against Fort Washington and its garrison of nearly 3,000 men. Warships pounded it from the river. Artillery hammered it from the land. Troops stormed ashore from the fleet, and Howe's soldiers from Westchester smashed at

The European view of the British seizure of New York is pictured in this series of colorful German engravings. The panel above shows the landing.

(Above) British troops enter New York City, 1776

(Below) The fire that soon swept through the city

91

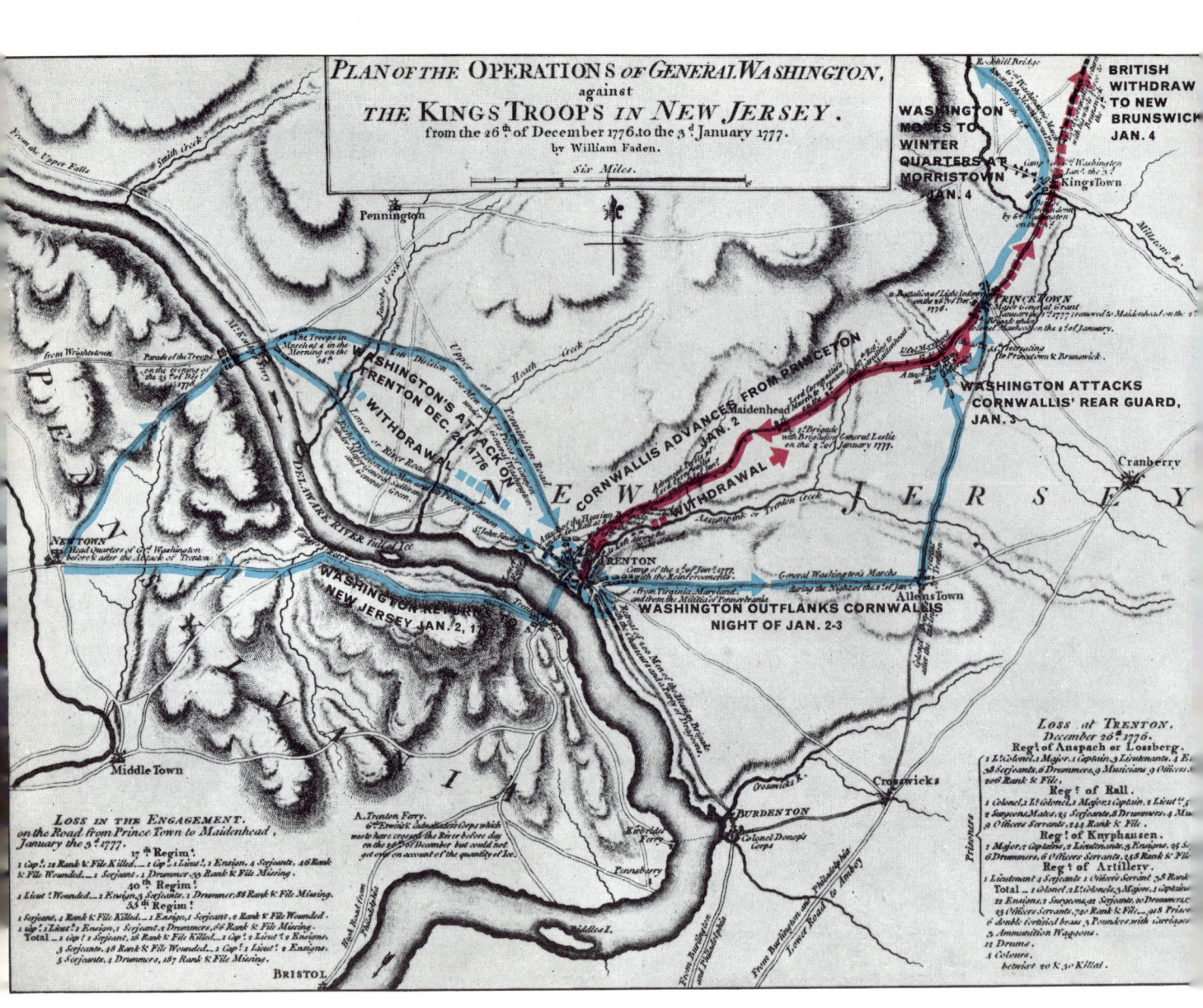

A British map of the period showing the routes of Washington's attack on Trenton and his later march to Princeton. American troop movements are shown in blue, British in red.

the landward bastions. The fort fell. Howe captured the entire garrison, 146 cannon, 12,000 rounds of artillery ammunition, 2,800 muskets and 400,000 cartridges. Four days later, he repeated the stroke, crossing the Hudson, scaling the Palisades and capturing Fort Lee. This time the Americans escaped, but they left behind them additional precious munitions and supplies.

Washington was now in a desperate way. His army was reduced by battle losses, capture, and desertions to less than 3,000 men. In the cold mist and drizzle of late November, they fled across New Jersey. The chase was led by Cornwallis, who, unlike Howe, believed in speed. He pushed his men at a pace of 20 miles a day. The Americans pulled out of Newark just as the Hessian jägers came storming into it. They left New Brunswick, as Washington reported to Congress, with the enemy "fast approaching, some of 'em in sight now." They had to burn their tents and baggage, because they could not carry them. The men were almost naked, and death and desertion swept their ranks. A British officer was shocked to see that "many of the Rebels who were killed . . . were without shoes or Stockings, & Several were observed to have only linen drawers . . . without any proper shirt or Waistcoat . . . they must suffer extremely."

Across the Delaware and into Pennsylvania the survivors went, and there finally they found a chance to pause and rest. Washington had seized or smashed every boat on the river as he put the water barrier behind him. And Howe, convinced that the rebellion was falling apart, called off the pursuit and began to garrison a string of posts across New Jersey.

Some reinforcements joined Washington. He could count perhaps 6,000 men, but many were "entirely naked and most so thinly clad as to be unfit for service." In a private letter, Washington confessed that unless he got more men "the game will be pretty near up." But the outlook was for fewer men, not more; at year end, enlistments would be up, and most of his soldiers would be leaving.

Winter closed down. Ice formed on the Delaware; then warm rains came, and, following these, a freezing, bone-chilling cold. The river was in full flood, jammed with great, massive sheets of ice that spun and swirled down from

A British army kettledrum West Point Museum

the upper reaches. Any soldier could tell at a glance that the river was impassable.

Safe beyond it, in Trenton, sat Colonel Johann Rall and his garrison of more than 1,000 Hessians. They were celebrating victory and Christmas. Washington, informed of their joy-making, began to plan a counter-stroke. "Necessity, dire necessity, will, nay must, justify my attack," he wrote, and for his army, he coined the watchword, "Victory or Death."

On the night of December 25, men in remnants of blue and white uniforms began to gather forty-foot Durham boats on the Pennsylvania shore. The "Web-Footed Infantry" of John Glover was at work again. The roads leading down to the river were astir with soldiers

Edward Hicks' conception of Washington at the crossing of the Delaware
Collection of Nina Fletcher Little; Courtesy *Life*

bending into gale-driven sleet, their path "tinged here and there with blood from the feet of men who wore broken shoes"—or no shoes.

The Durham boats shoved out into the dark, ice-choked flood. Huge slabs of ice crashed against their sides, lunged under their bows, ripped at their sterns; but Glover's boatmen rowed on, their hands stiff and freezing. Trip after trip they made, ferrying 2,400 men and 18 of Knox's cannon across the river. By four in the morning, the Americans were ashore north of Trenton, with nine long miles to cover before they could attack at dawn.

They set out in two columns. John Sullivan led one straight down the river road. Nathanael Greene took the Pennington Road, swinging inland to hit the city from the northeast. Their gunpowder was soaked; if it did not dry out in time, their muskets would be useless. Washington, who went with Greene, said grimly to an aide: "Tell General Sullivan to use the bayonet. I am resolved to take Trenton."

Ice had formed on the roads. Men slipped and fell in a clatter of equipment, were yanked to their feet, and went stumbling on. The eastern sky began to pale and the columns broke into what a soldier later called a "long trot."

Before them lay Trenton's hundred-odd houses. Ice glinted on picket fences, bowed the trees in orchards, glazed the stone barracks where the Hessians slept. A few of the Hessians were beginning to stir and moan with post-Christmas hangovers. Outposts were sleepy.

It was shortly after 7:30 that a Hessian lieutenant saw movement on the Pennington Road, then heard shots, running feet, shouts. A warn-

This print shows Washington leading one of the two American columns that charged into Trenton. Hessians in red coats are shown running from barracks and trying to form in this early stage of the battle.

Old Print Shop; Courtesy *Life*

The drama of a great moment in the Revolution—the surrender of the Hessians at Trenton—is captured in this painting by John Trumbull. Washington offers his hand to the fatally wounded Colonel Rall. General Nathanael Greene is on the white horse at right.

ing was cried—too late. Down by the river there was a horrible din where John Sullivan was going in with the bayonet. Henry Knox's field pieces began to slam out. Farther south, John Glover's men, tough, tireless despite their killing chore on the river, smashed across a little stream called the Assunpink and knifed into Trenton.

Washington and his staff stationed themselves on high ground at what is now Princeton Avenue. The commander-in-chief threw every man in his command into the battle. Captain William Washington and Lieutenant James Monroe (later to be President) led a charge that cut down the gunners around two Hessian field pieces. As powder dried out, muskets began to crack. Colonel Rall, still somewhat dazed from his holiday celebrations, raged up and down King and Queen Streets, bravely trying to rally his men. He was shot down, mortally wounded. The Hessian resistance collapsed, and the troops threw down their arms in a wintry orchard. Enemy dead and prisoners totaled more than 1,000, while Washington had just four men wounded.

The battle had taken less than three-quarters of an hour, but it had changed the course of an entire war. The rabble that previously had run away had turned tiger at last, and the impossible had been achieved. A garrison of sturdy Hessians, trained veterans of Europe's wars, had been surprised, beaten, and captured by amateurs in homespun rags. Never again, even in the darkest days ahead, would despair be quite so deep or hope so hard to find as it had been before the miracle of Trenton.

After the victory, Washington returned quickly across the Delaware. The year ended, enlistments expired. Officers went through the ranks, begging the men to stay. Enough signed up so that Washington still had an army, and he went back and re-occupied Trenton, hoping to strike another major blow.

Soon he was in a trap. Cornwallis, who had given up all thought of home leave after Trenton, was charging to the front with 8,000 well-

Princeton College's Nassau Hall and, at right, the college president's home. Both were looted by Hessians, and Nassau Hall was the last refuge of British in the Battle of Princeton.

equipped men. On January 2, he ringed Washington and his 5,000 scarecrows in Trenton, the river at their backs. That night, Cornwallis was confident he would "bag the fox" in the morning. But when daylight came, "the fox" was gone.

Beginning at one o'clock in the morning of January 3, 1777, Washington made his move. He left a skeleton force to keep the campfires well-stoked and burning steadily, for the unsuspecting Cornwallis to see. Then he led the rest of his men across the Assunpink and around the flank of the sleeping British army. The Americans went silently, gun wheels muffled in sacking, cannoneers holding the trace chains so that they would not clank on the icy ground. Dawn—"bright, serene and extremely cold, with a hoar frost" on everything—found Washington well behind the completely duped Cornwallis. The Americans were nearing Princeton when Lieutenant Colonel Charles Mawhood, bringing up the rear guard of Cornwallis' army, emerged from the town on the Trenton road. The two forces met head-on.

Mawhood's trained regulars charged with the bayonet. Hugh Mercer's slow-loading riflemen could not stand up to them, and Mercer himself was killed. The Americans began to panic. Another rout, like those of Long Island and Kip's Bay, appeared to be in the making, when Washington, mounted on a white horse, charged into the thick of bullets and bayonets. An aide, watching, flung his cloak over his eyes

William Mercer, deaf-mute son of the American General killed at Princeton, drew this battle scene. American artillery has just come on the field and is opening up with a heavy fire on the British.

to shut out the sight of his chief's death. But when he looked again, Washington was still there, his white horse plunging from one knot of fugitives to another, his tall and martial figure rallying his men, urging them back into battle.

The tide turned. Henry Knox's field pieces thundered across the frosted meadows. Over a ridge Daniel Hitchcock's Rhode Island and Massachusetts brigade and the hard-shooting Pennsylvanians of Edward Hand came running. Mawhood's lines shook, then broke away in flight. The British regulars, completely routed, pounded down the road to Trenton, with Washington yelling, "It's a fine fox chase, my boys!"

A long pursuit, however, would have been too dangerous. Washington called off his men and led them into Princeton. There he found a group of the enemy holding out in Nassau Hall. Up came Knox's guns again. Captain Alexander Hamilton fired a round at the college building, and the garrison, "a haughty, crabbed set of men," filed out and surrendered.

Princeton was no place to linger. Cornwallis, stung by the mauling of his rear guard, was back up the road from Trenton bringing an overwhelming force.

Washington led his men into the high hills around Morristown and went into winter quarters. How weak his forces were Howe and Cornwallis could not know. They dared not try to penetrate the snow-covered wilds in which the Rebels had holed up. Instead, Howe pulled in his outposts, uniting his forces about New York to avoid the risk of another Trenton. New Jersey was virtually free. The long retreat that had begun on Long Island had ended in a sudden turn-about, in brilliant victories. The new nation had showed its fighting mettle. The large Loyalist following in New Jersey was squelched, silent. Washington's six-weeks men went home, but recruiting throughout the country became easier, Continental currency gained circulation, supplies flowed a little more freely. Washington's army was still pitifully weak, but it had fought its way back from hopelessness.

Historical Society of Pennsylvania

Washington on horseback reviews his ragged troops at Valley Forge.

THE MAKING OF AN ARMY

"... you might have tracked the army from White Marsh to Valley Forge by the blood of their feet."

GEORGE WASHINGTON

Through the winter in the frosty hills of Morristown, the Continental Army suffered terribly. Clothes were worn to rags; there was little food; and smallpox broke out. Men sickened and died in their miserable log huts on the south slope of Thimble Mountain. Washington set up special isolation areas to keep the disease from sweeping the entire camp. Fearful that the army might rot in idleness, he set the men to building a fort for which there was no actual military need —a stronghold aptly named Fort Nonsense. Through the long cold weeks of winter, the army's only battle was to stay alive. Finally, spring came and, with it, supplies and fresh strength for the worn battalions.

In March the brig *Mercury*, out of Nantes, docked at Portsmouth, New Hampshire, with 1,000 barrels of fine powder and a heavy cargo of clothing and munitions. She was the first of 35 American ships that had sailed from French ports, laden with the supplies of war. With the new arms came men to use them. Some of the veterans back from prison in Canada, men like huge Daniel Morgan, joined up to serve again, and new recruits came in, swelling the ranks for the summer campaign. Here was strength such as Washington had not known before, but in that strength was weakness. Many of the officers had very little knowledge of war, and most of the troops could barely execute even the simplest maneuvers.

In Canada, British General "Gentleman Johnny" Burgoyne, commanding a powerful army, was driving southward down the chain of lakes and rivers, intent on splitting the colonies in half. Washington had to send Morgan and some of his best men north to meet the threat. Then, with his own forces weakened, he had to face the strong army of Sir William Howe, who had some 15,000 men available for battle in the field. British plans called for Howe to smash Washington and drive up the Hudson to join Burgoyne at Albany. But Howe did not follow the plan. He evidently decided that Burgoyne was strong enough to handle matters in the north alone, and he packed his 15,000 men into a huge fleet of 260 ships and headed out to sea, bent on a separate campaign of his own.

Washington could only guess at Howe's purpose. The British commander might strike a blow at any spot on the exposed Atlantic coast, but it seemed to Washington that the probable goal of such a huge expedition would be the

This 1777 handbill promises all Loyalist recruits 50 acres of land at the war's end.

The surprise night attack on Anthony Wayne's division at Paoli, near Philadelphia, became a slaughter. The British, using only bayonets, killed or wounded some 150 Americans and lost fewer than 10 men themselves.

Rebel capital of Philadelphia. And so Washington moved his army from Morristown into Bucks County in Pennsylvania, ready to meet the new threat.

In camp near Neshaminy Bridge, Washington and his army were joined by one of the most romantic figures of the war. He was Marie Joseph Paul Yves Roch Gilbert du Motier, Marquis de Lafayette. Not yet 20, he had become so wrapped up in the ideals of the American Revolution that he had left his wife and family and come to America to offer his services. Foreign volunteers had descended in droves on Congress. Some were men of real ability and value, such as the Polish Count Casimir Pulaski who joined Washington's army in 1777 and rose to Brigadier General and chief of cavalry. But many, demanding high rank and pay, were mere adventurers with shadowy military backgrounds. Lafayette at first was snubbed as just another self-seeker. But soon he met Washington, and from that meeting sprang a lasting friendship —one that was to stand as a personal symbol of the alliance between America and France.

Lafayette was just making his acquaintance with Washington's army when Howe finally reappeared. He had wasted an entire month of ideal summer weather on a ridiculously long sea voyage. But on August 22, 1777, his great fleet finally loomed out of the ocean mists, landing the British army at the head of Chesapeake Bay. Philadelphia was only about 50 miles away.

Washington moved south to meet the enemy, and Howe, after resting and refitting his sea-weary troops, drove north. The two armies collided on September 11 along a placid little stream known as Brandywine Creek, south of Philadelphia.

In the morning of that September day, four young girls "were walking in the road . . . close by Polly Buckwalter's lane." They saw horsemen riding through the fields under the tall elms. The troopers were a patrol sent out by General "Scotch Willie" Maxwell and his Jerseymen. A horseman called to the four, "Girls, you'd better get home . . . the British regulars are coming up the road." One of the girls, Elizabeth Coates, remembered looking down the road and seeing the redcoats "in great numbers." Then she and her friends scurried home.

Actually, the redcoats were not "in great numbers" at this particular spot, but Washington and his generals, like Elizabeth Coates, thought that they were. Howe was doing exactly what he had done at Long Island. He had thrown out a force in front large enough to keep Washington occupied, and he was taking the main strength of his army on a long sweeping march to circle the American lines and fall on their flank and rear.

Washington and his generals seem not to have remembered Long Island. They spent all morning preparing for an attack in the center, across a ford of the Brandywine. And all the time Howe was slipping away, crossing the unwatched upper fords of the creek and curving around the American right flank, commanded by New Hampshire's unlucky John Sullivan. It was late in the afternoon before the British got in position, but when the blow fell, it was shattering. British and Hessian troops crashed into the exposed tip and rear of Sullivan's line and put the Americans to flight.

Units broke and teamsters panicked. The uproar far off to his right finally alerted Washington to the danger, and he acted with swiftness and decision, but too late. He ordered Nathanael Greene and a whole division of Virginians to go to Sullivan's aid. Then he tore off across the fields, Lafayette galloping hard beside him, to take command at the point of danger.

Lafayette, his leg creased by a British musket ball, falls wounded at the Battle of Brandywine Creek.

Four miles of rough, broken ground lay between Greene's division and the battle, but "Joe Gourd" Weedon's leading Virginia brigade covered the distance in only 45 minutes. Without pause, it wheeled and plunged into battle in a narrow, wooded pass near the peaceful Birmingham meeting house. There the Virginians crashed head-on into the British veterans and for 45 furious minutes battled the enemy almost toe to toe and musket to musket. Lafayette was wounded in the thigh as he galloped back and forth across the fire-swept field, and as night fell the Virginians finally were forced to retreat. But they went fighting and in good order. By their gallant stand, they had saved the army.

The defeat meant, however, that Philadelphia could not be saved. The Continental Congress realized this and, after some hesitation, moved from the city to Lancaster and then on to York, which for the next several months was to be the capital of the United States. Howe, advancing slowly, occupied Philadelphia.

Emmet Collection, N.Y. Public Library

101

At Germantown, the Americans wasted precious time attacking a few British soldiers hiding in the Chew house (actually larger than shown here). Troops of Wayne and Sullivan, in background, advance along both sides of the Germantown Road.

Washington's army hovered near the city, posing a constant threat, but nothing seemed to go quite right for the Americans. Even one of their most alert and daring generals, "Mad" Anthony Wayne, allowed himself to be surprised in camp at Paoli by a British force that swept out of the night and put his men to the bayonet. The Americans cried "massacre," but the charge could not change the fact that again they had met with cruel defeat.

The string of disasters began to have its effect on American morale. The fall of Philadelphia had been a stunning shock at first, but men got over it. After all, the Congress was still functioning at York. The loss of the capital did not mean the loss of the cause. But the continuing defeats in the field were another matter. Civilians and even some of the best officers in the army began to look at Washington in doubt and ask the question: Is the right man in command?

Washington must have been aware of such rumblings, but calm and unshaken as ever, he concentrated on studying the British positions. And so, just at a time when even Nathanael Greene was agreeing with Washington's Adjutant General, Timothy Pickering, that the commander-in-chief did lack decision, Washington disproved the judgment by deciding to *attack*.

The British advance post was at Germantown, a village of small houses and stone mansions strung along the main highway leading to Philadelphia. Washington decided to strike it from two directions. A heavy column under John Sullivan would plunge straight down the Germantown Road; a second, led by Nathanael Greene, would swing to the east and crash in from that direction, joining Sullivan at a crossroads in the heart of the British-Hessian position. It was a daring plan if it worked, but it required precision and co-ordination—two columns of relatively unskilled troops would have to make a long night march and strike together from different directions at exactly the right time and place.

The advance began at 7 P.M. on October 3, 1777. The troops had to cover twenty miles before making contact with the enemy. By 3 A.M., Sullivan, accompanied by Washington, was inside the British picket lines. As dawn approached, an autumn mist rose from the land, a white and confusing blanket that was to prove a greater menace than British guns.

Valley Forge Historical Society

At Mount Airy, the Americans struck hard into the British camp. Sleepy grenadiers and light infantrymen, staggering into formation, were broken and swept back. Yelling and stabbing, the Americans rushed on, excited at the prospect of victory. British drums began beating out the call to retreat. Sir William Howe, riding to the front, was caught in a swirl of fleeing scarlet coats and beat about him with his sword, roaring, "For shame, Light Infantry! . . . it's only a scouting party." Just then, American gunners loomed through the fog and battle smoke and blasted off a hail of grapeshot. A British officer later recalled, "I never saw people enjoy a charge of grape more, but we really all felt pleased . . . to hear the grape rattle about the commander-in-chief's ears after he had accused the battalion of running away from a scouting party."

A big American victory seemed in the making, but just at the moment of success everything began to go wrong. East of the Germantown Road, the square stone mansion of Tory Benjamin Chew stood in the mists like a haunted castle. British stragglers from the 40th Regiment flung themselves into it, barricaded the doors, and turned its stout walls into a miniature fortress. "Scotch Willie" Maxwell's Jerseymen

103

The Howe brothers' inactivity in Philadelphia led to this cartoon. In the background, the Admiral's flagship Eagle *is abandoned as he and the General drowse over a punch bowl. France, Spain, and Holland are shown milking dry the cow of British commerce, while an American saws off its horns. At right, a suffering Englishman cannot rouse the sleeping British lion.*

tried to crash in, but were beaten back and began to fire at the windows. Common sense urged that a small body of troops be left to ring the Chew mansion and that everything else be hurled into the attack down the road, where the British were steadying and Sullivan was meeting with stiffer resistance. But the Americans did not listen to common sense.

Timothy Pickering, coming on the scene at the Chew mansion, found Washington and several other generals in a nearby field, debating the problem. Henry Knox, the most deeply read in military lore among the American generals, sought in his mind for a precedent—and came up with the wrong answer. "It would be unmilitary to leave a castle in our rear," Pickering quoted him as saying. And so, though the Chew mansion could hardly be called a castle in a strict military sense, more troops were flung against it, artillery was brought up and began to bang away—and Sullivan, in deep trouble, did not get the help that might have decided the day.

While the Americans were wasting their efforts on the worthless Chew house, Sullivan's drive had spent its force. Some of his men were

Howe's officers in Philadelphia gave him a gaudy farewell. The largest party of its kind ever seen in America, it was called the Mischianza. *Its theme was "a fantastic exhibition of sham chivalry."*

out of ammunition. Militia units became confused in the fog, fired on each other and fled. In the crisis of the battle, Nathanael Greene's men arrived on the field. They had had much farther to march than the headquarters staff had estimated and, as a result, were late getting into action. They struck finally into what they thought were the British lines. Both groups opened fire, and, too late, Greene's troops discovered that their opponents were Anthony Wayne's men, not the British.

Taking advantage of the Americans' confusion, the British hurled fresh troops into the battle. Greene's men struck hard, fought blindly in the mists, then fell back, losing prisoners and guns. Off to the west, Sullivan was in retreat. The cost of the daring attack had been heavy. American losses totaled about 1,000 men; the British, half that number. Yet it had been a near thing for the Americans. They had smashed into seasoned British and German formations on a far larger scale than at the Hollow Way, and had seen them run. Perhaps the next time ...

Missed chance that it was, Germantown had a lasting effect on the American cause. Foreign generals and statesmen, according to the British historian Sir George Otto Trevelyan, "were profoundly impressed ... that a new army, raised within the year and undaunted by a series of recent disasters, had assailed a victorious enemy in its own quarters and had only been repulsed after a sharp and dubious conflict."

The Battle of Germantown practically ended the year's campaigning. Howe did not follow up his victory, but spent a precious month clearing out American forts on the lower Delaware so that ships could come up the river to Philadelphia with supplies for his army. As for the Americans, they were not in much shape to fight. On November 15, the day the Rebels were planning to abandon the last of the Delaware forts, the Continental Congress meeting in York adopted the Articles of Confederation, the weak and loosely jointed pact by which the thirteen states were to be united and governed for the rest of the war. This done, most of the members of Congress went home. Washington and his army were on their own.

Although the army had been strengthened in numbers by brigades flowing down from the north, where a great victory had been won over Burgoyne at Saratoga, it was still in desperate physical shape. Tattered clothes had been patched and patched again. Blankets were scarce and shoes scarcer. Food could have been plentiful, but was not, as a result of poor transportation and a civilian tendency to hoard. On Thanksgiving Day, Lieutenant Colonel Henry Dearborn wrote "... God knows we have little to keep it with, this being the third day we have been without flour or bread."

N. Y. State Historical Association

Baron von Steuben, shown wearing European medals and the blue Order of the Cincinnati, was the expert Prussian drillmaster who swore at the Rebel troops in two languages—but turned them into soldiers.

Ragged American troops kneel in the snow at Valley Forge learning the basic principles of drill and maneuver from the exasperated, sternly pointing Baron von Steuben.

Since his army was too weak to attempt another attack, Washington looked about for a winter camp. The site he chose was 20-odd miles to the west and north of Philadelphia, where Valley Creek flows into the placid Schuylkill River. At the juncture of the two streams, the ground to the east of the creek rises steeply to a 250-foot crest, then rolls away into a two-mile plateau. An old forge gave the place its name—Valley Forge.

Here, in late December, the main army of the United States went into winter quarters. The men dragged themselves thirteen miles from their last camp at Whitemarsh, leaving bloody footprints in the snow. They built themselves squat log huts chinked with clay. There was no food, then there was a little, then none again. Soap was as rare as meat and flour. Bruised feet and chapped hands festered. Dirty rags, all that was left of clothing, brought on an itch that only soap and water could cure, and on the bleak plateau there was not even water. Some units had to send men on a two-mile round trip to fill heavy buckets at the creek and lug them back.

Starvation, nakedness, disease, death—these were the foes that swept through Valley Forge, reducing Washington's veterans to a scarecrow army. Officers mounted guard in old padded dressing gowns or wrapped in blankets. A soldier was seen keeping his post and presenting arms properly while standing on his hat to keep his bare feet out of the snow. Foreign officers were amazed. They had never seen endurance like this.

In late February, a valuable newcomer arrived in camp. He called himself Baron Friedrich Wilhelm Ludolf Gerhard Augustin von Steuben, late of the armies of Frederick the Great of Prussia. He described himself as a Lieutenant General, but actually he was a half-pay Captain who had been out of work for fourteen years. The deception did not matter. Washington liked von Steuben, and the Prussian quickly proved his worth. He was an expert drill master, and perhaps no army was ever in greater need of a drill master than Washington's.

On the bleak plateau of Valley Forge, von Steuben drove the troops from sunrise to sunset. He simplified the manual of arms, smoothed out such simple moves as right-face and left-face. He drilled squads, platoons, companies, regiments, then whole brigades and divisions, until heavy masses of men could march smoothly and maneuver together. Under von Steuben's strict taskmaster's eyes, a new army was born.

At right is a copy of Washington's requisition of supplies at Valley Forge in the winter of 1777.

As if to offset this good fortune, another general arrived in camp—the gaunt, ugly, sarcastic Major General Charles Lee. Lee had been a British officer and a Major General in the Polish army. His reputation for skill and daring had secured him a position second only to Washington on the list of American generals. Some, impressed by his service in Europe, felt that he should have been first, and Lee was inclined to agree with them. Arriving at Valley Forge, only recently exchanged after having been taken prisoner in 1776, Lee was critical of much that he saw. He sneered at von Steuben's drillmastering and drew up his own plans for "The Formation of the American Army," which called for less infantry and more cavalry. He said that he got on well with General Washington and added, "I am persuaded . . . that he cannot do without me."

This conceit was bad enough, but added to it was Lee's gift for nasty gossip. On one occasion he told an acquaintance that American troops were so badly trained and unreliable that they could never beat British regulars, no matter what the circumstances, and several times he sharply questioned Washington's military skill.

The bad feeling between Washington and Charles Lee cast a dark shadow over a future that seemed positively bright after the horror of Valley Forge. The outlook always seemed brighter for the Continental Army in the spring, but this spring of 1778, it seemed brighter than ever. For on May 5 Washington announced that France had joined the war. France was sending an army and a navy to the American coast. No longer did the ragged Rebels stand alone.

The entrance of France into the war had an immediate effect on British hopes and plans. Sir Henry Clinton, who had succeeded Howe in

> BY HIS EXCELLENCY
> # GEORGE WASHINGTON, Esquire,
> GENERAL and COMMANDER in CHIEF of the Forces of the UNITED STATES of AMERICA.
>
> BY Virtue of the Power and Direction to Me especially given, I hereby enjoin and require all Persons residing within seventy Miles of my Head Quarters to thresh one Half of their Grain by the 1st Day of February, and the other Half by the 1st Day of March next ensuing, on Pain, in Case of Failure, of having all that shall remain in Sheaves after the Period above mentioned, seized by the Commissaries and Quarter-Masters of the Army, and paid for as Straw.
>
> GIVEN under my Hand, at Head Quarters, near the Valley Forge, in Philadelphia County, this 20th Day of December, 1777.
>
> G. WASHINGTON.
>
> By His Excellency's Command,
> ROBERT H. HARRISON, Sec'y.
>
> LANCASTER; Printed by JOHN DUNLAP.

Historical Society of Pennsylvania

The troops at Valley Forge were almost shelterless, and Washington immediately put them to work building log huts.

New-York Historical Society

command in Philadelphia, was ordered by London to send thousands of his troops to the West Indies and to leave Philadelphia and unite his remaining forces in New York. The order posed a problem for Clinton. Since French warships might arrive at any moment off the coast, he could not ship his command back to New York by degrees. He had to move quickly, and he determined, after sending away all the fleet would hold, to cross the Delaware with his main army and march across New Jersey to New York.

It was a risky maneuver, but there was no other way the retreat could be carried out. Clinton began sending his troops across the Delaware at three o'clock in the morning of June 18, 1778, and in just seven hours, he had his entire command across the river, ready for its march through Jersey.

At his headquarters in Valley Forge, Washington had been debating what to do. He became aware of Clinton's intentions about June 1. He saw that there was a possibility of making an attack on Clinton's army while it was scattered along the roads in loose marching order, burdened with a long, cumbersome wagon train. He wanted to take advantage of the situation. But Charles Lee advised caution. If the army and Washington were captured now, he said, the American cause would be lost. It was most important, he argued, to preserve the army until the new French allies could send trained troops and naval vessels. Therefore, Lee favored only a limited attack. For the present, he felt, it would be enough to annoy the marching Clinton and try to wear him down.

Most of the other American generals agreed that it would be wiser to play safe. And so, on June 23, the Continentals crossed the Delaware in pursuit of the retreating British. They followed Clinton and his long train of 1,500 wagons, hoping for a favorable opportunity to strike him a damaging blow.

The weather turned tropical. The barrens of South Jersey steamed after savage downpours. American militia had broken down bridges over ravines and creeks, and Clinton's men had to rebuild them for the wagon train. Sometimes Clinton covered only six miles in a day.

The crawling march made Washington decide that the time to attack was now, while Clinton was tangled up in this hilly country. The question of who should command the advance, or striking force, now became a critical issue. Military etiquette required that such a post of honor go to Charles Lee, who was opposed to an all-out attack, but still the man who stood next to Washington in the table of organization.

Washington did what he felt he had to do: he offered the command to Lee. To Washington's relief, Lee scornfully turned it down. Washington then put Lafayette in charge, and the young Frenchman and Anthony Wayne moved forward to strike at Clinton. Then Charles Lee changed his mind.

New-York Historical Society

Lafayette (at left) was to lead the attack at Monmouth, but was replaced at the last minute by Lee.

Finding that Lafayette had an impressive force of some 6,000 men, Lee decided that the job belonged to him, and he wanted it. Washington yielded, and Lee galloped off to the American camp in Englishtown, where he snatched the command from Lafayette. It was now the night of June 27. The Americans could hear the rumble of the British wagon train passing them and moving on to the north out of reach beyond Monmouth Court House.

Morning of June 28 broke, and General Philemon Dickinson, commanding the New Jersey militia, reported that he was engaged with the British. Lee then sent Wayne with 600 Pennsylvanians and two fieldpieces to strike at what Lee supposed was the British rear. Wayne, handsome and eager, drove vigorously ahead, smashed through some loose British formations, then hit unexpected strength—practically the bulk of the British army. Wisely, Wayne took position along the edge of a swampy ravine and sent back to Lee for help.

But there was no help from Lee. He had received conflicting reports about what the British were doing and was now alarmed for the safety of his own forces. In actual fact, Clinton had been so stung by the harassing militia thrusts that he had turned against Lee with his main army. In the confusion, Lafayette enthusiastically urged an American attack and was taken aback by Lee's answer "Sir, you do not know British soldiers. We cannot stand against them." The young Frenchman replied that British soldiers had been beaten before, and that one must presume it was possible to beat them again.

Wayne fought on. He was joined by Scott's Virginians. But they were up against the flower of the British army. The Queen's Rangers struck them in a wild charge, the 19th Dragoons pounded down upon them. The Americans fired steady volleys, and repelled the British attacks. Nevertheless, they had to fall back, to keep in touch with Lee's main army, which was withdrawing to a stronger defensive position.

Monmouth County Historical Association

Washington (mistakenly pictured on a dark horse) relieves Lee of command at the Battle of Monmouth.

Meanwhile confusion was spreading in the American ranks. If Lee knew what he was doing, no one else did. Very few of his messengers were able to get through with orders to his subordinate officers. Some units retired in good order. Others fled aimlessly without any idea of what they were supposed to do. Insufferable heat made matters worse. It was ninety-six degrees in the shade, and officers and men began to collapse.

The whole effort was falling apart, when someone noticed a dust cloud swirling up on the road from Englishtown, and men stopped in their tracks to stare at a man in blue and buff on a huge white horse. Washington had arrived—and not a second too soon. He charged up to Lee and demanded to know the meaning of the retreat. Anger made him formidable. "Sir? Sir?" Lee stammered out in amazement. There are half-a-dozen versions of what happened next, but most accounts agree that Washington exploded in one of his rare bursts of wrath. Lee went to the rear in disgrace, and Washington took full command on the field.

Years later, Lafayette told over and over how Washington rode "all along the lines amid the shouts of the soldiers, cheering them by his voice and example and restoring to our standard the fortunes of the fight. I thought then, as now, that never had I beheld so superb a man."

It was a great demonstration of personal leadership. Men who had been fleeing minutes before rallied and went back into battle to fight as they had rarely fought before.

The British threw everything they had against the reforming lines—the 42nd Black Watch, light infantry, grenadiers, the Guards. The Dragoons drove in, smashing alongside the towering helmets of the Hessian grenadiers. But the American lines stood firm, and scarlet coats and blue littered the field, struck down by both heat and bullets. Late afternoon ended the action. Clinton flung one last charge at Wayne's lines, but it was beaten off, and the British slowly withdrew. Washington combed the field trying to round up enough fresh men for a counter-attack of his own, but on that day of fierce heat and fiercer fighting, no fresh troops were left. Utterly spent, men fell where they stood, and finally, late at night, the master of Mount Vernon collapsed under an apple tree, spreading his cloak over himself and the exhausted Lafayette.

During the night, Clinton moved off to Sandy Hook and the protection of the British fleet. He had saved his huge wagon train, made good his retreat. The Americans held the battlefield, but they had lost all chance of a major victory. And it was the last chance they were to have in the North. Though the war had five long years to run, never again after that hot June 28, 1778, were the two major armies to meet in battle.

At the Battle of Monmouth, General Washington, on his great white horse, rallied the confused troops. "Cheering them by his voice and example . . . never had I beheld so superb a man," Lafayette recalled.

Chicago Historical Society

Frick Collection

General John ("Gentleman Johnny") Burgoyne, painted by Sir Joshua Reynolds

Public Archives of Canada

Burgoyne's army gathered at St. John's on the Richelieu River in Canada. The two larger warships, the Royal George *(left) and the* Inflexible, *escorted the transports up Lake Champlain to Fort Ticonderoga.*

THE TURNING POINT

"I trust we have convinced the British butchers that the 'cowardly' Yankees can, and when there is a call for it, will fight."

MAJOR HENRY DEARBORN—September, 1777

On the morning of July 1, 1777, the waters of Lake Champlain were alive with motion, bright with color. A fleet was putting out from Crown Point on the west shore, its sails taut in the breeze that sifted down from the high lift of the Adirondacks. Ships almost as large as frigates, trim pinnaces, sloops, and ketches moved across the lake, towing countless bateaux behind them. The waters reflected the images of Indians, painted every color from green to blood red. They mirrored the scarlet coats of British regulars, the blue uniforms of Hessians and Brunswickers, the light green of the jägers. Major General John Burgoyne was setting out to conquer the Rebels.

"Gentleman Johnny" was a tall, handsome man whose face reflected the high living he enjoyed. He had toyed with playwriting, and he was known as a gay spirit, a jolly man given to bursts of rolling laughter. In an age when brutality was common in the ranks, he had a real concern for the well-being of his men, and, as one of his officers wrote, he was "idolized by the army . . . he was the soldier's friend."

The great plan of invasion was Burgoyne's. He had witnessed the slaughter of Breed's Hill, then he had gone back to England and drawn up his own plan of conquest. It called for joint action by three British armies driving from different directions to a meeting in Albany. Burgoyne himself was leading the main thrust straight to the south along the Lake Champlain-Lake George route. Sir William Howe was to come up the Hudson from New York. And from the west Lieutenant Colonel Barry St. Leger was to lead a strong force of British, Hessians, Tories, and Indians from Oswego on Lake Ontario across the state to Albany. With New York carved up by the three armies, all New England would be cut off from the rest of the colonies.

The plan should have worked, but from the start things were handled badly. London was late notifying Howe of the role he was to play, and even when the order was sent, it was not positive. Howe, given a chance to think for

113

The British thought the worst was behind them when they reached the Hudson after a hard wilderness march. Here they start out along the east bank of the river, transporting heavy baggage in barges.

himself, went off on the Philadelphia campaign, robbing Burgoyne of one of the three armies on which he had counted. This was bad enough, but worse was to follow. Burgoyne had drawn up a sound plan of campaign, but blundered when he tried to put it into action.

He began the series of errors on the day of his departure from Crown Point. He took with him 138 pieces of artillery. Burgoyne, with the nightmare of Breed's Hill still in his mind, was determined to smother the Americans with artillery fire if he found them dug in. But hauling this mass of metal through the wilderness slowed his advance to a crawl—and gave the Americans time to rally and throw up earthworks.

This first mistake did not seem so serious in the beginning. Only one American fort, Ticonderoga, stood in Burgoyne's way, and it fell quickly. It was held by only 2,000 poorly equipped troops, and its commander, Major General Arthur St. Clair, a former British officer, had neglected to fortify a peak known as Mount Defiance which overlooked the fort.

Burgoyne ordered his Indian allies to wage war in a civilized manner, but they did not heed his instructions.

St. Clair assumed Mount Defiance was too steep to climb, but Major General William Phillips, Burgoyne's second in command, was a determined man. His men hacked out a rough road, moved guns up the killing slope and established a secret battery on the top of Mount Defiance. St. Clair, discovering this, abandoned Ticonderoga and set out on a night retreat down the lake shore.

General Simon Fraser, a tough, seasoned British veteran, took up the pursuit. He drove his men at a furious pace and, at dawn of July 7, caught up with St. Clair's rear guard near a little hamlet known as Hubbardton in Vermont. A company of militia was surprised and scattered. But then a surprising thing happened. The rest of St. Clair's troops whirled and struck Fraser with such a hammer stroke that British dead began to dot the Vermont meadows and, for a moment, the British pursuit looked as if it might double about and become a rout. Just in time, Baron von Riedesel drove upon the field with his Brunswickers and saved Fraser.

The skirmish might have been taken as a warning of things to come, but "Gentleman Johnny" Burgoyne wasn't a man to take a gloomy view. Ticonderoga had fallen quickly; the Rebels in front of him were little more than a rabble. What was there to worry about?

Nothing, Burgoyne decided, as he settled himself comfortably in the fieldstone house of Philip Skene, late Major of his Majesty's forces and proprietor of Skenesboro. Here the British general studied his next move, and here he came to a puzzling, fatal decision. His own plan called for troops to follow the easy water route south from Lake Champlain to Lake George to the Hudson River. But now Burgoyne decided to ignore Lake George and strike directly overland through twenty miles of wilderness.

To do so, his army had to cut a road through virgin forest. It was steamy, mosquito-ridden work. General Philip Schuyler, the American area commander, added to its difficulty by sending expert woodsmen out ahead of Burgoyne's inching column. The axemen felled trees across existing trails, dammed brooks, and turned what had been solid ground into muck and swamp. Burgoyne's men had to build forty bridges, one of them two miles long, and it cost them twenty-six precious campaigning days to hack their way through those twenty miles of forest.

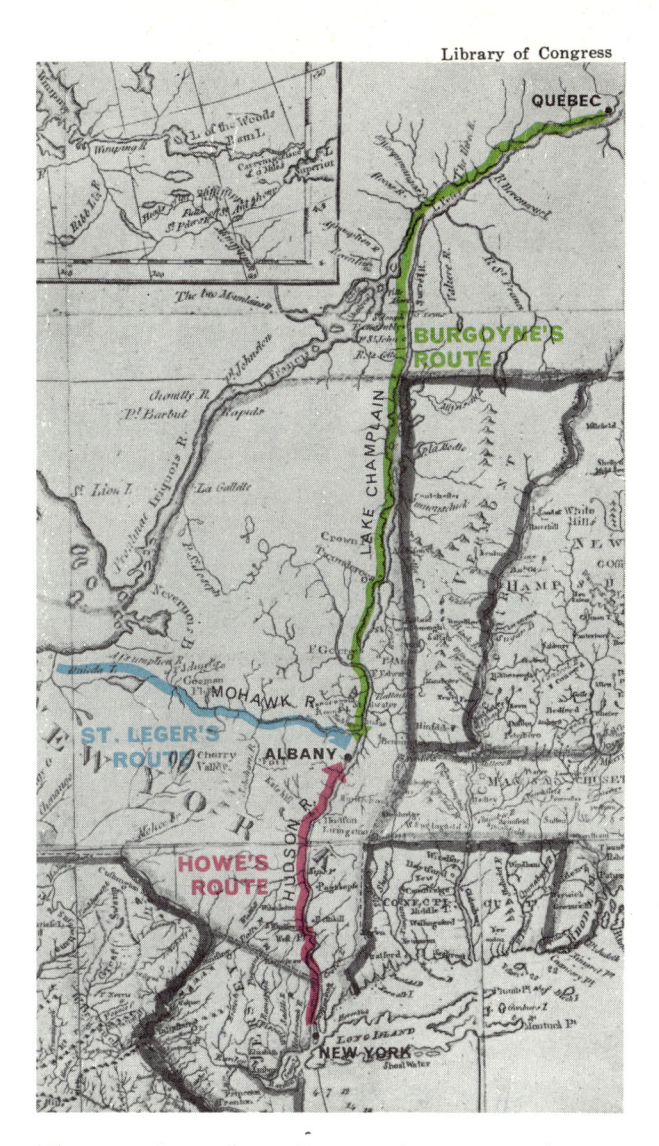

The map above shows Burgoyne's strategy. Arrows show how three armies were to meet at Albany.

While this back-breaking labor was going on, Burgoyne suffered another setback. He had tried from the first to keep his Indian allies under control. He had ordered them to make war only on troops, not on civilians, but such orders meant little to Indians on the warpath. One day a group of drunken young braves brought into camp a scalp whose beautiful hair was recognized as that of a pretty young woman

The scalping of Jane McCrea by Burgoyne's Indians turned many Americans against the British.

named Jane McCrea. From Burgoyne's viewpoint, the Indians could not have made an unhappier choice of victim. Jane McCrea had been the fiancée of Lieutenant David Jones of Colonel John Peters' little band of Tories. Worse, she had been staying with an elderly widowed cousin of General Simon Fraser, commander of Burgoyne's own Advance Corps. The decision of the British government to turn Indians loose on the colonists had already swung thousands of waverers away from the Crown; now, in the scalping of Jane McCrea, Burgoyne's Indians had provided the perfect lesson to sway any remaining doubters. With Indians on the warpath, not even Tories were safe. The Americans seized upon the issue to whip up sentiment and raise the countryside against Burgoyne.

With this tragedy and the horror of those twenty wilderness miles behind them, Burgoyne's columns finally burst into the open on July 29, 1777. Swift movement now might have made up for some of the lost days, but speed was not in Burgoyne. Again he blundered.

He waited long days while round-trips were made to drag his cannon up to the front. While he waited, Burgoyne settled himself comfortably in headquarters with a woman—the wife of his commissary officer. And though he ordered excess stores sent back to Ticonderoga, he still kept thirty carts to lug his own belongings, his traveling wine cellar, and Mrs. Commissary's extensive wardrobe.

This was making war in the grand style—a style completely unsuited to the grim events that were beginning to overtake Burgoyne. Even he must have begun to realize this on August 3, when he received a letter from Howe. The British commander in New York congratulated him on having taken Ticonderoga, then announced: "My intention is for Pennsylvania, where I expect to meet Washington. . . ." Howe was *not* coming north. Burgoyne was on his own.

He kept Howe's bad news to himself, and he refused to let it change his plan. A more sensible man might have turned back to Canada, but not Burgoyne. He always strutted a bit, like an actor upon the stage, and he decided now that his orders—which had been based upon the co-operation of Howe—allowed him to go to Albany, no matter what. *He* would *not* retreat. Besides, he could always rely on Barry St. Leger, moving across the state from the west.

But at that very moment Barry St. Leger was having troubles of his own. He had started out with 500 British and Hessian troops, about the same number of Tories, and some 1,000 Indians under the famed Mohawk chief, Joseph Brant, also known as Thayendanegea. St. Leger's first objective was old Fort Stanwix on the upper Mohawk, near the site of present-day Rome, New York, about 100 miles directly west of Burgoyne.

The fort had been in ruins, but Colonel Peter Gansevoort and Lieutenant Colonel Marinus Willett, of the 3rd New York, had worked miracles in repairing it. They had a garrison of

116

some 750 men, and they coolly turned down repeated demands to surrender, beating back every attack St. Leger hurled against them.

The battle for Fort Stanwix touched off one of the bloodiest clashes of the war, its fury accounted for, in part, by local feuds. With St. Leger were two much-hated Tory leaders, Sir John Johnson and Colonel John Butler. They had been huge landowners in the area and had ruled almost like feudal lords. The common people of the countryside hated them and hated the Indians whom Johnson and Butler had loosed against them. And so they joined up in a force of 800 men, headed by Brigadier General Nicholas Herkimer, to march to the relief of Fort Stanwix.

On August 6, 1777, Herkimer's Tryon County militia stumbled into an ambush carefully laid by St. Leger in a ravine on the south bank of the Mohawk near a place called Oriskany. All day long a fearful wilderness battle raged, with former neighbors and relatives on opposing sides. Before dusk, the Tryon County militia were in full retreat down the Mohawk, carrying the dying Nicholas Herkimer with them.

St. Leger had won the battle and he had prevented the relief of Fort Stanwix, but his Tories and Indians had been terribly mauled. When they returned to their lines around Stanwix, they found that in their absence Marinus Willett had sallied from the fort, raided their camps, and carried off all their goods and belongings.

Still Fort Stanwix was in a desperate way, and St. Leger drew the siege lines tighter around it. The American high command, however, realized the importance of the fort and sent Major General Benedict Arnold with a force of some 1,000 Continentals and militia to its relief. Arnold feared he was too weak really to challenge St. Leger in battle, but by a clever trick he spread the word among the Indians that he was coming with a mighty army of 3,000 men. Panic-stricken, the Indians deserted St. Leger, and the British commander had to retreat. As he did so, his own Indian allies turned upon him, slaughtering his straggling soldiers. The stroke from the west, on which Burgoyne had counted, was canceled out for good.

Back along the Hudson, Burgoyne made new plans. He had heard that there were great

This painting by Edward Buyck shows the raising of the Stars and Stripes over Fort Stanwix, August 3, 1777.

Rome (N.Y.) Historical Society

Tadeusz Kosciuszko, Polish soldier and statesman, was a volunteer in the American Army.

masses of Rebel stores to the east in Vermont, that his dragoons could get needed horses there, and, finally, that great numbers of Tories were eager to join him. A swift blow to the east could reap a three-way harvest, and Burgoyne decided to strike. But having so decided, he blundered again; he gave the job, which demanded speed, to some of the slowest and most cumbersome of his troops.

They were the dismounted German dragoons of Lieutenant Colonel Friedrich Baum. Each man wore boots that weighed twelve pounds a pair without spurs. Each was weighed down with a heavy saber, carbine, and equipment. And each carried a halter to secure the prize mount that would let him come riding back the way a good dragoon should.

This lumbering force of Baum's was backed up by Brunswick grenadiers, only slightly less encumbered than the dragoons, a picked handful of British light infantry, a few Tories, and a swarm of Indians. Baum swung away from the main army and marched toward Bennington in Vermont. There, on August 15, he was brought to bay by one of the strangest armies of the war.

It was a volunteer New Hampshire army, raised chiefly by John Langdon, Speaker of the General Court, who had pledged his personal fortune to meet its expenses. It was commanded by Brigadier General John Stark, the tough veteran of Breed's Hill and Trenton. Stark had quit the Continental Army in disgust, because lesser men had been promoted over his head, and he took command on just one condition—that there would be no foolishness about *this* army.

General John Stark directing his troops at the Battle of Bennington, August, 1777. German prisoners are at left.

Two mortally wounded commanders, Baum of the Germans and Pfister of the Tories, are carried from the field at Bennington.

Given his way, Stark surrounded Baum at Bennington, and in day-long fighting, completely crushed the Hessian force. Only the Indians and some nine dragoons escaped. Burgoyne, learning that Baum was in trouble, sent Lieutenant Colonel Francis Breymann and some additional slow-moving grenadiers to his relief. Before Breymann could get near, Stark had finished off Baum's force. At once, he whirled and attacked the relieving column, hitting it with such fury that Breymann lost a third of his men and had to retreat. In this one day, Stark and his men from the Hampshire Grants put some 900 of Burgoyne's solid, German veterans out of action for good.

Shaking off the setback, Burgoyne pressed on for Albany. At his front, resistance stiffened. A foraging party of thirty of his men was snapped up. Pickets had to be doubled, trebled. And off to the south could be heard the ghostly patter of distant drums. The Americans were massing.

The Americans also had problems. Philip Schuyler, who had done so much to slow Burgoyne's advance, had been relieved of command in favor of pompous Horatio Gates. Gates, with the help of the Polish engineer Tadeusz Kosciuszko, had thrown up strong earthworks on Bemis Heights near Stillwater, and there he waited for Burgoyne to come to him.

Burgoyne could have swept around Gates by keeping to the east bank of the Hudson, and could have forced action on open ground. But British tradition demanded that a challenge be met head-on. And so Burgoyne crossed the Hudson and headed for the American lines.

In doing so, he divided his army into three columns. One wing was led by von Riedesel, the other by Fraser, and Burgoyne himself commanded the center. His scouts had found wagon trails leading to the west. They led to a wide clearing, the abandoned weed-grown farm of a man named Freeman. To Burgoyne, the few

The painting above shows Benedict Arnold, on a white horse, leading a charge at the Second Battle

cleared acres apparently seemed like rolling countryside, where his troops could get out of the woods and fight in the open, in approved European style. Eagerly, he marched for Freeman's farm.

American scouts had watched his advance, and Benedict Arnold, ever a hot and eager fighter, wanted to strike while the British were split up into three separate forces. Gates preferred to sit in his trenches and do nothing. A furious argument developed between the two, and Gates finally permitted Daniel Morgan's riflemen and Dearborn's light infantry to go off to the front to see what they could do.

It was about 1 P.M. on September 19, 1777, when Burgoyne's leading files broke into the Freeman clearing and started across to the line of woods along the southern edge. Suddenly,

of Freeman's Farm in October, 1777. British General Simon Fraser is carried from the field.

in front, there was movement under the trees, made by half-seen men with fur caps and long rifles. Somewhere an unearthly turkey-gobbling broke out. Then came the crack of rifles, and every British officer in the advance force was shot down. Daniel Morgan's riflemen had struck the first blow of the Battle of Freeman's Farm.

More men poured into the woods south of the clearing. There were no stiff, formal lines for Burgoyne to charge. His cannoneers and gunnery officers were picked off before their pieces could be loaded. His men began fleeing back to the north woods. Morgan's riflemen and Joseph Cilley's New Hampshire Continentals headed after them. But the British, once in the shelter of the trees, steadied and fired back into the meadow. The Americans began to falter, and Morgan's turkey-call summoned his men back.

View of the British camp after the Second Battle of Freeman's Farm. General Fraser's funeral procession winds around the base of the hill at right.

For three hours the fighting raged. British losses swelled to frightening figures. Burgoyne rode among his men, and as bullets ripped his coat, he laughed and waved his hat. His men cheered—and continued to die.

In the end, Baron von Riedesel saved the day. He drove his German troops to Burgoyne's aid just as the British were almost on the point of collapse. Before this fresh force, the Americans drew off to the south. The British had survived, but they had lost more than 600 men.

Still Burgoyne refused to retreat. He dug his own entrenchments and waited, hoping that some other British forces might come to his relief. September passed, and October came, and Burgoyne realized that he would have to act alone.

On October 7, 1777, he assembled a force of 1,500 men in a wheat field beyond the Freeman clearing. It was a strange move, for the detachment was far too weak to deliver the kind of desperate attack that was Burgoyne's only hope. Perhaps "Gentleman Johnny" was just putting his men in position to see what would happen. If so, he soon found out.

Shortly after two o'clock in the afternoon, the Americans attacked. General Enoch Poor sent his brigade up the slope of the wheat field hill and charged in among the British grenadiers, putting them to rout. Dan Morgan's turkey-call was heard, and his riflemen and Henry Dearborn's infantry, having circled far, struck the British rear. In the center, Ebenezer Learned's brigade rocked back the German Brunswickers.

Soon all was confusion. Burgoyne threw back the first attack, but with difficulty. Morgan's riflemen took cover in the trees, and a deadly hail of lead swept the clearing. Simon Fraser, one of the most dashing of Burgoyne's generals, was shot from the saddle, fatally wounded, and the troops he had been trying to rally broke.

At the peak of action, Benedict Arnold came storming upon the field. Men cheered this strange, brave man who, in so short a time, was to become a traitor—and Arnold gathered up

At Saratoga (above), Burgoyne offers his sword to Gates, in surrender, as Morgan, in white, looks on.

units, as he swirled across the field, and hurled them at the enemy. He led a furious attack against the Balcarres redoubt. Driven back, he swung to the left, cleared out the light works between the main redoubts of the British line, and sent Morgan's riflemen charging at the Brunswick grenadiers. The Germans broke and fled. Breymann was shot down, and a British bullet smashed Arnold's leg, the same leg that had been hit at Quebec.

With his fall, the attack spent itself, and again, as night fell, the Americans withdrew. Burgoyne still had his army, but it was finished as a fighting force. The British drew back into fortifications around Saratoga. Gates was slow in applying pressure, but it made little difference. Americans, flocking to the kill in ever-growing force, surrounded Burgoyne, cut off his supplies, blocked his retreat. Only surrender was left.

On October 17, the British general surrendered with more than 5,000 crack British and German troops. It was the turning point of the war—the astonishing victory that led directly to the French alliance.

Benjamin Franklin, painted by Charles Willson Peale

THE QUEST FOR ALLIES

"Firmly assure Congress of my Friendship. I hope that this will be for the good of both nations."

KING LOUIS XVI—March 20, 1778

The course of events would probably have brought France into the war in any circumstances, but events were helped on their way by the wisest and ablest American of his day, the 70-year-old Benjamin Franklin. Franklin sailed for France on October 27, 1776, on the little armed sloop *Reprisal*. He had a double mission —to get increased aid for the embattled colonists and "to press for the immediate and explicit declaration of France in our Favour. . . ."

His great reputation as writer, thinker, and inventor, made Franklin an immediate sensation in France. Crowds followed him everywhere he went along the route to Paris. Balls and dinners were given in his honor. When he reached the French capital, he became the hero of the hour. Portraits, busts and statuettes of him appeared everywhere.

An admiring Frenchman lent Franklin a chateau in Passy on the right bank of the Seine, and in these fine lodgings, Franklin looked about him and saw the role that he must play. Wise in the ways of men, he understood as another might not have that he had been given a tremendous tribute simply because he happened to fit the French mood of the moment.

Jean Jacques Rousseau, the French philosopher, had glorified Nature. He had secured wide acceptance of the theory that man in his natural state was noble, possessed of the highest virtues and talents, and that only civilization and society made him weaker and meaner than Nature intended him to be. To the French, Franklin fitted almost perfectly into this conception. He was a brilliant man from a backwoods country. He seemed a living proof of Rousseau's theories.

The canny Franklin decided to play the part. Though he liked smart clothes as well as the next man, he dressed very plainly, wore a fur cap, and walked the streets carrying a long staff of apple wood. He wore his gray hair loose and falling nearly to his shoulders.

In this pose of rustic wise man, Franklin went to work, assisted by two American commissioners who had gone to France ahead of him, Arthur Lee and Silas Deane. Keeping clear of

Library of Congress

Benjamin Franklin, plainly dressed, receives a warm welcome at a fashionable French reception in 1778.

125

court intrigues, Franklin helped to increase the shipment of munitions cargoes to America. But when talk turned to the possibility of a formal alliance with France, Franklin craftily played hard-to-get. He let it be known that he was *not* eager for such an alliance, that he feared it might bind America beyond "its True interests."

Charles Gravier, Comte de Vergennes, the French Minister of Foreign Affairs, became all the more eager for the alliance. He began to wonder if Franklin could be *persuaded* to accept such an alliance, if it were offered!

Events now helped the wise old American. Germantown had impressed the French with the fighting ability of Washington's army; Saratoga showed them that the Americans could win. Final victory for the colonists would be a serious blow to England, and France might again become the leading power of Europe. But France would have to move quickly. Early in 1778, Lord North, the British Prime Minister, was proposing to Parliament a pact that would give the rebelling colonists every right for which they fought—and would keep them in the British family. There was no doubt that such a program, offered a few months earlier, would have been accepted gladly; it might still be accepted now if France did not counter it.

Such were the circumstances that led to the French alliance. Louis XVI himself made the final decision to go to war with Great Britain, and on February 6, 1778, Franklin and his fellow commissioners were called to Vergennes' office, where the Treaty of Alliance was signed. It was kept secret until March 20, when Louis XVI made it public by formally receiving the American commissioners at Versailles. The French had acted just in time. Congress turned down Lord North's proposals and eagerly ratified the French treaty on May 4, 1778, only two days after it was received.

America's new and powerful ally acted swiftly. A French fleet of 12 heavily armed ships under Admiral d'Estaing appeared off the Delaware Capes in early July, just a few days after Clinton had fought the battle of Monmouth Court House. D'Estaing found the British fleet clustered inside Sandy Hook, busy transferring Clinton's army across the bay to New York; but though the French had heavy superiority in ships, d'Estaing decided it would be too risky to cross the bar and attack the British.

There was still time to strike a blow, however, and Washington and the French Admiral mapped out a land and sea attack against British-held Newport, Rhode Island. Command of the land forces was given to John Sullivan, who promptly tangled in a hot-tempered argument with the French. Then a British fleet sailed from New York, threatening d'Estaing, who quickly took his ships out to sea. There they were battered by a hurricane, and d'Estaing gave up the whole Newport project. Sullivan's army, abandoned, found itself pinned on the northern part of Newport's island and would have been wiped out if John Glover's Web-Footed Infantry hadn't come to the rescue, rowing the troops away to safety across the harbor just as they had rowed Washington from Long Island.

The first fruits of the French alliance had been near-disaster at Newport, and many Americans, skeptical from the start of the wisdom of such foreign entanglements, were inclined to take a sour, I-told-you-so attitude. Soon, however, they had a more shocking topic to occupy their minds.

The British had never quite given up the idea that, if they could control the Hudson River, they could divide the colonies. In May, 1779, Sir Henry Clinton tested out the possibility by sending a force of 6,000 troops up the Hudson. They seized two partially completed American forts at Stony point on the west bank and Verplanck's Point directly opposite on the east. Washington concentrated his army around the heights of West Point, and on the night of July 15, sent Anthony Wayne with 1,300 picked men to storm Stony Point with the bayonet.

The first and last pages of the all-important Treaty of Alliance, between France and America, written in both French and English, are shown here. This document was signed in Paris in February, 1778.

Wayne slashed into the fort with such speed and fury that all of its defenders were either killed, wounded, or captured. It was one of the most brilliant enterprises of the war. Clinton, having lost heavily, fell back to New York and gave up for the moment—but only for the moment—the attempt to drive up the Hudson.

A year later, he tried again, this time not with an army, but with a traitor. The traitor was Benedict Arnold.

Washington had given Arnold military command of Philadelphia after Clinton left the city in 1778. There Arnold quickly displayed certain traits which had always made many men distrust him, despite his courage and his brilliance. He began to live almost like a king, taking over the huge mansion that had been Howe's headquarters, staging elaborate banquets, riding grandly about the city in a gaudy coach with liveried retainers. Since Arnold had hardly a

This French map of West Point, dated 1780, shows the iron chain that blocked passage on the Hudson.

Emmet Collection, N.Y. Public Library

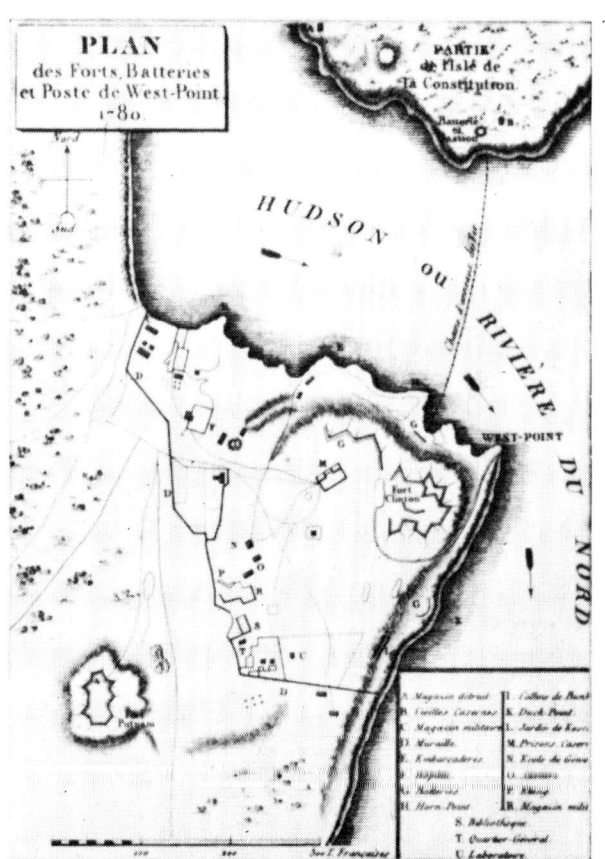

cent to his name, it seemed that his costly display could be financed only by outright thievery or profiteering from army stores, and today there is little doubt that Arnold was involved in many such practices.

Suspicion was focused not only on Arnold's high-flown manner of living, but on his friends. Amazingly, for a patriot general, he became most intimate with some of the leading Tory families of Philadelphia, and soon he took for his second wife the beautiful Tory, Peggy Shippen. Hardly had they married when Arnold, enraged by the action of Congress in investigating some of his doubtful business deals, began trying to sell his services to the British.

He made contact in New York with Major John André, the elegant, foppish adjutant to Sir Henry Clinton and one of Peggy Shippen's admirers during the winter of the British occupation of Philadelphia. During much of 1779, André and Arnold dealt through go-betweens, but the greedy Arnold wanted too much—a big money reward, high rank in the British army, possibly a title for his treason. Unable to meet such demands, André cut off the discussions.

But a year later in June, 1780, Arnold reopened the bargaining. He had completely recovered from his Saratoga wound, he had been demanding active duty, and Washington offered him the command of the left wing of the American army. Much to Washington's surprise, Arnold was still dissatisfied. What he would really like, he said, was the command of West Point. Washington gave it to him, and on August 3, 1780, Arnold went up the Hudson. He now had a valuable plum to barter. He would turn over West Point, the gateway to the Hudson, to Clinton and the British—for a price.

The Americans had no suspicion of this treachery until September 23, 1780. On that day, Major Benjamin Tallmadge, Washington's Chief of Intelligence, was out riding patrol with troopers of his own 2nd Dragoons. A close watch was being kept on the Westchester County-Fairfield County area in New York and Connecticut, because Washington had ridden that way to a conference in Hartford with the French general, Comte Donatien de Rochambeau. Washington was now returning, and Tallmadge was on the alert to see that the British and Tories did not cut off the commander-in-chief.

Washington's intelligence chief was also vaguely disturbed by recent strange actions of Benedict Arnold, the new commander at West Point. Arnold had been writing fawning, flattering letters to American officers—quite unlike his usual terse, rather angry style. Arnold had also asked Tallmadge for full details on all secret agents working under him—a demand the Major had side-stepped by saying that only Washington could give out such information. Finally, Arnold made a most curious request: that Tallmadge forward to him immediately one John Anderson from New York, should such a person appear in the Major's area.

Tallmadge, who disliked and distrusted Arnold, was puzzling over the general's actions when he returned from his September 23 patrol and found that a man named John Anderson had been picked up by militiamen close to the Westchester no-man's-land between the lines of the two armies. In Anderson's shoes had been found detailed plans of the West Point forts, data on ordnance, and digests of confidential orders issued by Washington. Some of the documents seemed to be in Arnold's handwriting.

Lieutenant Colonel John Jameson, Tallmadge's superior, had no idea what a bombshell had dropped into his lap. He had sent the mysterious Anderson, under heavy guard, to the headquarters of the commanding general, Benedict Arnold, and he had written Arnold a letter describing the strange papers that had been found on the man. The documents themselves he had dispatched to Washington.

Tallmadge was horrified. With his experience in intelligence, with his knowledge of Arnold's strange moves, he had no doubt that this was treason. He argued and pleaded with Jameson

Collection of Mrs. John Nicholas Brown
An English portrait of Benedict Arnold, painted in the year 1776, the result of widespread European interest in him after the ill-fated attack on Quebec.

for action. Jameson refused but agreed to call back the prisoner and his guard. However, Jameson insisted that the letter describing the man's capture must go to Arnold.

Arnold was just sitting down to breakfast with his officers in the Beverly Robinson house, on the east bank of the Hudson opposite West Point, when the letter from Jameson reached him. It must have been a fearful shock, but Arnold gave no sign. He excused himself from the table for a moment, bid a hasty farewell to Peggy, and plunged off down the slope to the Hudson. He was rowed downstream, where he boarded *H.M.S. Vulture*, riding at anchor, waiting for the passenger she had brought north.

129

Benedict Arnold's second wife, the beautiful Tory, Peggy Shippen, is shown here holding their child.

Emmet Collection, N.Y. Public Library

That passenger had been the mysterious John Anderson—in reality, Major John André. André had visited Arnold, and the two men had settled the terms for Arnold's treachery and the surrender of West Point. Then André, on Arnold's advice, had taken off his uniform and dressed in civilian clothes, trying to pass overland through the Westchester no-man's-land to New York. He had been on the last stage of his journey when he had been captured.

Washington, shocked and horrified when he learned what had happened, quickly strengthened West Point, and the British lost their last chance to split the colonies along the line of the Hudson. The conspiracy had failed.

For Benedict Arnold, there was nonetheless a reward from the British: a Brigadier General's rank in the British army, a cash payment of 6,315 British pounds, and a pension of 500 pounds annually for his pretty Peggy. Offsetting the cash was a future of disgrace—a life clouded by the hatred of the Americans he had sold out, by the scorn and distrust of the British who had bought him.

As for Major John André, General Clinton argued and stormed, demanding his release, but Washington stood his ground. André, he said, had been caught out of uniform within the American lines and, as a spy, must pay the penalty. A court martial tried him, convicted him, and sentenced him to hang.

If one were to judge from a man's appearance, one would have expected the dandyish André to crack and go to pieces at the prospect of being executed. But he did not. Instead, he exhibited a coolness and a calm courage that aroused the admiration of all the Americans who knew him. Benjamin Tallmadge expressed a general sentiment when he wrote to his friend, Colonel Samuel Webb: "By heavens, Colonel Webb, I never saw a man whose fate I foresaw whom I so sincerely pitied. . . . He seems to be as cheerful as if he was going to an assembly. I am sure he will go to the gallows less tearful of his fate and with less concern than I shall behold the tragedy."

And so it proved. Major John André died courageously—the victim of his general's search for an ally who could be bought and of Benedict Arnold's greed for rank and gold. The British had failed to buy their way into West Point, the gateway of the Hudson; while the Americans, through the skillful diplomacy of Benjamin Franklin, had gained in France a powerful ally whose help, in the end, was to make complete victory possible.

An effigy of Arnold, made by Charles Willson Peale, paraded through the streets of Philadelphia

Metropolitan Museum of Art

National Maritime Museum

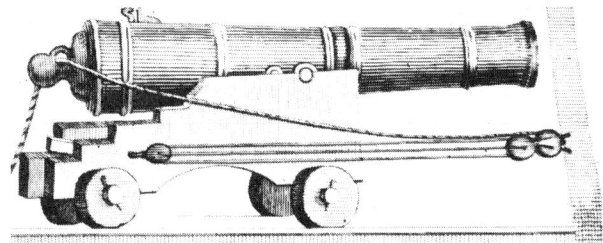

A typical naval gun

THE WAR AT SEA

The Revolution, fought so desperately on the land, was won in the end on the sea. Across the ocean lanes, the colonists were supplied with arms and reinforcements from France; and, finally, one moment of complete control of the sea proved to be worth many years of hard land fighting. It made Yorktown possible.

Despite this final victory in which sea power played so large a part, the naval warfare of the Revolution has been generally overlooked. When the war began, the Rebels had not a single warship and hardly any officers with regular naval training. This weakness made the war at sea largely a guerrilla conflict, lacking the drama of the large-scale collision of armies. Yet it was a war that had an intensity and a savagery all its own. For the rebelling colonists, with puny ships and unskilled fighters, daringly pitted themselves against the Royal Navy, the greatest sea power in the world.

The colonists were aided by a British blind spot: The English at first failed to understand that sea power, the basis of their national strength, could decide the outcome of the war. The government ignored the advice of men like Secretary of War Viscount Barrington, who felt that "the Americans may be reduced by the fleet, but never can be by the army." King George III and his ministers sent huge armies to America and found, after three years of fighting, that they had lost Burgoyne and all his men at Saratoga and that they were able to hold only ports like New York, where their troops could be supplied by the British fleet.

The final chapter might have been different had the British tried at the outset to strangle the American colonies by a tight blockade from the sea. Because they did not, a vigorous commerce was carried on throughout the war, and American privateers swarmed to sea, pouncing on British shipping and driving marine insur-

The Battle of Quiberon Bay, off France, one of the most famous naval battles of the age, broke French sea power in 1759. The French attempted to lure the British into shoal water in a November gale, but were outmaneuvered and crushed.

Life aboard a warship of the period is shown below in this cutaway view of a French two-decker. Captain's cabin (8) and officers' mess (14) are at the stern; crew's quarters (11) and mess (17), amidships. The brig, or jail (23), is deep in the hold, along with the ship's stores and powder magazine (26).

The Earl of Sandwich, head of the Royal Navy, was described as "Too infamous to have a friend, Too bad for bad men to commend." The painting at right shows the launching of the 74-gun British battleship Alexander *in 1778. A similar ship is at the right.*

ance rates to such high levels that the influential British merchant class complained loudly and bitterly. Not until France entered the war in 1778, followed by Spain a year later, did the British again begin to pay attention to that sea power which had made them strong. And by then it was too late. For now the Royal Navy had to escort merchant convoys from England to America, prevent invasion of the British Isles, and protect the rich trading areas of the Mediterranean, India, and the West Indies.

The British navy was poorly prepared for such a world-wide war. The fleet that had swept the sea at the end of the Seven Years' War in 1763 had been allowed to fall into ruin. The lazy and unprincipled Earl of Sandwich became First Sea Lord in 1771, and under him the proud Royal Navy decayed to a shadow of itself.

Meanwhile France built new and more powerful ships, restoring to full strength the navy that had been ruined in the last war with England.

The heart of the eighteenth-century navy was the ship of the line, the battleship of its time. A ship of the line mounted upwards of 64 guns, ranged in tiers up her sides. Such ships could hurl more than half a ton of metal in a single broadside. Vessels like the 90-gun *Sandwich*, which is shown on page 131, were the monarchs of the fleet, and they were supported by lighter-armed, fast-sailing frigates—the counter-part of today's cruisers—and by swarms of still smaller sloops-of-war.

134

National Maritime Museum

British Museum

The engraving at left shows a navy press gang kidnaping a London tailor, despite protests of his womenfolk. These gangs raided merchant ships and harbor areas for seamen; sometimes even "the gaols were swept."

135

Gabriel de Sartine (above) was France's Minister of Marine and played a key role during the Revolution.

The French alliance brought this kind of sea power into the war on the side of the colonists for the first time, but France's first choice of a naval commander for American waters was almost unbelievably bad. Comte d'Estaing was slow, timid, indecisive, and he bungled every opportunity. His fleet was much stronger than Admiral Richard Howe's, but d'Estaing, owing to his lack of initiative, lost his chance to destroy the British fleet in New York Harbor. Then d'Estaing made an attempt with the Americans against Newport, a campaign that failed disastrously; and finally, after his ships had been battered by a brush with the British fleet and an autumn storm, he sailed off to the West Indies, having accomplished nothing.

For the next two-and-a-half years, the French and British struck at each other's island bases in the West Indies. Island after island changed hands. In 1780, one of Britain's best admirals, George Brydges Rodney, smashed a Spanish squadron off Cape St. Vincent, Portugal, then sailed to the West Indies and captured the Dutch island of St. Eustatius. France strengthened her West Indian fleet and put it under the command of a far better man than d'Estaing, the Comte de Grasse.

It was de Grasse who made the great decision of the war. In July, 1781, he notified Washington that he was sailing for the Chesapeake with 28 ships of the line to trap Cornwallis. Samuel Hood, who had taken command of the British fleet while Rodney returned to England, learned of de Grasse's intentions and set sail in pursuit. But de Grasse followed such a little-used route that Hood actually passed him on the way without making contact. Finding the Chesapeake empty, Hood sailed on to New York and joined Admiral Thomas Graves.

Picture at right shows French naval architects at work designing the ships that outsailed England's.

136

Musée de Marine

Toulon (above) was the major French Mediterranean naval base. Ships' guns and cannon balls are in the foreground. France split her fleet between Toulon and the port of Brest, on the English Channel.

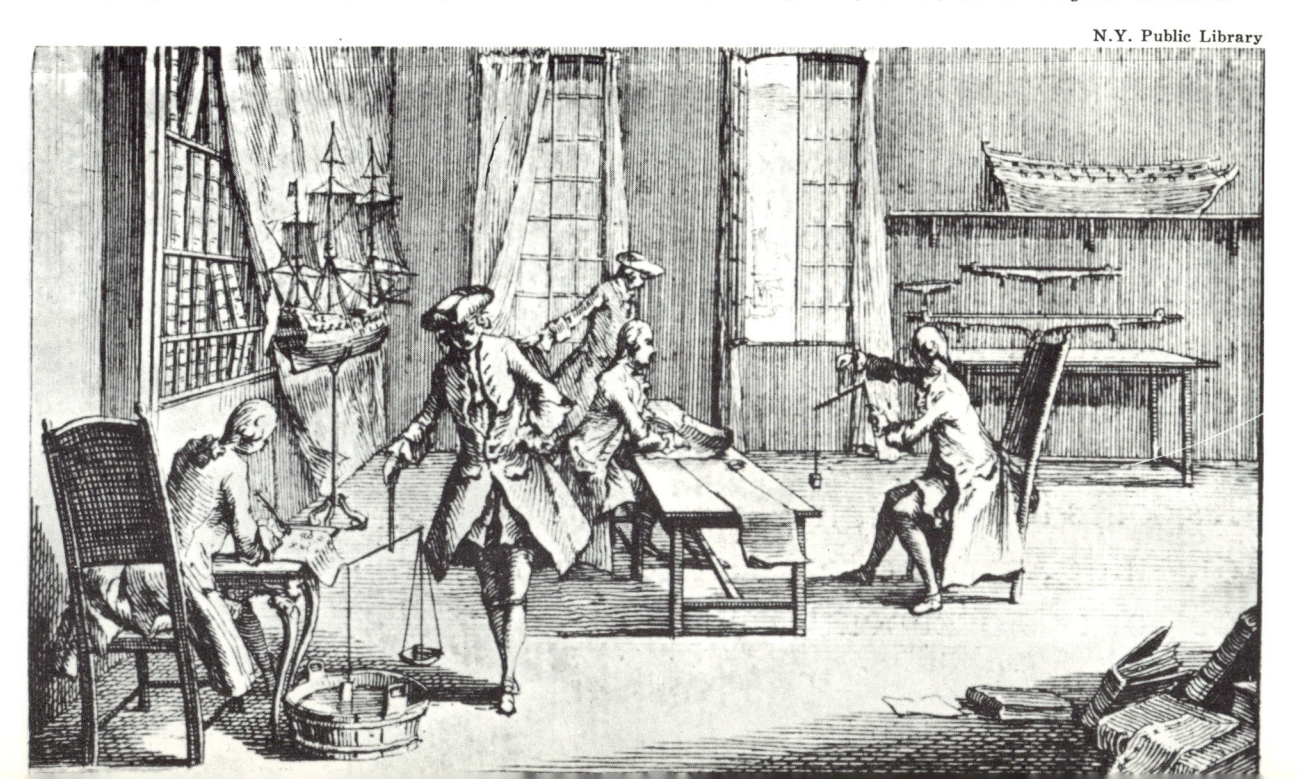

N.Y. Public Library

"Black Dick" Howe had a dark complexion, but Copley, in painting the portrait above, flattered him with light coloring. The Comte d'Estaing (below) was a good soldier but lacked naval experience.

This left the way clear for de Grasse. He slipped into the Chesapeake on August 30, blocking Cornwallis' escape by water, and landed 3,000 troops to help Lafayette ring the British on the land side until Washington could arrive with the main army. The operation was a masterpiece of strategy, but its outcome still depended upon de Grasse's ability to keep command of the sea.

Control of the ocean escape route from Yorktown was promptly challenged by Graves and Hood. They sailed from New York seeking the French, and on September 5 were startled to find "a number of great ships at anchor which seemed to be extended across the extreme of the Chesapeake." De Grasse sailed out to sea to meet them, and Graves formed his ships in line of battle, but bungled the attack. Only a part of his fleet got into action. For several days the two fleets sparred; but de Grasse, reinforced by another French squadron, now had 36 ships of the line to Graves' 18. The British, unwilling to tackle such odds, returned to New York, and Cornwallis was left to his fate.

After the surrender of Cornwallis, de Grasse sailed back to the West Indies, where in 1782 his fleet was badly beaten by Rodney in the Battle of the Saintes. This French defeat and France's continuing concern for the safety of her island possessions left the Americans without the support of the fleet and with nothing more than their own slender naval resources.

The Americans were stout seamen and good sea fighters, but throughout the war, they were hampered by the lack of powerful warships and experienced commanders. Washington, who early appreciated the importance of sea power, organized a small fleet of pint-sized raiders during the siege of Boston in 1775. These little cruisers snapped up some 35 British supply ships whose cargoes helped to outfit the ragged and poorly supplied American army.

In this same year, Congress made a start toward establishing a navy by ordering the construction of thirteen frigates and by buying

The seizure of Newport, Rhode Island (above), by Sir Henry Clinton in December, 1776, was a neatly executed assault from the sea. In this watercolor, landing barges wait in the harbor while five frigates lay down a barrage. The landing was unopposed.

Above, in the foreground, the French fleet lies off the entrance to New York Harbor in 1778. Howe's fleet lay behind Sandy Hook. The Comte d'Estaing made no attack, thinking his warships unable to get through the shallow channel at far right. Below, the 90-gun Languedoc, *dismasted by a storm that struck the opposing fleets off Newport, is pounded by the British* Renown. *Darkness saved d'Estaing's flagship from capture.*

139

James Nicholson (left) lost the navy frigates Virginia *and* Trumbull. *Nicholas Biddle (below) died on the* Randolph *(opposite page).*

Navy Department

Independence Hall

Esek Hopkins (left) commanded the first American fleet. This English print makes him look younger than he was, and shows the Rebel "Rattlesnake" and "Pine Tree" flags in the background.

Old Print Shop

a collection of merchantmen that could be turned into warships. Esek Hopkins was given command of the first American squadron. Early in 1776, he led it in a raid on Nassau in the West Indies. He captured the port and came home with munitions and supplies for Washington's army. But this was virtually the only planned major operation undertaken by the navy.

Of the thirteen new frigates authorized by Congress, several were burned before they could ever get to sea, to keep them from falling into the hands of the British when New York and Philadelphia were captured. Others, though fine ships, failed to accomplish much, largely because a succession of poor skippers was named to command them. Probably the finest ship ever built in America up to that time, the 32-gun frigate *Hancock*, was so mishandled by John Manley that she fell an easy victim to the 44-gun *Rainbow*, surrendering without firing a shot. Taken into the British Navy under the name of *Iris*, she became one of the fastest and best frigates the British had, and in August,

1781, she captured the last of her sister ships, the American frigate *Trumbull*.

Though men like John Adams and Robert Morris struggled to establish a navy, they were hampered by the constant lack of funds, by poor understanding in Congress of naval requirements, and by a system of competition in which privateers and the separate state navies drained away ships and men that could have been better employed in the national service.

The state navies especially were a doubtful asset. Eleven colonies established their own little fleets, operating a kind of sea militia to guard their coasts against English and Tory raiders. Such separate units were jealous of each other and, naturally, couldn't be expected to work together. And when they became too ambitious, disaster resulted.

A prime example of this occurred in 1779 when Massachusetts, owner of probably the most powerful state navy, organized an expedition of 19 armed ships and 20-odd transports to strike at havens the Loyalists had established

The 1779 Dutch water color below shows two American naval flags. The top one was flown by the Alliance, *the other by John Paul Jones' prize, the frigate* Serapis *(see page 147).*

Chicago Historical Society

Mariners Museum

Above, the Continental frigate Alliance *fights two British warships in 1781. The* Atalanta *(left) has surrendered; the* Trepassey *(right) is almost beaten.*

In March, 1778, off Barbados in the West Indies, the 32-gun Continental frigate Randolph *challenged a ship-of-the-line twice her size, the 64-gun* Yarmouth. *Captain Nicholas Biddle was punishing his foe severely when a shot struck the* Randolph's *magazine and blew her to pieces, killing Biddle and more than 300 of his men.*

Mariners Museum

141

British map (left) shows American fleet at Penobscot, Maine, and its retreat up Penobscot River.

in Maine's Penobscot Bay area. The American force failed to push the campaign swiftly and vigorously, and a British rescue squadron, led by a 64, bottled up the Americans in the bay. The Massachusetts fleet fled upstream, and every ship was either captured or destroyed. The disaster threw Massachusetts $7,000,000 into debt, nearly knocking the state out of the war.

The Americans did, however, develop a number of daring sea fighters. They were men like Joshua Barney, who escaped from a British prison and was given command of the little cruiser *Hyder Aly*, fitted out by Philadelphia merchants to protect their shipping on the Delaware. By a clever ruse, Barney lured the far more powerful British sloop-of-war *General Monk* into a helpless position under his guns and captured her. Another stout fighter was

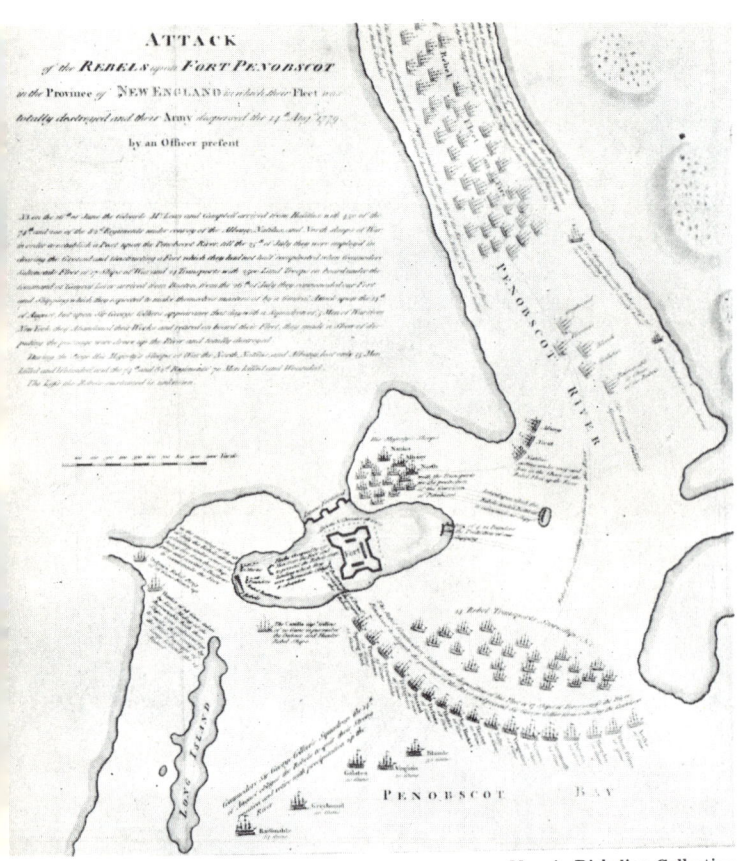

Manoir Richelieu Collection

Dominic Serres' painting below shows the British sailing into the Penobscot River as the Rebels burn their ships to prevent capture (background). The 64-gun Raisonnable *(left) pursues an American vessel and forces her to surrender.*

National Maritime Museum

142

John Barry, who in the Continental frigate *Alliance* fought two British warships at once in 1781 —and captured them. And above all, of course, there was John Paul Jones.

Jones had been a Lieutenant in Esek Hopkins' squadron during the first raid on Nassau. He later commanded the sloop *Providence* and the makeshift frigate *Alfred*. In both he skirted the New England coast under the noses of British men-of-war, taking prizes and nearly ruining the Nova Scotia fishing industry. In a few months, he established himself as the most daring and successful captain in the navy. Still, lesser men were given the command of frigates, and the best he could obtain was the 18-gun *Ranger*. In 1777, he sailed in her for Europe and his date with glory.

Jones understood sea warfare better than any other American commander. He used a warship to strike swiftly from the sea at exposed places on land. He attacked the British port of White-

Independence Hall

Joshua Barney, commander of the Hyder Aly, *was 25 years old when C. W. Peale painted this portrait.*

Barney, given command of the 16-gun Hyder Aly, *fights and takes the British sloop-of-war* General Monk *in Delaware Bay in 1782. A British frigate (left) and a brig (aground, right) failed to help the* General Monk.

U.S. Naval Academy Museum

143

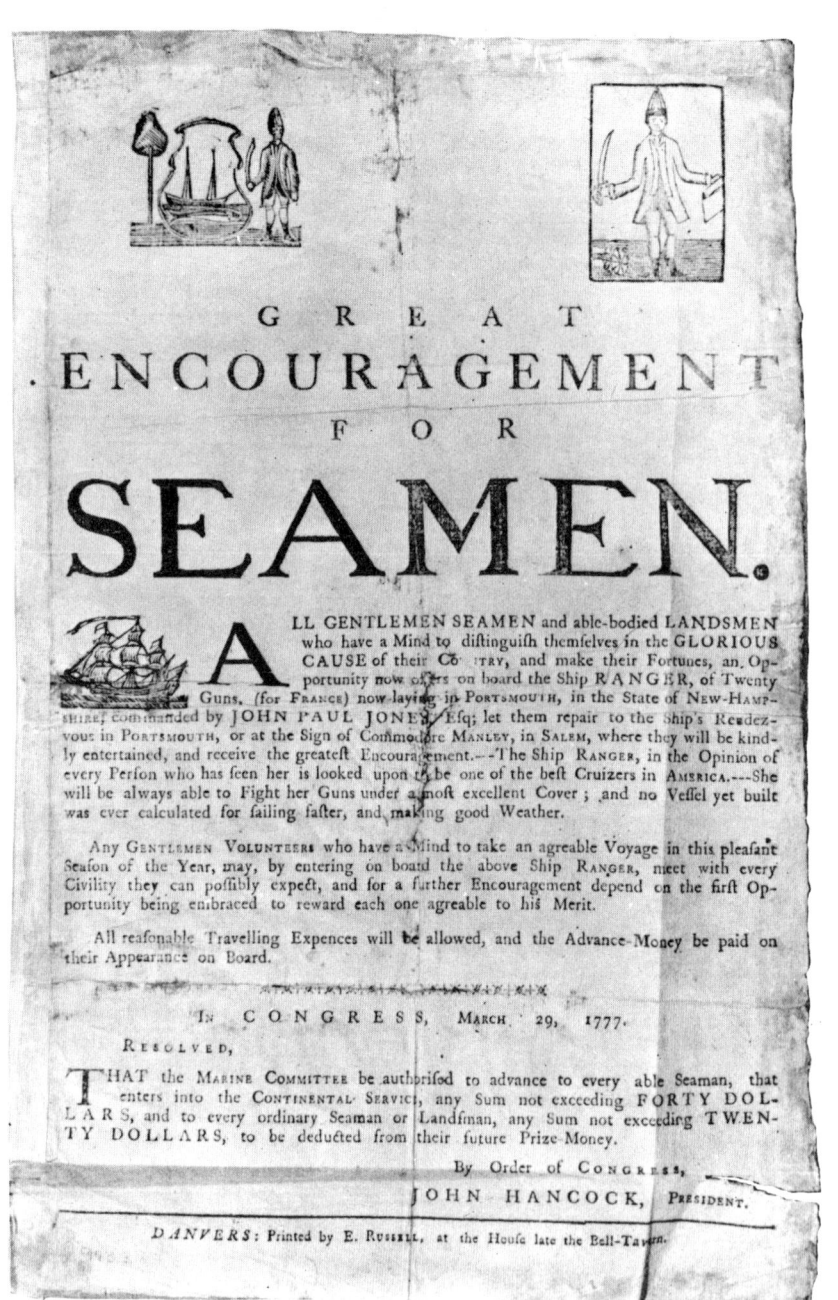

The print at right shows a handsome John Paul Jones. The bottom panel pictures the battle between the Bonhomme Richard *and the* Serapis.

Mariners Museum

Above is Gustavus Conyngham, American sea raider whom the British called the "Dunkirk Pirate." This 1777 poster, reproduced at left, called for "Gentlemen Volunteers" for Jones' Ranger.

Essex Institute

haven and set fire to some of its shipping; he raided the Earl of Selkirk's Castle; he made a complete sweep around the British Isles, and in the shadows of the English coast captured the British sloop-of-war *Drake*.

Sailing to France, Jones struggled for a year to get command of a ship large enough to battle a British frigate. Finally, with the help of Benjamin Franklin, he obtained a slow, rotting old East Indiaman which he converted into a warship named the *Bonhomme Richard*. In this flagship mounting 40 guns—some so old and rusted that they exploded on the first discharge —Jones sailed from L'Orient in August, 1779, at the head of a small squadron.

On September 23, off Flamborough Head in the North Sea, Jones sighted a British convoy escorted by the 50-gun *Serapis*. Despite the odds, he gave battle. The rotten sides of the *Bonhomme Richard* were soon riddled, and the ship was almost sinking when Jones maneuvered her close and lashed her fast to the *Serapis*.

The ships pounded each other "with unre-

144

J. PAUL JONES COMMODORE

VINDICATI LUDOVICUS XVI REMUNERATOR VINDICI
NARIS STRENUO

Collection of Mrs. John Nicholas Brown

This print above is based upon a legend that Jones killed a sailor who tried to strike the Richard's *flag.*

mitting fury." The broadside guns fired from the portholes almost muzzle to muzzle, and sharpshooters in the American tops swept the *Serapis*' deck with a hail of lead. At the height of the battle, though his own ship was a wreck beneath his feet, Jones refused demands to surrender and is reported to have shouted, "I have just begun to fight."

In the end, it was the more powerful *Serapis* that surrendered. Her captain testified that "the American ship was dominated by a commanding will of a most unalterable resolution." John Paul Jones had won a remarkable victory. He had reversed all the odds, had scored an astounding triumph, and had set for the American Navy of the future a glorious, fighting example.

At right, this colorful canvas shows the Serapis *on fire, her mainmast shot away, raked by the* Richard *at the climax of the battle. The shattered* Richard *had to be abandoned and sank two days later.*

146

U.S. Naval Academy Museum

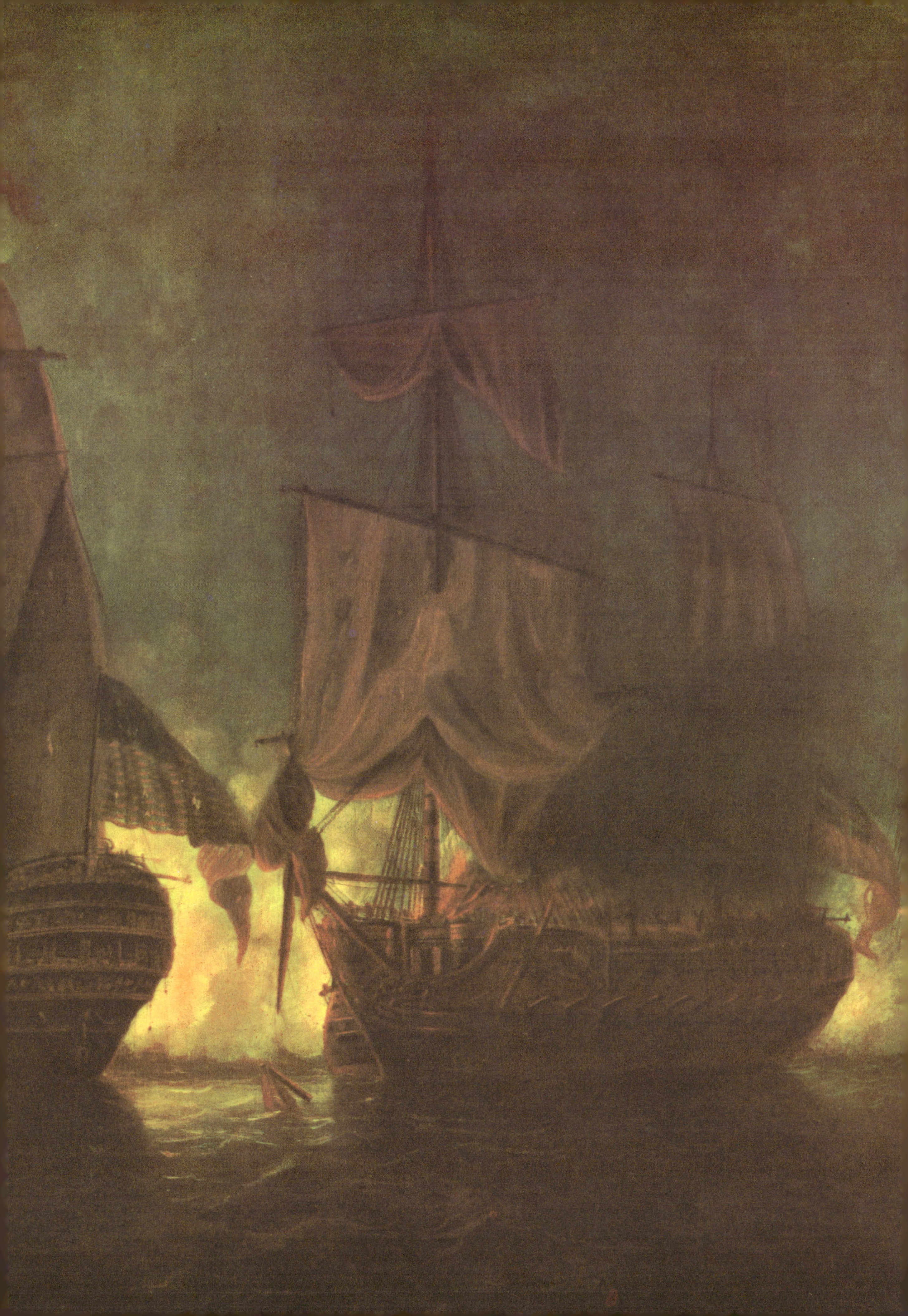

Francis Parsons' portrait of the Cherokee warrior Cunne Shote

FRONTIERS AFLAME

"At this moment I would have bound myself a slave to have had five hundred troops."

GEORGE ROGERS CLARK, 1779

Throughout the Revolution, there was a second war that was separate from the main war. It was a war that began before Lexington and Concord and continued long after Yorktown. It was the war on the frontier.

In the years before the Revolution, settlers had flowed west in ever-increasing numbers. They pressed into western Pennsylvania, into what is now West Virginia, and on into Kentucky, guided by Daniel Boone through the new-found Cumberland Gap and along Boone's Wilderness Road. These settlers were a hard-driving lot, intent on clearing the land and establishing farms. Farms meant the destruction of the wilderness—and of the Indians' hunting grounds. Fierce tribes battled the white men's invasion and when the Revolution came, the Indians found suddenly that they had a strong partner in the British along the Great Lakes.

The heart of the British power was a post at Detroit, commanded by Lieutenant Colonel Henry Hamilton, soon known to Americans along the frontier as the "Hair Buyer," for the scalps they accused him of purchasing. Hamilton supplied the Indians with arms, ammunition, rum, and blankets and sent them off to the south to raid the Kentucky settlements.

The outrages in Kentucky—known as the "Dark and Bloody Ground"—aroused the concern of Congress, and several times plans were made for expeditions against Detroit to wipe out the source of the Indians' supplies and power. But nothing ever came of these plans, and the Indians probably would have continued to raid unchecked had it not been for one man.

He was George Rogers Clark, a Virginia-

This view of Detroit was painted in 1794. A French outpost from 1701 to 1760, Detroit was held by the British for the next 36 years and was used after 1775 as a base for their attacks on the American frontier.

Detroit Public Library

George Rogers Clark, whose inspired leadership gave the U.S. control of the Old Northwest in 1779.

born surveyor who had gone into Kentucky. He was big, tough, red-haired, shrewd, and not much past twenty. A man of energy and vision, Clark lived through a series of bloody Indian raids, and he decided that the only defense for Kentucky lay in attack on the Indian country north of the Ohio.

Late in 1777, he went to Virginia and sought out Thomas Jefferson, George Mason, and Richard Henry Lee. He outlined for them his plan to strike at British-fed supply centers in the "Illinois country." This was a great area bounded by the Maumee and Miami Rivers on the east, the Illinois on the north, the Mississippi on the west, and the Ohio on the south.

Here, in what are now the states of Illinois and Indiana, there were several towns, originally settled by French traders who were living quietly under British rule, simply because the British, their old foes, were now in power. The main settlements were Kaskaskia on the Mississippi, about fifty miles south of St. Louis; Prairie du Rocher, about seventeen miles north of Kaskaskia; Cahokia, still farther north and just below what is now East St. Louis; and Vincennes, on the Wabash in what is now Indiana.

George Rogers Clark reasoned that a swift raiding force could seize these towns, win over the French who lived in them, and make friendly contact with the Spaniards across the Mississippi. Such a campaign, if successful, would rob the Indians of their bases and keep them from raiding Kentucky so freely.

Clark's plan made such good sense that Governor Patrick Henry of Virginia and the Virginia House of Burgesses gave him 1,200 British pounds to raise several companies of riflemen. The legislators were not told the full story, but voted the money under the impression that the rifle companies would be used to defend Kentucky, then claimed by Virginia.

Clark, of course, had much larger plans, but from the start he encountered obstacles that would have made a less determined man give up in despair. When he mustered his men at the Falls of the Ohio, near the site of present-day Louisville, he found that he had about 200 soldiers—a puny force with which to set out on a long wilderness march and attack a powerful enemy on his home grounds.

Common sense said Clark should have quit right there, but he was a man who believed that safety lay in daring rather than in caution. He embarked his men, shot the rapids on June 26, 1778, and rode the broad current of the Ohio to a spot nearly opposite the mouth of the Tennessee River. There he landed his men on the Illinois shore, hid his boats, and led his command across trackless prairie and forest.

It was a killing march, and at the end were two long, foodless days before the riflemen sighted Kaskaskia on July 4. The settlement was unguarded and fell without a shot fired. Clark at once sent Captain Joseph Bowman and a small band of riflemen on to Prairie du Rocher and Cahokia. Both towns were seized without the slightest resistance.

Clark was now the ruler of a wilderness empire, and he quickly proved himself a master of tact and understanding. His personal magnetism won the French almost to a man. Many of them cast off their allegiance to the British Crown and became firm allies. One, Père Pierre Gibault, volunteered to make the long trek overland to Vincennes on the Wabash, and to try to talk his fellow Frenchmen there into joining the Americans. He succeeded, and in August Clark sent Captain Leonard Helm and a small force to occupy Vincennes and the frontier post of Fort Sackville that guarded it.

Clark had been remarkably successful. He had taken every major town in the Illinois country without the loss of a man. Yet his situation was extremely perilous. His little force was far too weak to hold such a vast stretch of wilderness, and he was surrounded on every side by hostile Indian tribes. Again, all depended on Clark, and again, he showed his masterful way with men.

Through August and September, he met with chiefs and tribal delegates from such dreaded tribes as the Chippewas, Ottawas, Miamis, and Foxes. Speaking boldly but carefully, never making a promise he could not keep, he persuaded the Indians to agree to a truce, one that lasted for months and was strictly observed by both sides.

No sooner had the Indian threat been settled than Clark had to meet a new crisis. His own force, tiny at the start, was shrinking through expired enlistments and desertions.

Clark's men endured fearful hardships during their winter march to Vincennes, wading across a flooded plain with icy water above their hips. Under the inspired leadership of Clark, his men covered the 180 miles from Kaskaskia to Vincennes in 18 days.

Archives of American Art

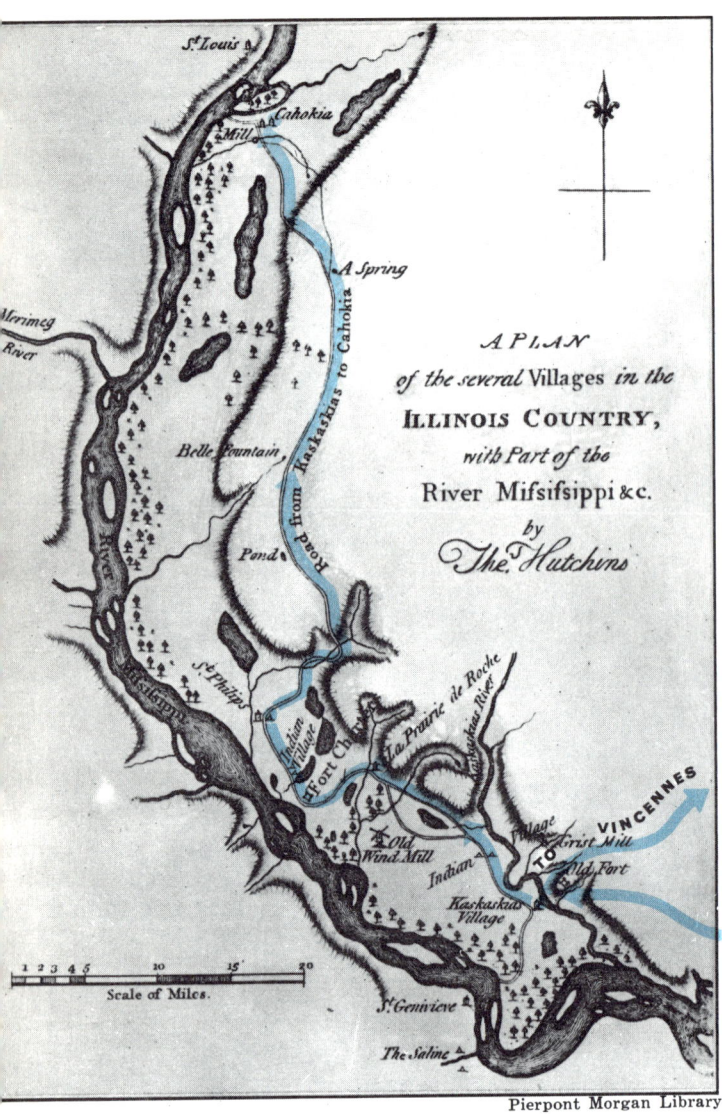

This 1778 map shows the area covered by Clark in his 1778-79 campaign. At right, Clark's Long Knives are shown firing on Fort Sackville at Vincennes.

Supplies were exhausted. Fortunately, Clark made contact with an American merchant, Oliver Pollock, in New Orleans, and Pollock dipped into his own private funds to send the soldier supplies by keelboats working up the Mississippi to Cahokia.

These arrangements took Clark over all the seemingly impossible hurdles except one—and that the most serious. It was the threat posed by Lieutenant Colonel Henry Hamilton, the "Hair Buyer," from his base at Detroit. Hamilton was a tough, energetic soldier, and as soon as word came to him of the loss of the Illinois towns, he prepared to strike back.

He scraped together a force of some 175 Europeans, mostly French militiamen, and 60 Indians. It was late in the year, and by all military rules Hamilton should have waited for spring and better campaigning weather. But Hamilton was not a man to wait. On October 7, 1778, he set out for Vincennes. His route was a rugged one, down the Maumee to the Wabash, and down the Wabash to southern Indiana. Boats had to be carried long distances overland between streams. Flood waters on the rivers swamped many of his barges and ruined provisions. But Hamilton held his men together, pressed forward and reached Vincennes on December 17.

Again the town changed hands without a struggle. The French residents decided they had made a big mistake in deserting England, the militia refused to fight, and Captain Helm and his few riflemen were captured. The victorious Hamilton started gathering supplies to strike west at the other posts Clark held. He decided, however, that he could not move until spring, for a mild winter had flooded the great flat stretches of land between Vincennes and the Mississippi with water ranging from inches to several feet in depth.

Hamilton's recapture of Vincennes had thrown the townsfolk of Kaskaskia and Cahokia into a panic. Clark had only about 100 men. Prudence called for him to flee while he could, but Clark always preferred boldness to prudence. Hamilton was at Vincennes some 180 miles away; he wouldn't be expecting a mid-winter attack. So Clark would *attack*.

Père Gibault helped him talk the townspeople out of their fear. Some local militia were persuaded to join the Kentucky riflemen, and by February 6, 1779, Clark had a force of about 180 men. With this tiny band, he set out on one of the most incredible marches in American military history.

Thaws and floods had turned much of the 180 miles he had to cover into one vast lake. The first part of the march was not so bad. The men were in high spirits, the water covering the land was only inches deep, and game was plentiful. By February 13, Vincennes was a mere twenty miles away. But now the flood waters deepened. The Little Wabash had swept over its banks, drowning the countryside, and two whole days were spent ferrying the expedition to wading ground on the east bank.

From here on, the march became increasingly rugged. Men pushed through icy, waist-deep floods. Game vanished, supplies ran low, and on the seventeenth, the Embarrass River, in high flood, blocked the line of march. Men floundered north and south along its banks looking for possible fords. By the eighteenth, the command was pushing on through slowly deepening water to the Wabash itself.

The river was in such flood that they could not cross it until February 20. Just beyond it,

Lieutenant Colonel Henry Hamilton, called the "Hair Buyer," surrenders his sword and troops to Clark.

they captured a stray Frenchman, and Clark learned from him that Hamilton in Vincennes had had no warning of the Americans' approach. Clark pressed on, but the water was so deep that in the whole day of the twenty-first he covered only three miles. The sick and exhausted were pulled along in canoes. Men half-waded, half-swam through shoulder-deep water, rifles and powder held high above their heads. The next day, the twenty-second, was even worse. They made practically no progress, and the men were exhausted and nearly starved.

On February 23, men began to hang back, croaking that they could go no farther. Clark settled the wavering in the ranks by personal example. "Follow me!" he shouted, plunging first into the water. He sent Captain Joseph Bowman with 25 riflemen to circle the rear and shoot any stragglers. Thus encouraged and threatened, the men followed him. The water was still shoulder-high. More and more men had to be towed in the canoes. Many tripped and

153

Sir William Johnson's large fortified house at Johnstown in upstate New York was the scene of frequent Indian councils. Johnson died here after speaking to visiting Mohawks in 1774.

fell in deep water, then clung helplessly to a rotten log or sunken tree until stronger comrades pulled them to their feet. Still they went on, and at last dry ground was reached—a tree-masked strip barely two miles from Fort Sackville, the key to Vincennes.

Boldly, they lit fires, dried out their clothes, ate the last of their scanty rations. They captured another Frenchman, and he gave them bad news. Some 200 additional Indians had joined Hamilton in the fort. And Clark's ammunition was almost gone.

But to George Rogers Clark every piece of bad news was a challenge. Clark sent the Frenchman back to Hamilton with a bold, magnificent message—he notified the British commander that he was going to take Fort Sackville that very night; he warned that friends of the United States in the town of Vincennes should stay quietly in their homes; that those holding with England should join Hamilton in the fort and resist him if they dared.

This is a testimonial issued by Sir William Johnson to Indian braves loyal to the Crown.

Clark followed up this bluff with action. He formed his men into two small divisions and marched them boldly into Vincennes and down the main street, drums beating. Once in the town, he split up his men and sent them swinging through the side streets and back to the main thoroughfare, then into the side streets again, to give the impression that he had sev-

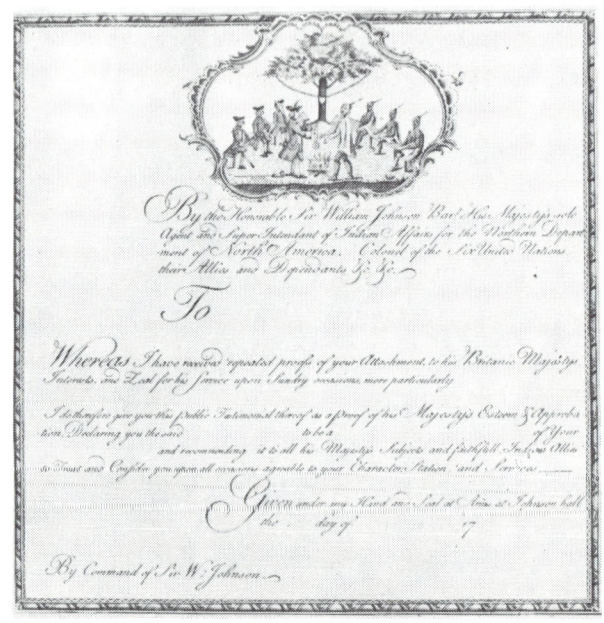

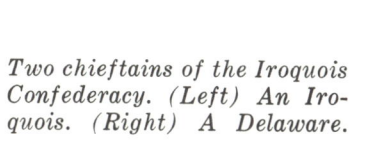

Two chieftains of the Iroquois Confederacy. (Left) An Iroquois. (Right) A Delaware.

Culver Service

eral times as many men as he actually had. The ruse worked. Again, the townsfolk were won over to what seemed to them the stronger side.

Friends guided Clark's men to secret stores of ammunition, and soon the riflemen were filling their nearly empty pouches and powder horns. Rumors about the great strength of the attacking American army reached the fort, and the Indians there, losing all interest in fighting for Hamilton, fled in all directions. Taking advantage of the panic he had created, Clark marched at sundown against the fort, drums still beating. His men scattered into the evening shadows and began to pepper the fort with rifle fire.

The fort was strong. A palisade, or wall of stakes, eleven feet high enclosed a space of three acres. At each corner, a wooden bastion towered a good twelve feet above the palisade, and each bastion mounted three fieldpieces. Inside the fort were 100 men, well-protected, well-armed, and well-supplied with food, water, and ammunition.

Clark set his men to work digging approaches to the fort. All night they worked, and when dawn came, they were within thirty yards of the walls. With the first light, Hamilton's cannon began to thud. Clark's riflemen lay low in their trenches and picked off gunner after gunner, until it became almost impossible to work the guns. At the end of the day, Hamilton surrendered.

It was a matchless victory, won by sheer courage and resourcefulness. And it gave America complete control of the huge Northwest Territory for the rest of the war. Partly because of George Rogers Clark and his little band, the area was ceded to the United States when the Treaty of Paris finally ended the war.

While Clark was battling the British and Indians in the west, another equally brutal frontier war was raging in the east, not far from Albany. Tories and Indians, led by the Johnsons and the Butlers and Joseph Brant, descended upon the Wyoming Valley in northeastern Pennsylvania and upon the Mohawk Valley in New York. Massacre followed massacre, and appeals for help went to Congress and to Washington.

The commander-in-chief was hard-pressed for men to meet the threat of the main British army in New York, but he did not turn his back on the needs of the frontier. In the spring of 1779, he drew up a plan for a two-pronged invasion of the central New York homeland of the Iroquois, or the Six Nations. The area to

(Continued on page 158)

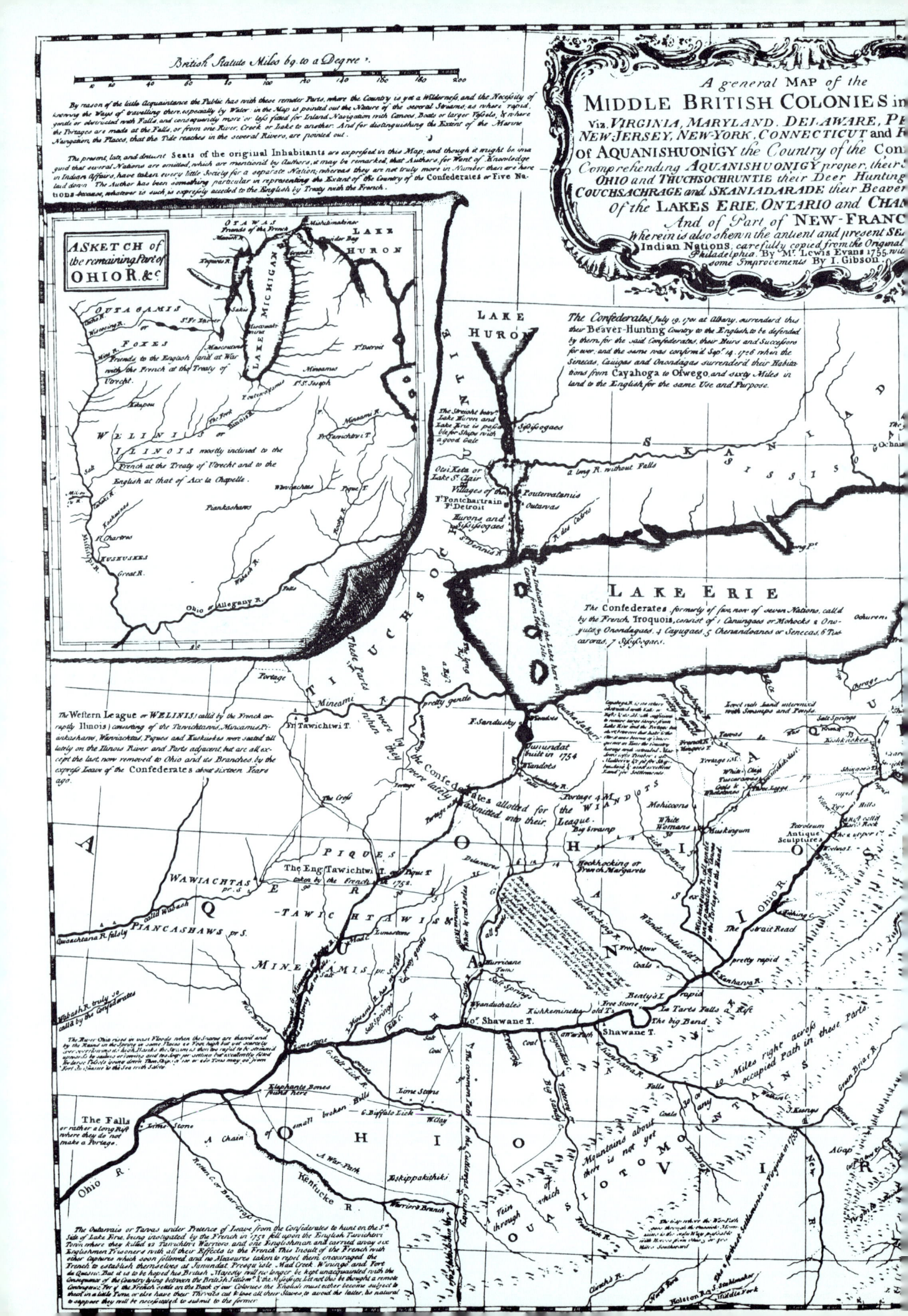

A general MAP of the
MIDDLE BRITISH COLONIES in
viz. VIRGINIA, MARYLAND, DELAWARE, PE
NEW-JERSEY, NEW-YORK, CONNECTICUT and R
of AQUANISHUONIGY the Country of the Con
Comprehending AQUANISHUONIGY proper, their
OHIO and THUCHSOCHRUNTIE their Deer Hunting
COUCHSACHRAGE and SKANIADARADE their Beaver
of the LAKES ERIE, ONTARIO and CHAM
And of Part of NEW-FRANC
Wherein is also shewn the antient and present Sea
Indian Nations, carefully copied from the Original
Philadelphia. By Mr. Lewis Evans 1755, with
some Improvements By I. Gibson

British Statute Miles 69 to a Degree.

By reason of the little Acquaintance the Public has with these remoter Parts, where the Country is yet a Wilderness, and the Necessity of knowing the Ways of travelling there, especially by Water, in the Map is pointed out the Nature of the several Streams, as where rapid, slow, or obstructed with Falls, and consequently more or less fitted for Inland-Navigation with Canoes, Boats or larger Vessels, & where the Portages are made at the Falls, or from one River, Creek, or Lake to another. And for distinguishing the Extent of the Marine Navigation, the Places, that the Tide reaches in the several Rivers, are pointed out.

The present, late, and antient Seats of the original Inhabitants are expressed in this Map, and though it might be imagined that several Nations are omitted, which are mentioned by Authors, it may be remarked, that Authors for Want of Knowledge in Indian Affairs, have taken every little Society for a separate Nation, whereas they are not truly more in Number than are here laid down. The Author has been something particular in representing the Extent of the Country of the Confederates or Five Nations, because, whatever is such, is expressly ceded to the English by Treaty with the French.

A SKETCH of the remaining Part of OHIO R. &c

The Confederates July 19, 1701 at Albany, surrendered this their Beaver-Hunting Country to the English, to be defended by them, for the said Confederates, their Heirs and Successors for ever, and the same was confirmed Sep'r 14, 1726 when the Senecas, Cayugas and Onondagas surrendered their Habitations from Cayahoga to Oswego, and sixty Miles inland to the English for the same Use and Purpose.

LAKE ERIE

The Confederates, formerly of five, now of seven Nations, call'd by the French, Iroquois, consist of 1 Caniungaes or Mohocks 2 Onoyuts 3 Onondagas, 4 Cayugas 5 Chenandoanes or Senecas, 6 Tuscaroras, 7 Skyhsogaes.

The Western League or WELINIS, call'd by the French corruptly Ilinois, consisting of the Tawichtawis, Mincamis, Piankashaws, Wawiachtas, Piques and Kuskuskies were seated till lately on the Illinois River and Parts adjacent, but are all except the last, now removed to Ohio and its Branches by the express Leave of the Confederates about sixteen Years ago.

OHIO

The Outawais or Tawas under Pretence of Leave from the Confederates to hunt on the S Side of Lake Erie, being instigated by the French in 1752 fell upon the English Tawichtwi Town where they killed 14 Tawichtwi Warriors and one Englishman and carried away six other Captives which soon followed and no Measures taken to repel them encouraged the French to establish themselves at Sanandski Presqu'ile, Mud Creek Weneango and Fort du Quesne. But it is to be hoped his British Majesty will no longer be kept unacquainted with the Consequence of the Country lying between the British Settlem'ts & the Missisipi's let it not this be thought a remote Contingence. For if the French settle on the Back of our Colonies, the English must either become subject to them in a little Time, or else have their Throats cut to save all their Slaves, to avoid the latter, as natural to suppose, they will be necessitated to submit to the former.

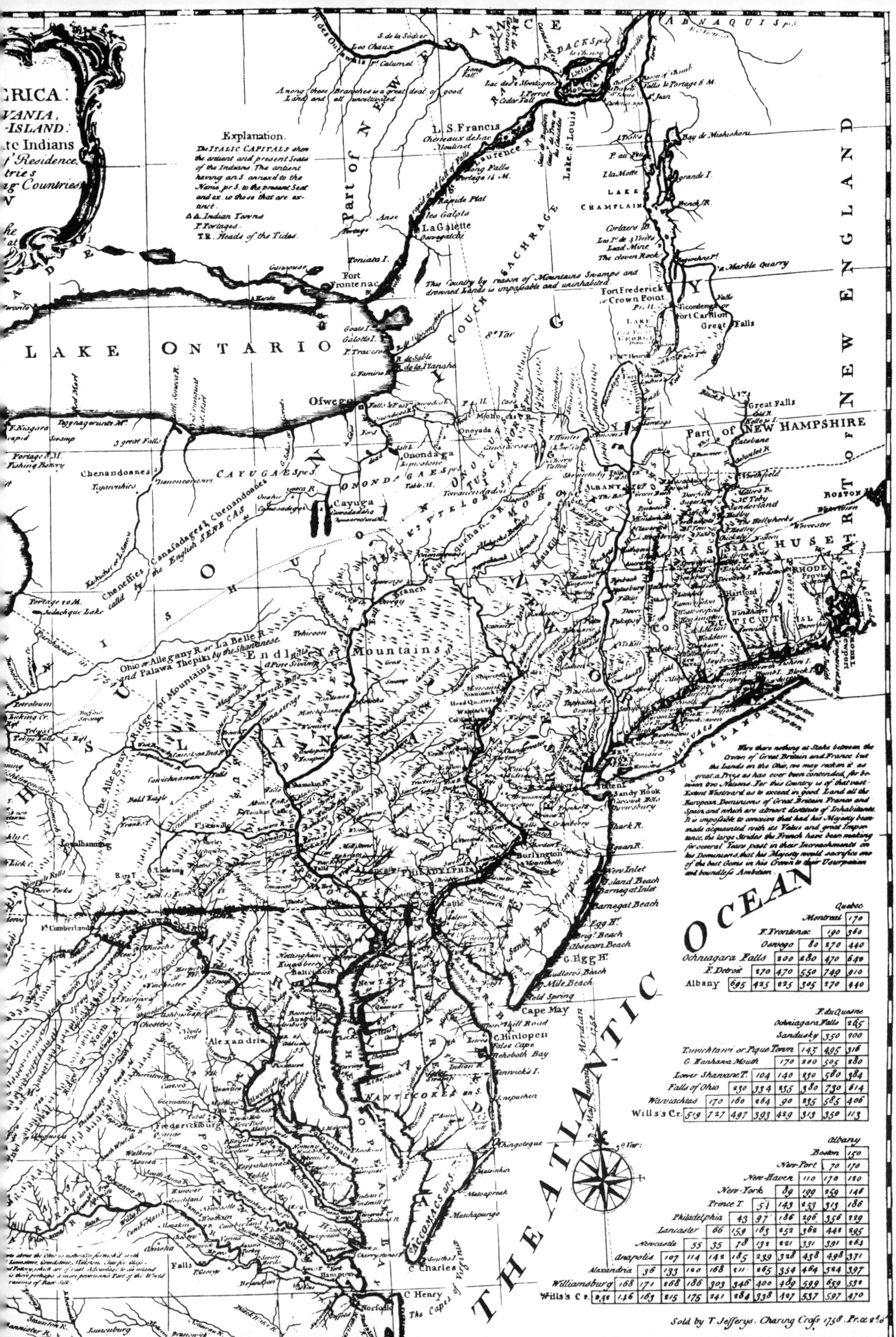

The Mohawk leader Joseph Brant had been educated by Eleazar Wheelock, founder of Dartmouth College.

be invaded stretched from Lake Ontario south to the Susquehanna River, from the Catskills on the east to Lake Erie on the west. Here the Six Nations had built their towns, studded with good houses made of stone with glazed windows. They had well-developed orchards and fine farms, all tended by the women while the men hunted and raided the frontier settlements.

Washington's plan called for "the total destruction . . . of their settlements and the capture of as many prisoners . . . as possible." He stressed that prisoners of all ages and sexes should be held as hostages in the hope of forcing the Indians to good behavior in the future.

To accomplish all this, two columns of veteran troops were fitted out. The stronger force was led by Major General John Sullivan, still smarting from his defeat at Newport the previous year. Sullivan was to start out from Easton, Pennsylvania, and drive north into New York. At Tioga, he was to be joined by the second force, headed by General James Clinton of New York. Each column was supplied with pack horses and artillery, and each was weighed down with what seems to have been too much heavy equipment for the job at hand—a lightning-fast invasion of the Indian country.

Instead of speed, there were long delays. Sullivan reached Easton on May 7, 1779, but supplies were slow in coming, and he had to hack out a road through some 23 miles of wilderness to transport his guns, wagons, and the herd of cattle that was taken along to supply meat for the troops. It was June 23 before he set up field headquarters at Wyoming, and it was July 31 before he set out for Tioga.

Clinton, in the meantime, had organized his own column at Canajoharie on the Mohawk. He had more than 200 bateaux and a three-months supply of rations. On June 17, he began to batter his way across wooded, hilly country, crossed by only a few bad roads. By June 30, he had reached Otsego Lake twenty miles away and was ready to set out to join Sullivan.

Sullivan was so late getting started that the water level in Otsego had fallen to a point that would not float Clinton's bateaux. A resourceful general, Clinton built a dam, raised the level of the water, and set out again. Meanwhile, Sullivan's troops had entered the Indian village of Chemung. Here, as one of them wrote, they found "between 30 & 40 Houses, some of them large and neatly finish'd; particularly a Chapel and a Council House." There was no resistance, and Chemung flamed up in a "glorious Bonfire and wide fields of grain and vegetables were ruin'd."

The burning of Chemung was a sample of what was in store for all the Iroquois country. Frontiersmen who had lived through the horrors of Indian raids were getting their revenge by destroying the homes of the raiders. Village after village was found deserted and was put to the torch.

But Sullivan and Clinton seem to have forgotten Washington's instruction that hostages be

Benjamin West painted Colonel Guy Johnson and his Indian ally, Chief Joseph Brant, in London in 1775. Succeeding his father-in-law as Indian agent, Johnson joined Brant in ruthless frontier war.

Mellon Collection, National Gallery of Art; Courtesy *Time*

The routes followed by Clinton and Sullivan in their punishing raid on the Six Nations are seen on Guy Johnson's 1771 map of the area. The advance is shown in blue, the return in brown.

taken. They made no attempt to surprise the Indians, though this was the only way large numbers could be captured, the only way that the tribes could be wiped out as a fighting force. Instead, the expedition made its way through the forest with a maximum of noise to advertise its coming. A cannon was touched off each morning to mark reveille. And when the troops set out on the day's march, regiments kept strict formation, drums beating, colors flying, and fifes playing.

This manner of march invited the kind of ambush that had wiped out General Braddock and most of a British army in the French-and-Indian war. But the skilled riflemen of Daniel Morgan and a small group of friendly Oneida Indians managed to protect Sullivan's flanks, scouting the countryside well ahead. They found no signs of resistance until the expedition was near what is now Elmira, New York. There, on August 29, 1779, the retreating Tories and Indians laid an elaborate ambush in an effort to destroy the American columns.

Fortunately, scouts spotted the trap. The Tories and Indians were quickly routed, and many were slain. The victory cost the Americans only three men killed.

Kanadaseagea, a Seneca town of eighty houses set in flourishing orchard country, went up in flames. So did Schoyere and Canandaigua, Honeoye and Kanagha. At last Genesee, a town about twenty miles south of the present Rochester, was reached and 128 buildings were put to the torch. This marked the farthest point reached by the expedition. After burning Genesee, Sullivan turned back and returned to Easton on October 15, 1779.

He reported that "there is not a single Town left in the Country" of the Six Nations, except one village far to the west of Genesee. Sullivan, Washington, and nearly everyone connected with the expedition seems to have considered it a great success. From one standpoint, it was. Sullivan's army had indeed performed a difficult feat, marching through dense forests, across mountains, and into dangerous Indian country. It had inflicted great damage upon the Indians, had caused them great suffering and loss. But it had not done what an army is supposed to do: it had not killed or captured the enemy; it had not wiped out the enemy as a fighting force.

The Indian tribes had been sent reeling back to the borders of Canada. They were now completely dependent on the British for food, for clothing, for ammunition and supplies. And with their homeland in ruins, they were more angry, more desperate, more vicious than ever. The British gladly supplied the aroused Indian warriors with food and powder and guns, and all through 1780 and 1781, Indians and Tories, acting both singly and together, struck at the Mohawk settlements with a savagery that made everything that had gone before seem mild by comparison.

By late 1781, the towns on the New York frontier lay in ashes and ruins, as had the Indian villages raided by Sullivan. Then the settlers found a new champion. He was Colonel Marinus Willett, the partner of Gansevoort in standing off St. Leger at Fort Stanwix in 1777. Willett raised a little army and caught up with a large raiding party of Walter Butler's Tories and Indians at Jerseyfield near West Canada Creek. Though badly outnumbered, Willett put the enemy to flight in a running battle fought in a blizzard. Walter Butler was killed, his force broken. And with this victory by Willett the New York frontier, like the Kentucky frontier, was finally made secure.

The horrors of Pennsylvania's Wyoming Massacre are the subject of this painting by Alonzo Chappel. Colonel John Butler's Tories and Indians are shown killing and scalping fleeing militiamen. Butler claimed 227 scalps at Wyoming, while he lost only three men.

Chicago Historical Society

Collection of J. Lewi Donhauser

A cavalry skirmish after the American victory at the Battle of Cowpens in South Carolina in 1781

STRUGGLE FOR THE SOUTH

"We fight, get beat, rise, and fight again."
GENERAL NATHANAEL GREENE—March 18, 1781

The Revolutionary fighting began in the North and ended in the South. In the first years, the hostilities were mainly in Massachusetts, in New York and New Jersey and Pennsylvania. Except for the futile British attack on Charleston in 1776, the South was quiet, hardly touched by the war. But with the French alliance and the Battle of Monmouth Court House in 1778, everything changed. London decided to try to knock the Southern colonies out of the war and to conquer them.

The first step in the new campaign was taken early in 1779. A British force under General Augustine Prevost moved up the coast from British Florida and entered Georgia. The force was strengthened by British, Hessian, and Tory units brought down the coast in transport ships from New York. The combined army swept through Georgia—Sunbury, Augusta, and Savannah fell, and the military government actually set up a new Georgia legislature loyal to the British Crown.

The patriots had no way of meeting the new threat. Across the Savannah River in South Carolina, Major General Benjamin Lincoln of Massachusetts tried to build up a force of Continentals and militia strong enough to attempt the recapture of Savannah. The task seemed hopeless, for the South was sparsely settled and had nothing like the manpower that had fed the northern armies. Besides, there was no way of sealing off Savannah from the supplies that the British could ship into it by sea.

Then someone thought of Admiral d'Estaing and the powerful French fleet lying in the West Indies. Word was sent to d'Estaing, and he replied promptly. He would sail for Savannah with a strong fleet of warships and transports carrying more than 6,000 French regulars. Benjamin Lincoln and the Americans were delighted. At last, it seemed, the great alliance with France was about to bear fruit.

On September 12, 1779, d'Estaing arrived off the Georgia coast and began unloading troops for the attack on Savannah. An immediate attack almost certainly would have carried the city, for Prevost and his British army were struggling desperately to repair the ruined old earthworks. But d'Estaing, the prisoner of old-fashioned military custom, did not strike at once. Instead, he sent the British a formal demand to surrender.

The British stalled—and worked frantically on the defenses. General Lincoln, arriving with a small American force, was snubbed by d'Estaing, who seems to have had a knack for making himself disliked by every officer with whom he had to deal. It was not until September 23 that d'Estaing finally broke ground for his siege train, and it was not until October 9, almost a month after his arrival, that a joint attack was launched on the Savannah lines.

By that time, the busy Prevost had made the originally weak defenses truly formidable. The attack was a terrible failure. The British, at a loss of only 100 men of their own, inflicted casualties of more than 800 on the attackers. Among the dead on the American side was the brilliant Pole, Casimir Pulaski.

A French-American force is shown ringing Savannah in 1779. The effort to retake the city failed.

Lincoln wanted to renew the assault, but d'Estaing had had enough. The crews of his ships were ill, the hurricane season was near, a British fleet might appear at any moment. Offering these excuses, he re-embarked his men and sailed to the West Indies. Lincoln and his little army trudged back to Charleston. Again, as at Newport, the French-American alliance had produced only discord and disaster.

Even worse, the whole affair had served to advertise the weakness of the Americans in the South. The miserable failure of Lincoln and d'Estaing before Savannah practically invited the British to come in force and hammer at a weak spot, and up in New York, Sir Henry Clinton read the message correctly. He abandoned Newport, pulling back 3,000 troops that had been idling there, and early in 1780 set sail for South Carolina.

Avoiding the mistakes that he and Admiral Sir Peter Parker had made in 1776, Clinton did not try to pound his way directly into the city past the harbor forts. Instead, he landed his troops down the coast and began to circle leisurely inland, cutting off Charleston on one side while his fleet blockaded it on the other.

These tactics forced General Lincoln to choose between two courses. He could either fall back from Charleston, drawing Clinton inland, far from the strength of the British fleet; or he could hole up in Charleston and, with his poorly equipped 5,000, try to beat off the attack of

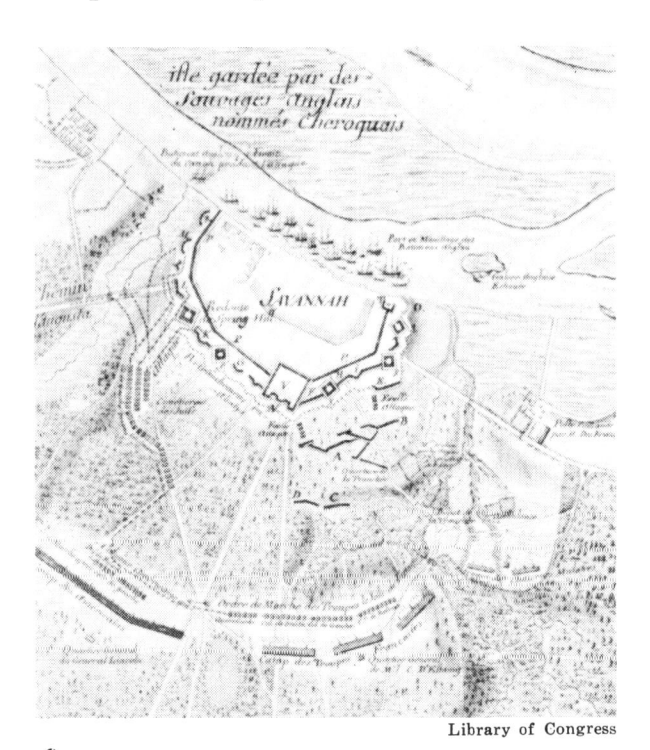

Contemporary map detail by Ozanne, showing the French-American lines of siege at Savannah

Clinton's seasoned 10,000. Lincoln, perhaps influenced by Carolinians who did not want to see their prize city lost, made the wrong decision. He decided to stay in Charleston.

Disaster came swiftly. Lieutenant Colonel Banastre Tarleton, who had landed with his finely trained and well-equipped Tory Legion, smashed into 500 American cavalry under General Isaac Huger at Monck's Corner, some 30 miles from Charleston. Tarleton practically wiped out Huger's force, seized 100 fine dragoon-mounts, and slammed shut the last escape route from Charleston. Clinton drew his siege lines tighter, and his ships bombarded the city. On May 12, 1780, Benjamin Lincoln surrendered with all his army.

More than an army had been lost. The greatest city in the South had fallen. Huge quantities of supplies had been destroyed. Nearly all the patriot leaders of South Carolina, both political and military, had been taken prisoners of the British. The Americans had suffered their worst setback of the war, and Clinton moved quickly to take further advantage of it.

Flying columns spread out over the whole of South Carolina—north to Camden along the Wateree, west to oddly named Ninety-Six, northeast toward the North Carolina border. There was nothing anywhere to stand in their way. The few patriots who tried to fight met with defeat. Colonel Abraham Buford of Virginia tried to make a stand at the Waxhaws near the North Carolina border. Tarleton, with his hard-riding Tory cavalry, cornered Buford in May, 1780. Buford tried to surrender, but Tarleton, perhaps deliberately, misinterpreted his signals, and a horrible butchery followed. Even the wounded received no mercy. From that day on, Tarleton, with his almost womanish good looks and his streak of cruelty, became known to the Americans as "Butcher."

On June 8, 1780, Clinton turned the Carolina command over to Cornwallis and sailed back to New York with 4,500 of his troops. He believed, a bit too optimistically, that the rebellion had

Independence Hall

Major General Nathanael Greene, by C. W. Peale

been crushed in the Carolinas for all time. As for Cornwallis, he built a chain of forts across South Carolina, then turned to meet a new force coming at him from North Carolina.

A small American army had started south, originally in the hope of relieving the pressure on Lincoln at Charleston. Low in numbers, the troops were high in quality. Among them were the always reliable, always staunch Delaware and Maryland Continentals. These were backed by an infantry-cavalry Legion commanded by the mysterious Frenchman known as Colonel Armand. Leading the force was the huge, physically powerful Baron de Kalb, a soldier of fortune who had come to America with Lafayette in 1777 and had turned into a real patriot. With de Kalb were such capable officers as General William Smallwood and Colonel Otho Holland Williams.

These were some of the best men in the army, but Congress decided that it would not do for de Kalb, a German, to command the only American army in the South. Furthermore, Congress wanted a leader known throughout the land,

165

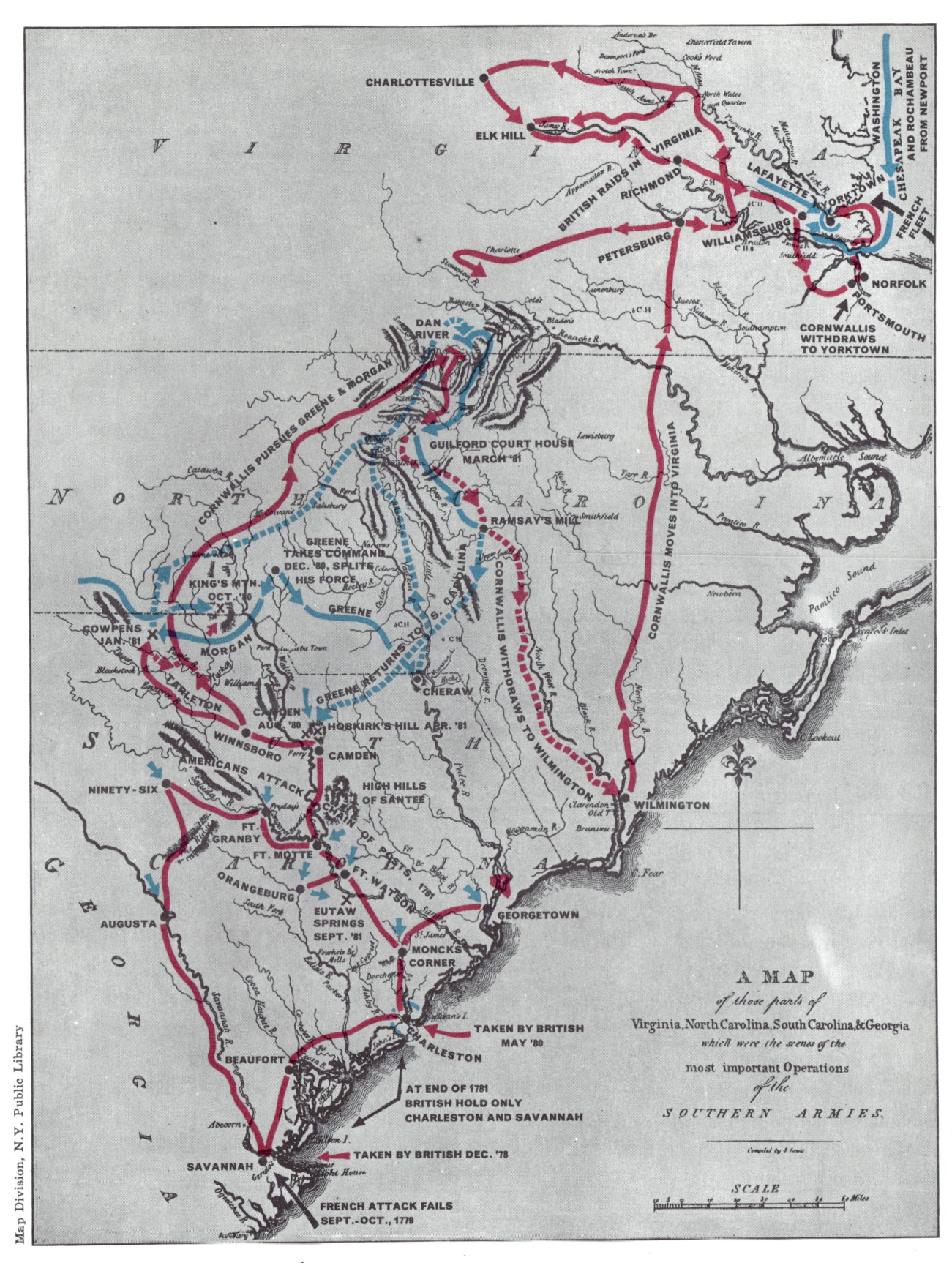

The major movements and battles of the armies during the war in the South are traced on this map. The routes of the British forces are shown in red, those of the American forces in blue.

someone whose name would make the public feel confident of victory. The politicians had always been impressed with Horatio Gates, the victor of Saratoga, and now he was given the command.

Gates took over from de Kalb in late July, 1780, on the Deep River in North Carolina. Some militia had come in, and Gates set out for the South to find Cornwallis. On the way, he met a shabby little troop of South Carolinians, whom he described as "distinguished by small black leather caps and the wretchedness of their attire; their number did not exceed twenty men and boys, some white, some black, and all mounted, but most of them miserably equipped." Their leader was a small, dark man who rarely talked and who limped from a still-healing ankle fracture—Lieutenant Colonel Francis Marion, soon to be known as the "Swamp Fox." Gates sent Marion and his men south to seize the Santee River crossings behind Camden, South Carolina, hoping to cut off Cornwallis' communications with his base at Charleston.

This done, Gates hastened on south, committing many errors along the way. He had a choice of two routes to Camden, where Cornwallis was. The longer of the two routes led through a rich countryside where patriot sentiment was strong; the shorter, through a barren waste where there were no provisions for the army and where the Tories were strong. Gates chose the shorter way. Colonel Otho Williams, one of the most capable officers in the South, pointed out that the army consisted of only 3,000 men, most of these militia and miserably equipped; Gates insisted he led 7,000. When Williams politely tried to show his commander that nearly all units had fallen in number to half strength or less, Gates cried out: "Sir, there are enough for our purpose."

On the night of August 15, Gates sent out his green troops, many of them sick, half-starved, and exhausted, on a night march to surprise and strike Cornwallis.

The British commander, who had not been napping, had exactly the same idea at exactly the same time. His veterans, marching through the night to strike Gates, crashed into Armand's Legion and scattered it. There was some confused fighting in the dark; then Cornwallis drew back and waited for dawn.

Gates still had time to retreat. De Kalb and Otho Williams, who had learned from British prisoners that Cornwallis had some 2,200 veterans at his command, privately expected him to do so, but Gates accepted the view of one officer that it was now too late. "We must fight, then," he said. "To your commands, gentlemen."

The British struck at dawn. The American left and center caved in. The raw, exhausted militia broke and fled from the British bayonets in utter, senseless panic. With the first charge, the Battle of Camden was lost.

Only on the American right, where de Kalb commanded, was there stiff resistance. There the veteran Marylanders and Delawares, a bare 600 troops, stood like a wall of iron, battling the entire British army. For more than an hour, thinking they were winning, they kept up the unequal fight. They charged with the bayonet, reformed, and charged again, rallying always around the huge figure of de Kalb, as around a battle standard. Cornwallis had to call off the pursuit of the shattered militia and throw the bulk of his army at the gallant 600. Then de Kalb was struck down, dying from his eleventh wound of the day. Tarleton's Legion charged, and the Delawares and Marylanders at last were routed.

The wreckage of Gates' army streamed north from their defeat at Camden. Officers like Otho Williams and William Smallwood and Armand stayed with the troops, struggled with them, restored some kind of order. They protected the rear as the beaten columns straggled north to Charlotte, North Carolina. And there at last they caught up with their commander, Horatio Gates.

While de Kalb was fighting and dying, while Williams and Smallwood were trying desper-

This scene shows the "over-mountain men" from the Watauga settlement in Tennessee, gathering before marching to attack the Tory forces massed on King's Mountain.

ately to hold the command together, Gates had leaped upon a horse and led the way to the rear. He galloped sixty miles before he stopped in Charlotte, a performance that led Alexander Hamilton to remark bitingly that Gates' speed did "admirable credit to the activity of a man at his time of life."

Never had American fortunes in the South been brought so low. The army that Gates had numbered at 7,000 men in mid-August now mustered less than 700. It was in wretched shape, without equipment, arms, blankets, artillery, ammunition, or food. All of South Carolina had been crushed by Cornwallis; even North Carolina and Virginia were menaced.

This was the darkest hour in the South, a moment comparable to the disasters in New Jersey before Trenton. There were only a few bright spots. One was provided by Francis Marion on August 20. A mixed band of British and Tories was convoying a column of Americans captured at Camden back to prison in Charleston. Suddenly, at daybreak, out of the swamps a mounted band burst upon them, struck hard, freed the prisoners, and captured the captors. The British and Tories were ashamed to find that they had been overwhelmed by Marion and only 16 followers.

The Americans left their horses behind and scrambled up King's Mountain. The Tories fired too high, over the heads of the attackers, and were overwhelmed.

168

The second blow at British power in South Carolina was far more important. Cornwallis, trying to protect his left flank by cleaning out the western section of the state, sent Major Patrick Ferguson, one of his best officers, into the western mountain country with a force of more than 1,000 Tories. The invasion stirred up the "over-mountain men" of the Watauga settlements, of modern Tennessee, who rallied around their leaders, Colonels Isaac Shelby and "Nolichucky Jack" Sevier, and trapped Ferguson's force on a long, wooded hill known as King's Mountain.

Some 900 of the best-mounted frontiersmen were sent ahead. They tethered their horses and swarmed up the mountain slope to the attack, taking cover behind trees and rocks as they went. All the time they sprayed the crest with deadly rifle fire. Behind this blanket of bullets, they gained the top with slight loss. Then the end came quickly.

Ferguson was shot down. His men were surrounded, and the loss was almost total. Only some 200 men, whom Ferguson had sent out on a foraging expedition before the Battle of King's Mountain, managed to stumble east to Cornwallis and safety.

Staggered by the loss of his left wing, angered by the raids of Marion and Thomas Sumter and Andrew Pickens, Cornwallis changed his plans. He had been thinking of an easy march north to the Potomac. Now he saw that he still had problems in South Carolina, and he went into winter quarters at Winnsboro, well to the west of Camden.

Still, the plight of the Americans was desperate. Even Congress recognized that the army no longer had any faith in Horatio Gates, and it empowered Washington, whose advice previously it had refused to seek, to name a new commander. Washington promptly selected the man he had wanted to see in charge in the South in the first place—his own strong right arm in all the major campaigning in the North, Major General Nathanael Greene.

The death of Major Patrick Ferguson, who was killed while trying to rally his men at King's mountain

Greene, a man of great modesty, seems to have had some doubts about his fitness for the command, but he agreed to take it. He succeeded Gates at Charlotte on December 2, 1780, and officers of the Southern army were amazed at the difference one man could make—almost overnight, at that. Colonel William Polk of North Carolina exclaimed that Greene "by the following morning understood [supply problems] better than Gates had done in the whole period of his command!"

Greene's task was truly staggering. He had but 2,300 men—and only 800 of these fit for duty. They had only three-days' rations. Clothes were in tatters, shoes lacking. The camps were filthy, badly placed; morale was low. And Greene's assignment was to defeat Cornwallis' powerful army and reconquer three states.

The job seemed impossible, but Greene saw strength where another man might have overlooked it. He knew the value of those solid Continentals from Delaware and Maryland. His sound soldier's mind quickly placed the right value on men like Otho Williams; Colonel Wil-

A painting based on a legend that Lieutenant Francis Marion once offered to share his "usual fare" of potatoes and water with an amazed British officer who was in his camp under a flag of truce.

liam Washington, a tested cavalry leader and a distant cousin of the commander-in-chief; Lieutenant Colonel Edward Carrington, an artillery expert who had smashed a British attack at Monmouth; and John Eager Howard, one of the best officers in the Maryland line.

These were leaders on whom a general could rely, and soon two others, even more important, joined Greene. One was a huge figure in fringed buckskin, creaking and groaning with arthritis—the "Old Wagoner," Daniel Morgan. Morgan had been in retirement since 1779, because of his resentment over the failure of Congress to reward his great services with promotion; but he had been made a Brigadier at last and had come out "to crack his whip once more." Also joining Greene was a famous cavalry leader, Lieutenant Colonel Henry "Light-Horse Harry" Lee. Lee brought with him a green-jacketed, helmeted Legion of some 300 finely equipped and trained men.

Greene considered his strengths and his weaknesses and saw the whole picture with the eye of genius. He knew that his army, already discouraged, would rot away if he sat in winter quarters doing nothing. He saw that his army, as a single unit, was too weak to accomplish anything. If Greene kept his force together in one place, Cornwallis could keep his iron grip on all of South Carolina, and could drive on into North Carolina to crush the one army that still stood in his way. To prevent such a move, Greene decided to go against the rules of all the military books. He decided to *divide* his already weak force.

Even now, the move seems almost like madness until one stops and thinks it out the way Greene did. He sensed at once the value of guerrilla leaders, such as Francis Marion. The day after he took command, he wrote Marion at the latter's camp on Snows' Island in the Great Pee-Dee River in South Carolina. Greene pointed out that the guerrillas and the regular army could team up to help each other. The guerrillas could harass Cornwallis with swift raids against his far-flung outposts and long lines of communication; at the same time, Greene's army could pose enough of a threat so that Cornwallis would not risk turning all his power upon the raiders.

It was a new and brilliant idea for the conduct of war in the South, and Greene's first major move as commander was to put it into effect. Instead of attaching Lee's Legion to his main army, as another commander almost certainly would have done, he sent Lee south to join Marion and step up the raids against Cornwallis' supply lines.

Old Print Shop; Courtesy *Life*

Next, Greene daringly divided his own army. The part under his own command he moved just across the South Carolina border to a camp in the Cheraws. The rest, a scant 600 men, he placed under the command of Dan Morgan for a sweep far to the west. Greene hoped that he could tempt Cornwallis into dividing the British forces, and that Cornwallis would send in chase of Morgan a detachment that, just possibly, Morgan might have a chance of beating.

Cornwallis did just what Greene hoped he might do. He sent Tarleton at the head of a force of 1,100 men to track down Morgan. The Old Wagoner, kept advised of Tarleton's movements by Andrew Pickens' roving men, picked his battlefield with care. Morgan, too, had a keen military instinct that led him now to throw away the rule book and to adopt new tactics to fit his own situation. He decided to give battle on a park-like tract that had been used by drovers to rest and graze their cattle on the way to market—a place known as the Cowpens, in the very shadow of King's Mountain.

Two low hills commanded the pasture. Behind the hills was the Broad River, a deep stream that would cut off all escape if Morgan were beaten. The book said a commander should never invite such disaster, but Morgan reasoned that, with the Broad River at their backs, his militia would *have* to fight. To make sure, Morgan placed the militia out in front, with the veterans of the Continental line drawn up on the first of the low hills behind them, with Washington's cavalry hidden behind the second hill. Before the battle, Morgan went among the militia, commanded by Pickens, and told the

171

Francis Marion's guerrilla fighters pole their way across the Pee Dee River to raid the enemy in South Carolina. British Colonel Tarleton said that "the devil himself could not catch" the wily Marion.

men exactly what he expected of them. They were to fire two volleys, Morgan said, and he told them to aim first at the British officers. "Look for the epaulets!" he said. "Pick off the epaulets!" Their two volleys fired, the militia could break and fall back behind the Continentals on the first hill. It was a daring and decidedly different battle plan.

On January 17, 1781, Tarleton drove straight into the Cowpens pasture. The helmet plumes of his dragoons tossed in the wind as they charged into the sights of the militia and riflemen. Fire crackled along the skirmish line, and the dragoons fell back. In the center, the British and Tory infantry charged straight forward. The militia fired once, fired again, then fell back according to Morgan's plan. But Tarleton did not see a plan; he saw only the panicked flight of clumsy Rebels. Rashly, he charged forward with everything he had—and crashed head-on into the solid wall of those Delaware and Maryland Continentals, commanded by John Eager Howard.

There was hard, desperate fighting on the slick, brown grass. Howard, fearing his line was about to be turned, bent it back, and Tarleton, again thinking the Americans were breaking, charged furiously. And again he was surprised. Morgan was there roaring at the men along that shifting line; the ranks steadied, and suddenly the Americans plunged downhill with the bayonet. Tarleton's charge was broken, thrown into confusion, and instantly the battle picture changed.

Pickens' reformed militia, backed up by Kirkwood's Delawares, swept out around the flank of the first hill, circled and struck the British on their left and rear. At the same time, William Washington's cavalry charged around the other side of the hill and smashed into the right rear. Tarleton's whole force was trapped.

In blind fury, Tarleton tried to rally his dragoons, but Washington crashed through them and engaged in a saber duel with Tarleton himself. Washington's horse was wounded, and Tarleton, with a small knot of riders around him, galloped away down the road. Behind him, his men threw down their arms. The patriots had lost 12 killed, 60 wounded; the British, 100 killed, 800 prisoners. Virtually all of Tarleton's command was wiped out at the Battle of Cowpens, in what has been called the most brilliant, best-fought action of the entire war.

Cornwallis was shocked, and he lashed out

in fury. He started after Morgan, but that clever fighter had lost no time. Immediately after Cowpens, he had turned and fled toward the fords over the Catawba River, 100 hard miles to the northeast. Cheated of quick revenge, Cornwallis prepared for a long chase. He burned all surplus wagons, baggage, supplies, and equipment so that he could move faster, and on January 28, 1781, he set out to catch Morgan and Greene before they could reach the fords over the Dan River leading into Virginia. If he could get to the Dan first, he could cut off the Americans' retreat and force them into battle with his greatly superior army.

But Greene had reacted to the news of Cowpens as swiftly as Cornwallis. He started at once on a march across state to join forces with Morgan and get across the Dan. Greene seems to have had amazing foresight into exactly what Cornwallis would do, and he planned accordingly. He sent Lieutenant Colonel Edward Carrington ahead to snap up every boat on the Dan River, and he called back Light-Horse Harry Lee, who had been raiding with Marion along the Congaree River.

Combining Lee's Legion with Washington's cavalry, some Continental infantry and militia riflemen, Greene formed a rear guard of less than 700 men under the command of Otho Williams. Williams' job was one of the most difficult in war. He had to strike at Cornwallis' advance, led by General O'Hara of the Guards; he had to fight it, halt it, delay it—and yet never fight it so hard that his whole command became involved in a pitched battle or got itself surrounded. Williams carried out his assignment to perfection, while O'Hara lashed out furiously and strained every nerve to pin him down. And all the time this fierce feinting went on, the two main armies raced for the Dan. Sleet stung their faces, then changed to a wet and sticky snow that lay on the roads. Men and horses died of exhaustion. Rations ran out. And still the gruelling race went on.

Colonial Williamsburg

This primitive painting shows Peter Francisco wielding his sword against nine of Tarleton's men. Francisco, a legendary Southern fighter, reportedly routed the nine as a troop of 400 approached.

Reynold's portrait of Colonel Banastre Tarleton, the cruel raider whom Americans called "the Butcher"

Greene won it, finally, by the narrowest of margins. On February 13, he got his forward lines across the Dan, and by midnight of the fourteenth, the last man of Lee's Legion—the rear guard of the rear guard—was ferried over to the Virginia shore, just as the spearhead of O'Hara's column burst from the woods on the south bank and stared down at the bridgeless flood before them.

Cornwallis had driven Greene out of North Carolina, but what was he to do now? He had lost over 200 men during the long pursuit to the Dan; he had destroyed wagons and supplies —and in the end, all for nothing. He needed to re-equip, so he turned back to Hillsboro, North Carolina. There he issued a call for all loyal Tories in the region to join up, and recruits began to flock in.

Across the Dan, safe after a retreat that had been worth a battle, Greene went right back into action. He did not want Cornwallis reinforced by Tories, and he at once stepped up the guerrilla warfare. Lee's troopers swooped down on Tory formations heading for Hillsboro. Kirkwood's Delawares snapped up supply parties, seized local leaders. Andrew Pickens' men raided day and night. And near Alamance, Lee surprised the mounted company of Tory Colonel Pyle and massacred them with a ferocity that matched Tarleton's bloodiest exploits. Suddenly Tory enthusiasm cooled, and Cornwallis' recruits drained away to a trickle.

Almost at once, Greene went back on the attack with his regular army. Baron von Steuben had sent him some troops from Virginia, and he now had some 4,000 men under his command. About 1,600 of them were Continentals, many never tested in battle. With this new-found strength, Greene went south, the cavalry of William Washington and Henry Lee screening his advance and brushing Tarleton aside. By March 14, Greene had brought his army to a spot he had carefully picked out, during his retreat to the Dan, as a promising battle site.

It was only a dot on the map, with a hill and a brick building known as Guilford Court House. Greene had studied Morgan's tactics at the Cowpens, and the Old Wagoner himself, forced by bad health to leave the army, had written advising Greene to put his militia in the front and center "with some picked troops in their rear to shoot the first man that runs." Greene followed this advice, spotting the militia in the flat woodland approaches to the court house hill, with picked men in a second line behind them, and the cream of his troops in a third line on the crest.

.On the fifteenth, Lee's cavalry, raiding south down the wood road, crashed into the British advance. Cornwallis was coming. The British forward lines charged straight up the road toward the court house hill. Greene's North Carolina militia fired the two volleys he had asked of them, but then they broke and fled. Virginians in the second line behind them were entangled in the woods and the fleeing troops; suddenly, panic spread.

O'Hara's Guards drove on with the bayonet, smashed through the second line, plunged on across the crest of the hill, and seized the guns planted there. Then they were met by the counter-shock of John Howard charging headlong with his hardy Delaware and Maryland troops. The veteran Guards were rocked back, split for a moment, and in that moment William Washington led a cavalry charge that pounded over and back again through the shredding British ranks.

Americans and British were tangled in wild fighting all over the slope of the court house hill. Cornwallis, in desperation, wheeled up his artillery. The wounded General O'Hara, understanding his intention, was horrified and pleaded with Cornwallis not to open fire on his own men. But Cornwallis, iron-faced, gave the word to his gunners and turned loose a murderous hail killing friend and foe alike.

This brutal measure saved the day for Cornwallis. The Americans fell back. One final charge by Greene might have taken the field, but if it had failed, it might have cost his army. Greene was never prepared to pay such a price. He knew that, at whatever sacrifice, he must always keep his army intact in the field, ready to fight. And so he ordered a retreat, and Cornwallis was left in possession of the ground around Guilford Court House—left with a technical victory that was worse than defeat. He had taken 1,900 men into action, and he had lost more than a quarter of them in killed and wounded. He was left with an army so weakened that it was in poor condition to fight again, and Greene, who had lost only 78 killed and 183 wounded, was almost as strong as ever.

Cornwallis could only retreat, and he did, taking his battered army off to Wilmington on the coast. There he refitted and set out on the march that was to lead to a little village named Yorktown in Virginia.

William Washington's troopers (in blue) smash Tarleton's Legion in the furious charge that turned the tide at the Cowpens.

Mabel Brady Garvan Collection, Yale University Art Gallery

Greene had whittled down the main British army and chased it out of the Carolinas. Now the time had come to win back what had been lost. Messages went out to Francis Marion and to Sumter and Pickens. Lee's Legion again rode south. One after another, the British posts, strung out in a T-shape from Charleston to Ninety-Six, came under fierce guerrilla attack. Greene made certain that the guerrillas had a free hand by leading his own army to engage the principal British force, commanded by Lord Rawdon at Camden, South Carolina.

Greene and Rawdon met in battle on April 25, 1781, on a small rise known as Hobkirk's Hill near Camden, almost on the site of the field where Gates had been so disastrously defeated. Greene placed his troops in the familiar Cowpens-Guilford Court House pattern, with the militia out in front, and it seemed for a time that the Americans would be victorious. But some units were mishandled; William Washington rode into the British camp and so overloaded himself with non-combatant prisoners that he was useless when most needed. And again Greene, unwilling to risk all on a final charge, drew off with his army. "We fight, get beat, rise, and fight again," he wrote—a sentence that describes perfectly his entire campaign.

The fights and the beatings were never in vain. Each time they cost the British so heavily that the result, in the end, was victory for the Americans. Lord Rawdon, after Hobkirk's Hill, found himself in very much the same position as Cornwallis after Guilford Court House. He had suffered so heavily that, on May 10, he abandoned Camden, burning a great quantity of military stores, and marched south to try to protect his outposts, now being hammered by Marion and Lee.

This fighting team captured Fort Motte. Then Marion went off to harry the Georgetown area, and Lee with some Marylanders struck at Fort Granby. Greene himself swung west and lay siege to the farthest outpost, Ninety-Six. The siege lasted from May 22 until mid-June, when

Lee's Legion skirmishes with the enemy in the early stages of the Battle of Guilford Court House.

Lord Rawdon charged up to the fort's relief. Again Greene had to retreat, but again he gained his objective.

Lord Rawdon, finding his lesser posts falling to Marion and Lee, realized he could not hold Ninety-Six. So he burned the post and marched back to Charleston. Even today, the almost complete reversal of British fortunes in six short months seems astounding. In December, 1780, Nathanael Greene had inherited the wreck of an army from Gates; and by late June, 1781, after a campaign in which Greene had not won a single major battle, British power in the Carolinas had been broken, their entire chain of posts had been swept away, and they held securely only the area immediately around Charleston. It was an achievement that still seems little short of magic.

In the tropical heat of a South Carolina summer, Greene rested his marched-out, battle-weary troops in the High Hills of Santee and planned his next move. Lord Rawdon, broken in health and thoroughly disgusted, gave up the British command and sailed back to England. He left a capable officer, Lieutenant Colonel Alexander Stuart, in charge of the British army. Greene, studying these changes, went back to his familiar guerrilla-regular army, two-way attack.

Sumter and Marion and Lee struck at the British supply depot at Monck's Corner, just outside of Charleston. They carried the post and brought off 150 prisoners, 200 horses, and a long string of wagons. Then in late August, 1781, Greene moved out of the High Hills of Santee, crossed flooded plains, and advanced on Stuart's army, camped at Eutaw Springs. Marion and his guerrillas joined the main army and were put in the front line for the approaching battle.

On September 8, 1781, Greene struck. Lee led the attack, crashing into Tory cavalry and infantry that had been sent to feel out the American advance. He broke the enemy and drove them before him in rout. Greene's whole command followed closely and smashed into Stuart's surprised line. The entire British left wing collapsed, the center folded, and British troops took to their heels down the road to Charleston. A major victory seemed in the making, but off on the British right, a tough major named Marjoribanks stood his ground with his grenadiers and light infantry.

He beat off every attack Greene sent against him. William Washington charged with his cavalry and saw his troopers shot down. Greene tried to mass his infantry for a crushing blow, but the Americans now were as out of hand from victory as the British were from defeat. The famished, poorly-clad Americans had entered the well-stocked British camp, and the lure of plunder and rum was too much. They broke ranks.

Stuart sensed the changed situation. He rallied his troops and charged to Marjoribanks' relief. Somehow he reformed a battle line, and Greene knew that he would have to risk his whole army in one all-out charge if he were to dent it. Again Greene refused the gamble. Once more he drew off, this time leaving the British in possession of the battlefield at Eutaw Springs, but once more Greene was the final victor.

Stuart, like Cornwallis and Rawdon before him, found that he had paid so heavy a price he could not keep the battleground that he had won. He buried his dead, including that stout fighter, Marjoribanks, and took his badly mauled army back to the safety of the Charleston fortifications.

Nathanael Greene followed and drew a tight line around the largest city in the South. In all the Carolinas and Georgia, which at the beginning of the year the British seemed to have won completely, the only places where the British flag still flew were over the ports of Charleston and Savannah, protected by the guns of the British fleet. Nathanael Greene, who never won a battle and never lost a campaign, had saved the South.

A scene at the Battle of Eutaw Springs in 1781

Washington, Lafayette and aide Tench Tilghman at Yorktown, by Charles Willson Peale

THE WORLD TURNED UPSIDE DOWN

"I propose a cessation of hostilities for twenty-four hours ... to settle terms for the surrender."

LORD CORNWALLIS—October 17, 1781

On September 30, 1768, a British fleet had arrived in America to occupy Boston and, ultimately, to bring on the war. Almost twelve years later, on July 11, 1780, another fleet felt its way through a thick blanket of fog into the harbor of Newport, Rhode Island. This fleet was to bring victory.

It was a French fleet, and it brought Lieutenant General Comte Donatien de Rochambeau and nearly 5,000 of France's best soldiers to fight at the side of Washington's army—and under Washington's command. There were seven mighty ships of the line, four frigates, and thirty-odd transports. They had sighted the American coast three days before, at the end of a long sea voyage. Then fog had clamped down, and the ships had had to feel their way carefully toward the land. The mists lifted just enough for the fleet to find its way into harbor, then had closed down again, hiding ships from shore.

Rochambeau and his officers were eager to land. The discomforts of the seventy-day voyage, the deaths from scurvy, were behind them. And now, on shore, their new American partners would give them banquets and a warm welcome. It would be a joyous occasion.

Boats put out from the sides of the ships and rowed to the shore. But there was no welcoming party. No senior American officer was present to whom Rochambeau could report. The French general and his staff wandered through the streets of the pretty little seaport. Nobody paid any attention to them. Rochambeau later wrote, "There was no one about in the streets; only a few sad and frightened faces at the windows." Finally, after much difficulty, he managed to find a few town officials and identify himself.

National Portrait Gallery

This portrait of Major General Cornwallis was painted by Gainsborough after the Yorktown defeat.

179

POTOWMARCK RIVER
St. Marys
Falmouth
Pt. Tobacco
Tappahanck
Raphannock River
BAY
MAR
Fairfield
Lewis
Mockjack Bay
Rosewel
YORK
JAMES Cty
WILLAMSBURG
Glocester
YORK-TOWN
R I V E R
YORK COUNTY
Long Island
Egg I.
Back Bay
Halfway House
Burwell
Bray
Burwell
Hog I.
JAMES RIVER
ELIZABETH Cty
Rascow
Hampton
CHESAPEAK
Fort George
Comfort Pt.
Warrasqueak
WIGHT Cty
I. OF
Graney I.
Willowbys Pt.
Smithfield
NORFOLK Cty
Lamberts Pt.
PRINCESS ANN Cty
Norfolk
Cape Henry
Armée Navale de France aux Ordres du Cte. DE GRASSE avant la Victoire remportée sur
l'Amiral GRAVES faisant le Blocus de la Baye de Chesapeak

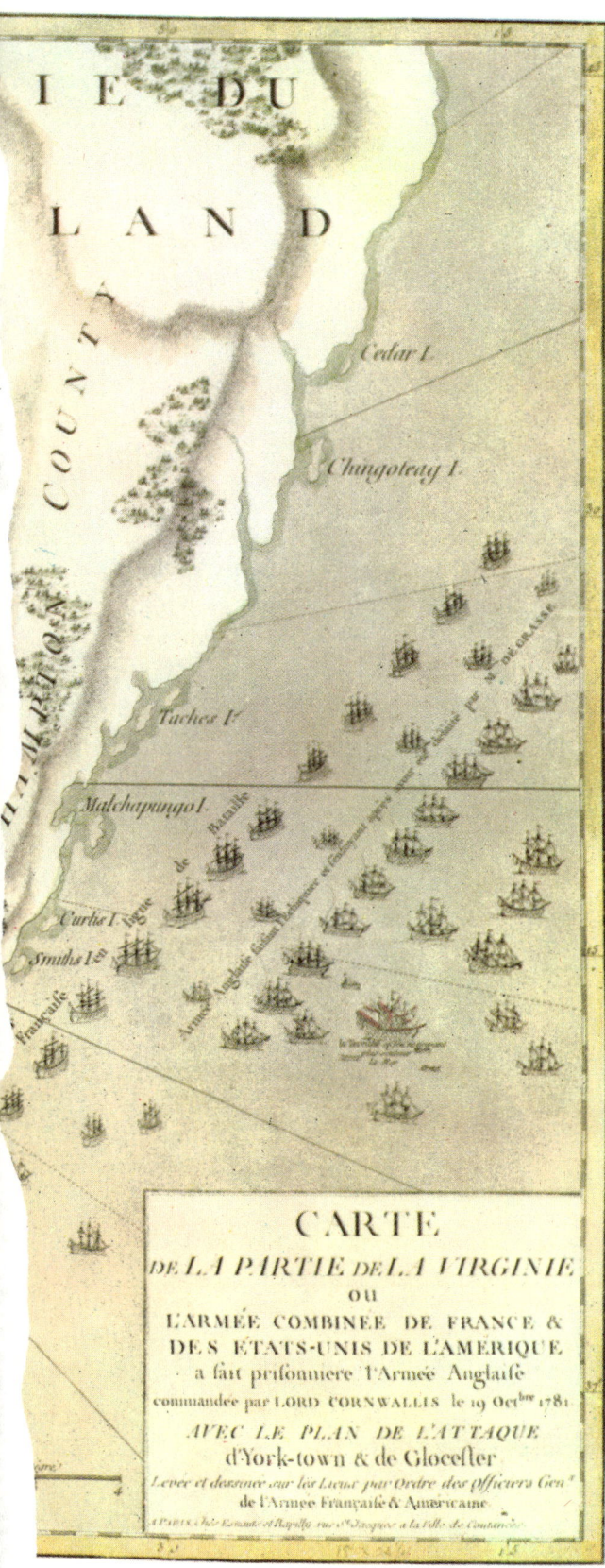

A chillier reception for a new and gallant ally would be hard to imagine. Fortunately for America, Rochambeau was a truly fine and remarkable man. In the months ahead, he was to prove his worth many times, but perhaps no test ever showed his quality more clearly than this—that the unfriendly reception did not lessen his enthusiasm for the American cause.

Fortunately, too, General William Heath of Roxbury, Massachusetts, a veteran who had been in the field since 1775, soon arrived in Newport to act as Washington's deputy. Heath had been delayed on the roads, but once he reached Newport, he tried to make up to the French for the manner in which they had been greeted. Heath dashed everywhere, securing proper camp sites for the troops, locating water supplies, arranging for the purchase of provisions, and smoothing over the disagreements that cropped up between the townsfolk and the newcomers.

The French soon made a deep impression on the citizens of Newport and Providence, who watched the steady ranks parade past, beautifully equipped in natty white uniforms with crimson, green, and black facings. They were especially struck with the 300 Legionnaires of Armand-Louis Gontaut Biron, Duc de Lauzun, riding past with their long lances and great, curved sabers. No doubt about it, these French looked like magnificent fighters, good men to have on our side.

Yet for some time the French were almost ignored by the American command; they were given nothing to do, nobody to fight. Not until mid-September did Washington ride to Hartford to meet Rochambeau for the first time. And Rochambeau made no secret of his disappointment that, even then, the American com-

This map shows the allied siege of Yorktown, the French ships blocking Chesapeake Bay, and the later Battle of the Virginia Capes. (Above and below) Water colors from a French logbook show the two lines of warships firing broadsides in the battle.

181

This contemporary map shows the disposition of the French and American forces besieging the British at Yorktown.

mander spoke only in generalities and extended no invitation to French officers to ride over to the Hudson and have a look at the American army.

Washington was not really to blame for this coldness. His army was in very bad shape, few in numbers, lacking in equipment. He may have feared that one look would discourage the French so much that they would climb back on their ships and sail for home.

The result was that the French settled down in Rhode Island, wasting idle months, growing bitter at their new American allies. Rochambeau was impatient, but, from the first, he seems to have understood many of Washington's problems. As one observer wrote, Rochambeau seemed "to have been purposely created to understand Washington and to be understood by him and to serve with Republicans . . . his example more even than his authority obliged us scrupulously to respect the rights, properties and customs of our allies."

Rochambeau's example must indeed have been of the finest, for there seem to have been few, if any, fights or disputes between the French troops and the townsfolk. It was amazing that 5,000 French soldiers could settle down in what was to them a foreign countryside and cause so little trouble.

As the winter of 1780–81 dragged on, Washington and Rochambeau began to plan the summer campaign, and as they did, the situation in Virginia claimed their attention. Virginia had been almost untouched by war since 1776, but it was one of the wealthiest of the colonies, and it had contributed heavily to the patriot cause in men and supplies. The British knew that if Virginia could be knocked out of the war, the patriots would be crippled, and so in January, 1781, Sir Henry Clinton in New York decided to strike at the Tidewater region.

A British fleet sailed up the James River and put ashore a raiding force of 1,200 men, headed by the traitor, Benedict Arnold. Arnold swept inland, captured Richmond, and spread havoc

Alexander Hamilton in the trenches at Yorktown

and destruction through the eastern part of the state. Then he retired to Portsmouth and went into winter quarters. Washington, studying Arnold's situation, thought that there might be a chance to trap the traitor, and he sent Lafayette south with a picked force of 1,200 New England and New Jersey troops.

Before Lafayette could reach Virginia, however, the British forces against him were greatly strengthened. Major General William Phillips, who had been Burgoyne's second in command in 1777, was sent to Virginia with 2,600 more men to take over the command from Arnold. And in May, Lord Cornwallis, having refitted

On the night of October 14, 1781, two of Cornwallis' redoubts anchoring the left of his Yorktown lines were stormed, one by the French, the other by the Americans. This scene shows the Rebels under Alexander Hamilton overwhelming the redcoats and raising the Stars and Stripes over the parapet.

State Capitol, Richmond

his army in Wilmington after the battle of Guilford Court House, came up from the South with 1,500 more men. Clinton sent an additional 1,500 troops, and suddenly the British army in Virginia under Cornwallis totaled some 7,200 men.

Lafayette was hopelessly outnumbered. Even when he was joined by Anthony Wayne and was reinforced by local militia, he could count only some 3,000 troops. A single mistake on his part could have led to disaster, but the young Marquis, in his first independent command, quickly proved that he had a cool head. He skirmished with Cornwallis' superior army, but he always managed to keep out of the Britisher's reach. He played the game of fight, retreat, and fight again, very much the way Greene had played it in the Carolinas, annoying Cornwallis, never letting himself be drawn into a pitched battle.

Despite his far greater strength, Cornwallis had his problems. Up in New York, Sir Henry Clinton could not make up his mind what he wanted to do. He was alarmed by signs that Washington and Rochambeau might be planning an all-out assault against Manhattan Island, and about the first day of July, he ordered Cornwallis to ship back 3,000 regulars to help him meet this supposed threat. Cornwallis tried to lure Wayne and Lafayette into a trap along the James River before these troops departed. Wayne plunged into battle, but Lafayette smelled the trap, and the Americans managed to break off the action. Cornwallis, in disgust, marched to Portsmouth to ship the 3,000 soldiers to Clinton.

Even then, Clinton could not reach a decision. He sent Cornwallis conflicting orders almost daily. The 3,000 troops were to be shipped; then they were not to be shipped. The soldiers boarded transports, got off transports, boarded transports again. Finally, on July 20, Clinton decided the troops should stay with Cornwallis after all. And he ordered Cornwallis to take up a position on the coast where a

185

This painting by a French eyewitness, Louis Van Blarenberghe, shows a column of white-uniformed French troops marching into the siege lines around Yorktown. At center, officers discuss the situation.

naval base might be established. Clinton suggested Hampton Roads, where Fortress Monroe now stands. But he also suggested Yorktown, and since Cornwallis preferred this dying old tobacco port on the York River, he took his army there.

While this maneuvering had been going on in Virginia, Washington and Rochambeau had been trying to map out a campaign in the North. They conferred in Connecticut in late May about the courses open to them. Rochambeau's orders all but commanded him to join Washington in an attack on New York. This was Washington's dream. If New York could be captured, the war might be ended. But the difficulties and dangers were enormous. The British fleet controlled the waterways surrounding New York on every side; the defenses of the city were strong. Rochambeau, while willing to follow Washington anywhere, had serious doubts about the wisdom of trying to take New York, and seems from the first to have favored striking a blow in Virginia.

To do this, however, it would be necessary to have command of the sea. Otherwise, even if Cornwallis were penned up in Yorktown by land forces, he could simply board a British fleet and sail away. This meant that Washington and Rochambeau themselves could not make the decision; they would have to have the help of a French fleet. It was agreed, therefore, that Washington, backed by French troops, should continue sparring with the British in New York, testing their defenses. And in the meantime, messengers from both Washington and Rochambeau would go to the West Indies, where a new French Admiral, Comte Francois Joseph Paul de Grasse, was planning a blow against the British-held islands.

So it came about that de Grasse made the great decision. Word of it reached Washington by a hard-riding courier on August 14, 1781. The French Admiral had sailed with 28 ships of the line and a swarm of transports. He was heading for the Chesapeake, where he would land his troops and use his fleet to bottle up Cornwallis in Yorktown. All doubts now vanished, and Washington and Rochambeau moved quickly.

One problem had to be solved immediately. The American treasury was bare; Washington

Musée de Versailles

could not finance such a campaign. But Rochambeau, loyal as always, opened his own war chest and gave Washington half the money in it. By doing so, he made it possible for the Americans to fight.

The next hurdle was a military one and the most hazardous of the entire expedition. French and American troops had to cross the Hudson in the face of Clinton's strong army and strong fleet in New York. If Clinton struck while the army was divided by the river, disaster would result. But Clinton did not strike. He seems to have been completely deceived by Washington's earlier stabs at New York, completely convinced that the blow was about to fall on him. Not until Washington's forward files were crossing the Delaware did Clinton finally wake to the great plan that was afoot.

Once clear of Clinton, the march south was pressed with great speed and efficiency. Washington's tattered but hardy veterans led the way, followed by the well-equipped, sturdy French. The marching schedule was rigidly kept; there was little disorder, almost no straggling. On the way, word came that de Grasse had reached the Chesapeake and had landed 3,000 troops to join forces with Lafayette and Wayne. The good news cheered the marching files; they stepped out faster. By early September, the leading columns had reached Head of Elk in fine shape, ready to embark for a quick voyage down the Chesapeake to Williamsburg.

The complicated plan was working out perfectly, but Washington and Rochambeau still had one serious worry. Could de Grasse keep command of the sea? Suppose the British Navy smashed the French fleet and cut off a second fleet under Admiral Barras, coming down from Newport with the heavier French ordnance and tons of salt beef for the armies? That would mean disaster. On September 15, however, this worry vanished. Before dawn, word reached Washington that de Grasse had beaten off two English Admirals, Thomas Graves and Samuel Hood, in an action at sea off the Chesapeake Capes. The British, their ships badly battered, had sailed back to New York; Barras' all-important fleet from Newport had slipped into the Chesapeake while the sea battle was being fought; and now de Grasse himself was back in the bay, blockading Cornwallis.

With this one naval action, so little noted in history, the fate of Cornwallis was practically decided. Washington and Rochambeau marched out of Williamsburg and swept down the peninsula to join Lafayette and Wayne before Yorktown. The allied army, increased by militia, numbered some 16,000 men. Cornwallis had only a little more than 6,000, and he had only one faint hope of getting out of the trap in which he found himself.

Across the York River from Yorktown lies Gloucester Point. Cornwallis had erected fortifications there. Washington and Rochambeau realized that if Cornwallis could ferry his army across the York, he might burst out of the lines on Gloucester Point and begin a long march up the coast to rejoin Clinton in the North. Therefore, additional allied troops were sent to Gloucester Point, and on October 3, 1781, the Marquis de Choisy, commanding the allied forces on the peninsula, knocked out the British outposts. In the battle, Banastre Tarleton's troopers were routed, and Tarleton himself was nearly slain in a fight with the Duc de Lauzun. De Choisy closed his lines about the Gloucester works, forming a barrier that blocked Cornwallis' last escape route.

On the Yorktown side of the river, Washington and Rochambeau dug their trenches ever closer to the British fortifications. Their massed cannon pounded Cornwallis night and day. On the night of October 14, the allied cannonade was stilled for a moment. Then six guns barked out in rapid succession. It was the signal for a night assault on Cornwallis' lines.

Picked companies of French regulars stormed from the allied left; from the right swept lean American light infantry, commanded by Lieutenant Colonel Alexander Hamilton. The two attacking columns struck with deadly swiftness, using the bayonet. The next day, Cornwallis wrote sadly to Clinton, " . . . the enemy carried two advanced redoubts by storm. . . . My situation now becomes very critical. . . ."

With this success, allied artillery pushed up closer to the front. Heavy 24-pounders and 18's and 16's, squat mortars and little coehorns roared full blast. At least 100 guns were work-

The surrender at Yorktown, painted by Van Blarenberghe. As the British bands played "The World Turned Upside Down," redcoats marched between French and American ranks to stack their arms.

ing over the British, and there was no answer from the British lines. At about ten o'clock on the morning of the seventeenth, the fourth anniversary of Burgoyne's surrender, the cannoneers paused for a moment to let the powder smoke clear so that they could better train their sights on their targets. Suddenly, off on the great curved mound inside the British lines known as the "Horn Work," there was movement.

One small figure stood alone on the parapet—a little British drummer boy, gun smoke curling about his thin legs. Bravely, he hammered out a message on his drum. Fire slackened as the little scarlet figure, his shabby bearskin cap erect, drummed on. The French were the first to recognize the drum beat. Then others caught it. It was a request for a parley, and Lieutenant Ebenezer Denny of the 4th Pennsylvania wrote that he had "never heard a drum to equal it—the most delightful music to us all."

Minutes later, an aide, red-faced with excitement, burst in upon Washington. The commander-in-chief had been writing letters to be sent back to Williamsburg. His aide handed him a note. Washington broke the seal and read: "I propose a cessation of hostilities for twenty-four hours, and that two officers may be appointed by each side, to meet at Mr. Moore's house to settle terms for the surrender of the posts at York & Gloucester. I have the honor to be Sir Your most obedient and most humble Servant, Cornwallis."

It was the end. On October 19, 1781, the capitulation was signed, and that afternoon, the British army marched out of its works, passed through lines of French and American troops, stacked its arms and surrendered. General Charles O'Hara of the Guards, the fighter who had pressed the Americans so hard in the race for the Dan, made the formal surrender on behalf of Cornwallis. Washington named General Benjamin Lincoln—who had suffered the shame of surrender at Charleston—to receive O'Hara's sword.

A tremendous victory had been won, the war in effect had been decided; but no one could be quite sure of that at the time. Cornwallis'

Musée de Versailles

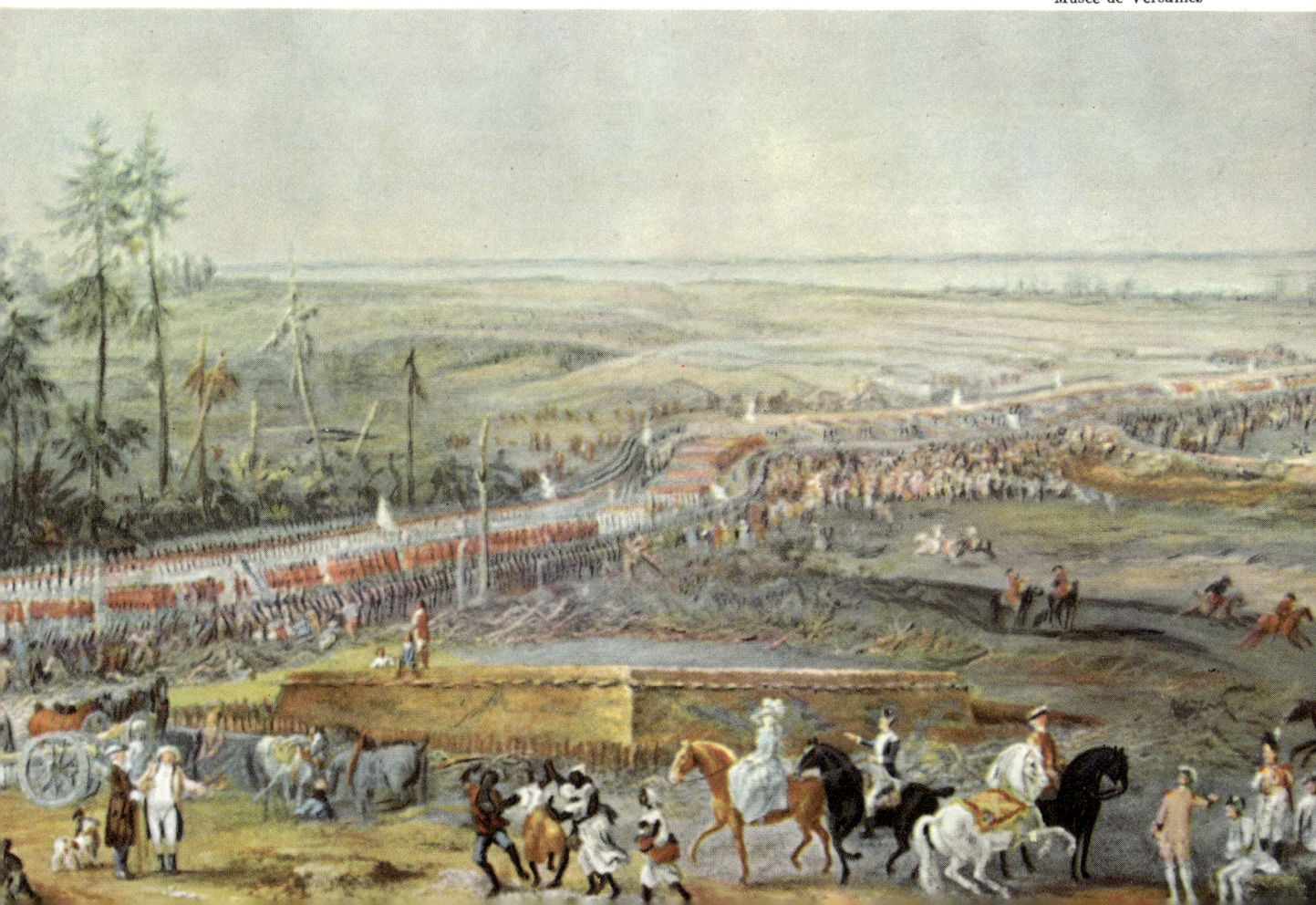

An inaccurate but delightful French view of Cornwallis' surrender. Yorktown appears as a medieval town, de Grasse's fleet is at the water's edge, and the French dominate the field of battle.

men went off to prison camps; Washington and Rochambeau marched back north. Then followed two long weary years of waiting. In New York, Sir Guy Carleton replaced Clinton and, late in 1782, called back the troops that had been holding Charleston and Savannah. In Paris, French and American commissioners met with the British in peace discussions that dragged on for long, endless months.

Washington's army almost wasted away with the waiting. The great danger had passed, and men saw little reason to sacrifice their personal interests to stay in the lines and watch the British in New York. But enough did stay so that Washington was able to keep an army together until April, 1783, when the final treaty recognizing American independence was received and quickly ratified by Congress.

Even then, there were more wearisome delays. It was not until September 3 that England finally agreed to peace with France and Spain; not until the end of November that Carleton finally gave up New York and sailed away. General Henry Knox led the American army into the city close on the heels of the departing enemy, and New York once more, for the first time since 1776, was an American city.

One more farewell was left, the hardest and the saddest of all. On December 4, 1783, Washington's officers gathered at Fraunces' Tavern in New York to bid farewell to their chief.

Washington entered, gestured at the laden tables, put some food on a plate, picked up a fork—but could not eat. As he filled a glass, his hand shook, and he bowed his head. Then, in an odd, tight voice, he spoke. "With a heart full of love and gratitude, I now take leave of you," he said. Slowly and carefully he added: "I most devoutly wish that your later days may be as prosperous and happy as your former ones have been glorious and honorable."

He raised his glass. Here and there a man stammered out a response. Then again the commander-in-chief spoke, his face glistening unashamedly with tears. "I cannot—" he stopped, and then went on again—"I cannot come to each of you but shall feel obliged if each of you will come and take me by the hand."

Henry Knox moved across the room, his hand out. Washington started to take the hand, but then threw his arms about his faithful artillery chief in an embrace that seemed too little to express his affection. One by one, the others came forward to be greeted in the same way, with heartfelt warmth and sadness.

"Such a scene of sorrow and weeping I had never before witnessed, and hope I may never be called upon to witness again," wrote Major Benjamin Tallmadge, Washington's handsome young Chief of Intelligence. "Not a word was uttered to break the solemn silence . . . or to interrupt the tenderness of the . . . scene. The simple thought that we were then about to part from the man who had conducted us through a long and bloody war, and under whose conduct the glory and independence of our country had been achieved, and that we should see his face no more in this world, seemed to me utterly insupportable. But the time of separation had come, and waving his hand to his grieving children around him, he left the room. . . ."

It was not, of course, the final parting that it seemed. The country turned again to George Washington for leadership. As the first President of the United States, he bound together the new nation which, in time, was to become the bulwark and the beacon of the free world.

When Benjamin West began painting the signing of the peace treaty, he started with portraits of (left to right) John Jay, John Adams, Benjamin Franklin, Henry Laurens, and Franklin's grandson, William Temple Franklin, secretary to the American delegation. However, the British commissioners refused to pose, and the picture was never finished.

Du Pont Winterthur Museum

INDEX

Page numbers in **bold face** refer to illustrations.

Acts of Trade and Navigation, 43
Adams, John, 9, 13, 15, 28, **47**, 50, 55, 65, 140
Adams, Samuel, **11**, 13-15, 18, 19
Albany campaign, 113-123
Alexander, William (Lord Stirling), 85-86
Allen, Ethan, 23
American long rifle, 60
André, Maj. John (John Anderson), 128-130
Armand's Legion, 165, 167
Army, Continental *see* Continental Army
Army of Observation, 17
Arnold, Benedict, 23, 25, 117, 183
    Canadian campaign, 34-38
    at Freeman's Farm, 120-123
    West Point conspiracy, 128-130
Articles of Confederation, 105
Artillery, **62-63**
Baltimore, **41**
Barney, Joshua, 142, **143**
Barras, Admiral, 187
Barrington, Viscount, 132
Barry, John, 143
Baum, Lieut. Col. Friedrich, 118, 119
Bennington, Battle of, 118-119
Biddle, Nicholas, **140**
Bonhomme Richard, 144-145, **146-147**
Boone, Daniel, 149
Boston, occupation of, 9-29, 47
Boston Harbor, **9**
Boston Massacre, **8**, 12-14
Boston Port Bill, 15, 17, 47
Boston Tea Party, **15**, 47
Bowman, Capt. Joseph, 151, 153
Brandywine Creek, Battle of, 100-101
Brant, Joseph, 116, 155, **158**, 159
Breed's Hill, Battle of, 25-29
Breymann, Lieut. Col. Francis, 119, 123
Brooklyn Heights, 83-88
Brunswick, Duke of, 76
Buford, Col. Abraham, 165
Bunker's Hill, 25, 28
Burgoyne, Gen. John, 99, **112**
    Albany campaign, 113-121
    surrender at Saratoga, **122-123**
Butler, Col. John, 117
Camden (South Carolina), Battle of, 167
Campaigns
    Albany, 113-123
    Canadian, 31-38
    Carolina, 38-39
    Kentucky frontier, 149-155
    New Jersey, 92-97, 108-110
    New York, 81-91
    New York frontier, 155-161
    Pennsylvania, 99-107
    Southern, 163-177
    Yorktown, 179-189
Camps, military, 66-67
Canada, conquest by England, 42
Canadian campaign, 31-38

Carleton, Sir Guy, 32-38, 190
Carolina campaign, 38-39
Carrington, Lieut. Col. Edward, 170, 173
Caswell, Col. Richard, 38
Charleston
    Battle of, 38-39
    siege of, 164-165
Charlestown Heights, 22, 25
Chesapeake Bay, 100, 138
Chew, Benjamin, 103
Cilley, Joseph, 121
Clark, George Rogers, 149, **150**, 151-155
Clarke, Reverend Jonas, 18
Clinton, Sir Henry, 38-39, 81, 190
    Charleston, siege of, 164-165
    New Jersey campaign, 107-110
    West Point, 126-130
    Yorktown campaign, 183-187
Clinton, Gen. James, 158
Committee of Safety, 17
Committees of Correspondence, 14
Common Sense, 48, 49
Concord, 17-20
Concord Bridge, Battle of, 21, **22**
Congress
    first Continental, 47
    Massachusetts Provincial, 17-18
    second Continental, 28, 31, 41, 47, 49, 55
    Stamp Act, 46, 47
Continental Army, 6, 28
    artillery, 62-63
    camps and prisons, 66-67
    fortifications, 64-65
    infantry, 70-71
    militia, 57
    regulars, 72-73
    training, 57-58
    uniforms and equipment, **68-69**
    weapons, 60-61
Continental Congress
    first, 47
    second, 28, 31, 41, 47, 49, 55
Cornwallis, Lord, 81, 138, **179**
    New Jersey campaign, 92-97
    Southern campaign, 165-175
    Yorktown campaign, 183-189
Cowpens, Battle of, 171-172, **175**
Davis, Capt. Isaac, 21
Deane, Silas, 125
Dearborn, Col. Henry, 105, 120, 122
de Choisy, Marquis, 188
Declaration of Independence, **51-55**, 76
    drafting committee, **40**
Declaration of Rights and Grievances, 46
de Grasse, Comte, 136-138, 186, 187
de Kalb, Baron, 165, 167
De la Place, Capt., 23
d'Estaing, Adm., 126, 136, **138**, 163-164
Detroit, 149
Dickinson, John, **47**, 55
Dickinson, Gen. Philemon, 109

Drake, 144
East India Company, 14
Eutaw Springs, Battle of, 177
Ferguson, Maj. Patrick, 169
Flintlock musket, 60
Fort Lee, 91-92
Fort Moultrie, 38-39
Fort Nonsense, 99
Fort Sackville, 151, 154-155
Fort Stanwix, Battle of, 116-117
Fort Ticonderoga, 23, 65, 114-115
Fort Washington, 91-92
Fortifications, **64-65**
France
    aid to colonies, 49
    entry into war, 107, 125-126
    Seven Years' War, 42
Franklin, Benjamin, 17, 48, 50, 55, **124**, 130, 144
    in France, 125-126
Fraser, Gen. Simon, 115, 119, 122
Fraunces' Tavern, 190
Freeman's Farm, Battle of, 120-123
French and Indian War, 42, 65
Gadsden, Christopher, 7, 39, 46, 48
Gage, Gen. Thomas, 17, **18**, 19, 23, 28
Gansevoort, Col. Peter, 116
Gaspée, burning of, **14**
Gates, Gen. Horatio, 119-120, 167-169
    Burgoyne's surrender, **122-123**
Genesee, burning of, 160
George III, 9, **10**, 42, 49, 76, 81, 132
Germantown, Battle of, 102-105
Gibault, Père Pierre, 151, 153
Glover, John, 81, 87, 91, 93-95, 126
Graves, Adm. Thomas, 136, 138, 187
Greene, Col. Christopher, 34, 36, 37
Greene, Gen. Nathanael, 34, 94, **165**
    Pennsylvania campaign, 101-105
    Southern campaign, 169-177
Guilford Court House, Battle of, 174-175
Hamilton, Alexander, 97, **183**, 188
Hamilton, Col. Henry, 149, 152-155
Hancock, John, 17, 18, 19, 41, **46**
Hancock, 140
Hand, Edward, 97
Harlem Heights, Battle of, 88-89, **90**
Haslet, John, 72, 81, 86
Heath, Gen. William, 181
Helm, Capt. Leonard, 151-152
Henry, Patrick, 45, **46**, 150
Herkimer, Brig. Gen. Nicholas, 117
Hessians, 49, 76-77, 81
    at Trenton, 93-95
Hitchcock, Daniel, 97
Hobkirk's Hill, Battle of, 176
Hood, Adm. Samuel, 136, 138, 187
Hopkins, Esek, **140**, 143
Howard, John Eager, 170, 172, 175
Howe, Adm. Richard, 136, **138**
Howe, Gen. Sir William, 113, 116
    at Breed's Hill, 26, 28
    at Harlem Heights, 88-90
    at Long Island, 83-87
    New Jersey campaign, 91, 93, 97

Pennsylvania campaign, 99-107
Huger, Gen. Isaac, 165
Hutchinson, Israel, 86
Hutchinson, Thomas, 10, 13
Indian warfare, 31, 115-117, 149-160
Infantry
   American, 70-71
   British, 74-75
   French, 78-79
   uniforms and equipment, **68-71**
   weapons, **60-61**
"Intolerable Acts," 47
Jameson, Lieut. Col. John, 129
Jefferson, Thomas, 50, **55**, 150
Johnson, Col. Guy, **159**
Jones, John Paul, 143-146
Kentucky frontier campaign, 149-155
King's Mountain, Battle of, 169
Kip's Bay, 88
Knowlton, Thomas, 27
Knox, Gen. Henry, 29, 62, 65, 104, 190-191
   at Harlem Heights, 88-89
   New Jersey campaign, 94-97
Kosciuszko, Tadeusz, **118**, 119
Lafayette, Marquis de, 100, **101**, 178
   at Monmouth Court House, **108**, 109
   Yorktown campaign, 183-188
Langdon, John, 118
Lauzun, Duc de, 181, 188
Lauzun's Legion, 78
Learned, Ebenezer, 122
Lee, Arthur, 125
Lee, Maj. Gen. Charles, 107-110
Lee, Lieut. Col. Henry, 170, 173-177
Lee, Richard Henry, 150
Lexington Green, Battle of, 18-19, **20**
Lillington, Col. John Alexander, 38
Lincoln, Maj. Gen. Benjamin, 163-165, 189
Livingston, Robert, 50
Long Island, Battle of, 82-87
Louis XVI, 78, 125, 126
Loyalists, see Tories
Marion, Lieut. Col. Francis, 39, 167-170, 176-177
Mason, George, 150
Mawhood, Lieut. Col. Charles, 96, 97
Maxwell, Gen. "Scotch Willie," 101, 103
McCrea, Jane, 116
McQuarters, Sgt. Hugh, 37
Mercenaries see Hessians
Mercer, Gen. Hugh, 96
Minutemen, 17
Mohawk Valley, 155-161
Monck's Corner, 165
Monmouth Court House, Battle of, 109-111
Monroe, James, 95
Montgomery, Gen. Richard, 30, 33, 36, 37
   Montreal, fall of, 33-34
Moore's Creek Bridge, Battle of, 38
Morgan, Capt. Daniel, 34, 37, 99, 160
   at Saratoga, 120-123
   Southern campaign, 170-174
Morris, Robert, 140
Morristown, 67, 97, 99
Moultrie, Col. William, 39
Mount Defiance, 114-115
Musket, flintlock, 60
Naval warfare, 132-146
New Jersey campaign, 92-97, 108-110

New York, **44-45**
New York campaign, 81-91
New York frontier campaign, 155-161
Newport, Battle of, 126
Nicholson, James, 140
Ninety-Six, siege of, 176
North, Lord, 126
Northwest Territory, 149-155
O'Hara, Gen. Charles, 173, 175, 189
Old North Church, 18
"Olive Branch" petition, **50**
Paine, Thomas, 31, **46**, 48, 49, 81
Paoli, Battle of, **100**, 102
Parker, Capt. John, 19
Parker, Adm. Sir Peter, 38, 39
Pennsylvania campaign, 99-107
Percy, Lord, 17, 22
Philadelphia, occupation of, 100-101
Phillips, Maj. Gen. William, 115, 183
Pickens, Andrew, 169, 171, 172, 176
Pickering, Timothy, 102, 104
Pitcairn, Maj. John, 19-22, 26
Pollock, Oliver, 152
Poor, Gen. Enoch, 122
Prescott, Col. William, 26
Prevost, Gen. Augustine, 163
Princeton, Battle of, 96-97
Prisons, military, 67
Privateers, 132, 140
Provincial Congress, Massachusetts, 17-18
Pulaski, Count Casimir, 100, 163
Putnam, Israel, 83, 86, 88-89
Quebec, **31**; Battle of, 34-37
Quiberon Bay, Battle of, **133**
Rall, Col. Johann, 93, 95
Ranger, 143
Rawdon, Lord, 176-177
Revere, Paul, **18**
   midnight ride, 19
Rifle, American long, 60
Rochambeau, Comte de, 78, 179-190
Rodney, Adm. George, 136, 138
Rousseau, Jean Jacques, 125
St. Clair, Maj. Gen. Arthur, 114-115
St. John's, siege of, 33
St. Leger, Col. Barry, 113, 116-117
Saintes, Battle of the, 138
Sandwich, Earl of, **134**
Saratoga, surrender at, **122-123**
Sartine, Gabriel de, **136**
Savannah, siege of, 163, **164**
Schuyler, Gen. Philip, 31, 33, 115, 119
Sea power, 132-146
Serapis, 144-145, **146-147**
Seven Years' War, 134
   see also French and Indian War
Sherman, Roger, **47**, 50
Shippen, Peggy, 128
Six Nations, 155-161
Smallwood, Gen. William, 72, **73**, 86, 165, 167
Smith, Col. Francis, 19-21
Sons of Liberty, 13, 17, 18
Southern campaign, 163-177
Spain
   aid to colonies, 49
   entry into war, 134
   Seven Years' War, 42
Stamp Act, 45
   Congress, 46-47
Stark, Gen. John, 27, **118**, 119
Stirling, Lord (William Alexander), 85-86

Stuart, Lieut. Col. Alexander, 177
Sugar Act, 46
Sullivan, Maj. Gen. John, 83, 86, 126
   New York frontier campaign, 158-161
   Pennsylvania campaign, 101-105
   at Trenton, 94-95
Sumter, Thomas, 169, 176, 177
Tallmadge, Maj. Benjamin, 128-130, 191
Tarleton, Col. Banastre, 165, 167, 171-174
Taxation, 9, 10, 14-15, 43-45
   without representation, 46
Tea, tax on, 14-15
Ticonderoga, Fort, 23, 65, 114-115
Tories, 6, 38, 97, 118, 165, 167, 174
Toulon, **136-137**
Townshend Acts, 46-47
Treaty of Alliance (1778), **127**
Treaty of Paris (1763), 42
Treaty of Paris (1783), 190
   signers, **191**
Trenton, Battle of, 93-95
Uniforms
   American, **68-71**
   British, **74**
   French, **78-79**
   Hessian, **76-77**
Valcour Island, **36-37**
   Battle of, 38
Valley Forge, 66, **98**, **106**, 107
Vergennes, Comte de, 126
Vincennes, Battle of, 152-155
Virginia Resolves, 45
Volley firing, 60
von Riedesel, Baron, 115, 119, 122
von Steuben, Baron, **105**, 106-107, 174
Ward, Gen. Artemas, 22-23, 25, 28
Warren, Dr. Joseph, 18, 27, 28
Washington, George, 28, 57, 66, 67, 72, **80**
   captures Boston, 29
   crossing Delaware, **93**
   at Monmouth Court House, **109**, **110-111**
   New Jersey campaign, 91-97, 108-110
   New York campaign, 81-90
   New York frontier campaign, 158-161
   Pennsylvania campaign, 99-108
   retirement, 190-191
   and Rochambeau, 181-183
   at Trenton, **94**
   at Valley Forge, **98**
   Yorktown campaign, 183-189
Washington, Capt. William, 95, 170-177
Wayne, Gen. Anthony, 102, 105
   at Monmouth Court House, 108-110
   at West Point, 126, 128
   Yorktown campaign, 185, 187-188
Weapons, **60-61**
Weedon, "Joe Gourd," 101
West Point, Battle of, 126-130
Whipple, Abraham, 14
Willett, Col. Marinus, 116, 117, 161
Williams, Col. Otho, 165, 167, 169, 173
Wolfe, General James, 42
Writs of Assistance, 47
Wyoming Massacre, **161**
Yorktown campaign, 179-189

193

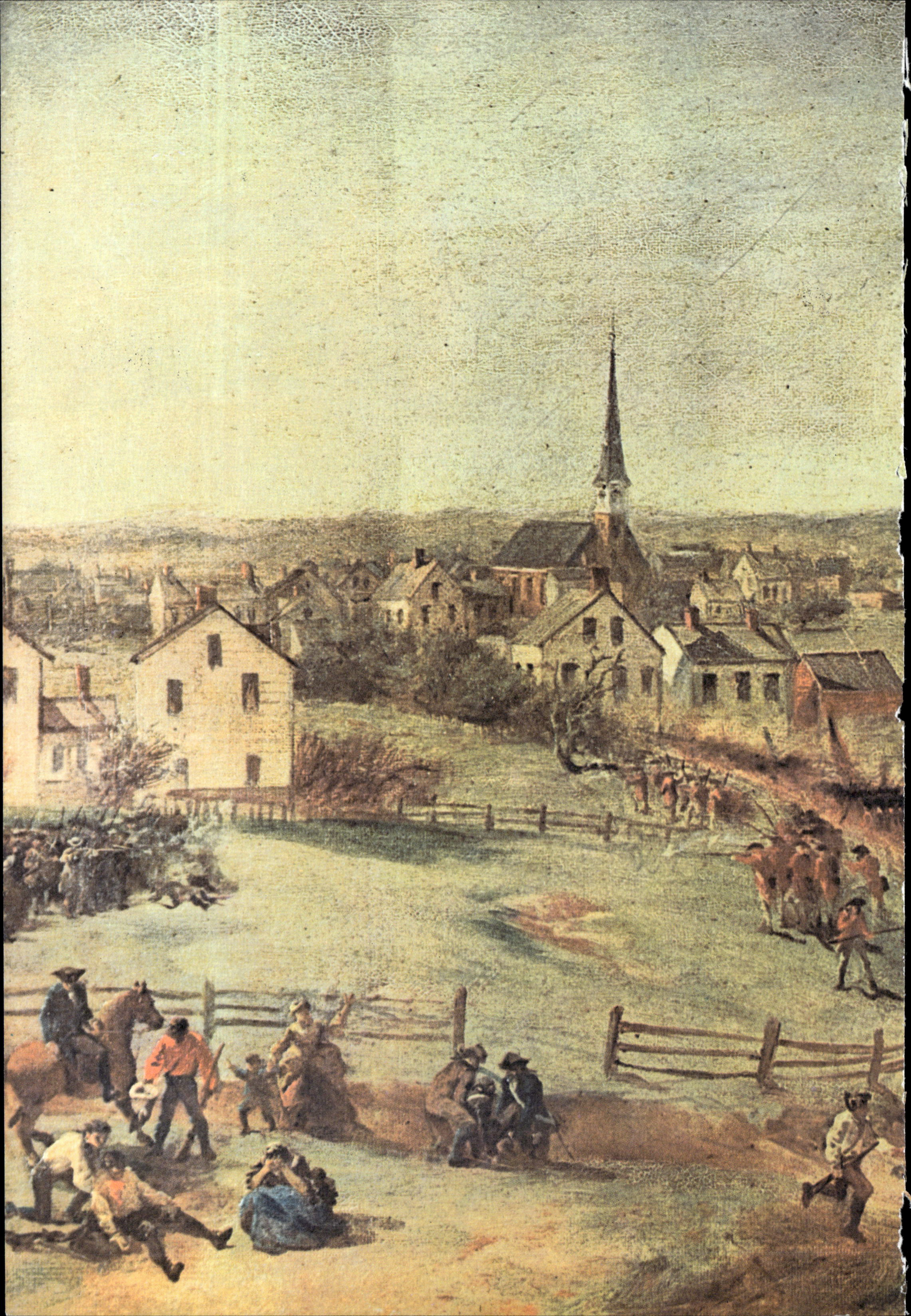